HENLEY UNION
WORKHOUSE
The Story of Townlands

The author would like to acknowledge the grant
kindly provided by The Greening Lamborn Trust.
The Greening Lamborn Trust's objective is to
promote public interest in the history, architecture,
old photographs, and heraldry of Oxford and its
neighbours by supporting publications and other
media that create access to them.

HENLEY UNION
WORKHOUSE
The Story of Townlands

VALERIE ALASIA

BREWIN BOOKS

BREWIN BOOKS
56 Alcester Road,
Studley,
Warwickshire,
B80 7LG
www.brewinbooks.com

Published by Brewin Books 2016

A CIP catalogue record for this book is available from
the British Library.

ISBN: 978-1-85858-540-6

Printed and bound in Great Britain
by Bell & Bain Ltd.

Contents

List of Illustrations

List of Tables

References

1 National Archives, Kew: Poor Law Union correspondence for Henley, MH. 12/9681-9701, sequential by date.

2 Oxfordshire History Centre, Cowley: Poor Law Union – Henley Minute Book, PLU4/G/1A1/6-18. Previously Oxfordshire Record Office (ORO) and Oxfordshire Archives (OA).

3 Local Press:
Reading Mercury, July 1723-December 1950.
Henley Advertiser, May 1870-January 1908.
Henley Chronicle, January 1904-December 1913.
Henley and South Oxfordshire Standard, September 1892.

Acknowledgements

FIRSTLY, my grateful thanks go to Stella Kendall, without whose time, dedication and IT skills my untidy typescript would have remained unpublished.

The late David Pitt of Henley U3A encouraged my early work and Joan Dils of Reading University was my guru and gave me my foundation in local history.

I thank Graham Jones of Henley Archaeological & Historical Group for the inclusion of the work on Henley censuses; Nicholas Cooper of gbs Architects for sharing his work on Henley Workhouse for the Victoria County History and John Whiting for his reproduction skills.

I am indebted to Carol Richmond for allowing me to copy her list of workhouse employees and to Old Maps and Ordnance Survey for permission to include the 1976 site plan.

Henley Town Council kindly allowed me to photograph paintings by Lucy Cooper hanging in the Mayor's Parlour.

My thanks to the *Henley Standard* for authorising me to reproduce newspaper photographs.

My thanks also to Anthony Taylor for allowing me to use photographs taken in 2009 for Assendon e-museum.

HENLEY UNION WORKHOUSE CENSUS ANALYSIS								
	1841	1851	1861	1871	1881	1891	1901	1911
Total Inmates	131	227	186	192	203	90	95	121
Paupers - Male	64	112	96	98	105	48	47	73
Paupers - Female	67	115	90	94	98	42	48	48
Staff	5	7	10	11	11	9	11	12
Vagrants	-	2	-	11	-	7	4	3
Men 65 +	15	24	25	31	14	17	16	43
Women 65 +	6	9	11	9	12	10	9	17
Men 15 - 64	22	35	23	26	40	16	10	23
Women 15 - 64	26	42	33	41	36	18	23	23
Boys 7 - 14	23	32	31	36	40	8	13	2
Girls 7 - 14	22	40	29	30	41	11	8	1
Boys under 7	4	21	17	5	11	7	8	5
Girls under 7	13	24	18	14	9	3	8	7
Scholars in School	N/A	86	79	79	98*	27	28	-
Boys	-	39	37	41	32	12	15	-
Girls	-	47	42	38	31	15	10	-
Children under 4	-	25	19	8	6	4	9	12
Paupers born in Henley	N/A	45	42	53	58	25	25	-
Oxfordshire	102	99	104	99	78	41	29	-
Berkshire	-	4	4	7	6	3	13	-
Buckinghamshire	-	19	17	26	6	11	8	-
Married	-	21	9	12	16	4	8	14
Unmarried	-	59	54	61	59	26	28	55
Widower	-	20	20	21	16	14	8	21
Widow	-	3	8	10	16	10	7	13
Unmarried mothers	6	3	17	17	4	2	1	3
& Children	12	22	24	31	5	3	1	4
"Imbecile / Idiot" etc	-	-	15	19	10	3	5	-
"Blind/ deaf /dumb" etc	-	1	7	3	2	-	4	-
Paralysis	-	-	-	-	-	-	3	-
Epileptic	-	-	-	-	-	1	2	-

*Scholars at Uxbridge & Brentford = 35

Census Analysis 1841-1911.

A Walk Around Henley Workhouse

which became Townlands Hospital in 1948

WHEN we were able to walk around what was until 1930 Henley's workhouse[i], <u>no longer possible because of redevelopment</u>, we would start at West Hill, Henley-on-Thames, around 6 pm in the 19th century. Not a place to be, with all those vagrants queuing up outside the workhouse waiting to be let in. The 7 ft high wooden gates to the workhouse are shutting them out until 6 o'clock, but the Red Cow beerhouse is right next door if there are any pennies left to spend. Tramps are not allowed to take any money into the workhouse anyway; otherwise they are expected to pay for a bed outside, perhaps in a neighbouring run-down slum cottage. Nobody else comes up here because word goes around town that you don't want to be going up **there**.

The penalty for vagrants found with any money on them is to be put before the Magistrates for falsely gaining relief at Henley Union workhouse and could result in 21 days hard labour in Oxford Gaol and forfeiting the money. However, a sympathetic occupant of a cottage in West Hill might, for a small cut, have the money overnight for safe-keeping.

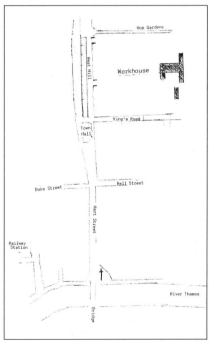

Location of Henley Union Workhouse.

At 6 pm the Gatekeeper appears from the porter's lodge, No. 78 West Hill, and proceeds to open the gates for admission into the Casual Wards. The vagrants may, in fact, be wayfarers – men and/or families walking to a new place in search of a job.

---

i   Some buildings were still in use as a hospital until the 1980s, now to be redeveloped as sheltered residential accommodation.

On admittance they and their clothing are all put through the disinfectant bath by the Gatekeeper (or his wife for the separated families), after being questioned about having any money or food on them. Access is limited to the designated Tramp Wards at the front of the site for an overnight stay in a hammock. Sometimes this does not go down well, resulting in tramps appearing before the Magistrates next day accused of tearing up their allocated workhouse clothing or refusing to carry out the allotted tasks in the hope of being given a better replacement suit. Indeed, experienced vagrants often found conditions in prison (where such indiscipline led them) to be more congenial than a life on the road.

Otherwise, general access to the workhouse for long-stay inmates has to be strictly controlled so as to admit only those poor people who are deemed eligible after assessment by the Relieving Officer. What the workhouse is not intended for is the able-bodied poor, despite the low level of wages paid locally, making mere survival difficult for families.

View of Townlands Hospital site, 2013.

Once inside those 7 ft gates to West Hill, there opens up an area of six acres (see picture above), with boundary walls along the length of it. Most is put down to garden, where the male paupers can earn their keep by working a 12-hour day, under the direct supervision of the Gatekeeper, acting as Superintendent of Labour (see page 72). The produce serves to supplement the strict diet provided by the workhouse kitchen. At the western boundary, parallel to Hop Gardens, there is a smallish greenhouse for early seed-growing and perhaps some tomatoes.

In the middle of the site, away from everyone, sits the Pest House. This was built early on to isolate infectious diseases like smallpox, typhus, scarlet fever and even itch cases (scabies). With 150 inmates in the poor house (1790-1835), it was imperative that contagious and infectious diseases should not be passed around.

Interestingly, in 1794 it is recorded that two troopers of the King's Light Dragoons occupied this solitary hut, which has four windows and little else. These men had been left behind by their regiment to look after themselves when one of them was "sick of the confluent smallpox" and the other was covered with ominous spots. Thomas

Hardy[i] wrote that we do not know the name of the trooper who had the smallpox, but the one covered with spots was called Comberbacke – later to be revealed as Samuel Coleridge, the poet.

So let us move on to the main building at the north end of the site (see cover), built in 1790 (as confirmed by the plaque over the north wing) to house 150 of Henley's poor. Previously, Henley Poorhouse had existed in New Street on the site of what is now the theatre but by 1790, with shortages incurred by the Napoleonic Wars, times were hard and more accommodation was needed. Most of this site had been acquired by the Town for the benefit of the poor in 1654 and known as the Town Lands, had been held in reserve. Now, in 1790, the time had come to make use of it and John Strange, a Henley builder, was commissioned along with the architect, William Bradshaw, to construct suitable premises.

The northern block of grey and red brick still in 2015 housed an active hospital kitchen (once preparing three meals a day ultimately for 382 people) and the facilities for an extensive laundry. This became where the able-bodied females were put to work.

Two wings run north-south from a central range containing an arcaded ground floor. The side wing along the western boundary from 1847 contains the men's day room downstairs, with their dormitories above (see page 16). Men and women are strictly segregated. Alongside are a series of dry goods stores for clothing, malt and hops, brooms, coal and even coffins. In the wing opposite is the dining hall/chapel, with the Master's office alongside. The women's wing backs on to this, facing east.

Adjoining Stores.

Fronting the women's day rooms are two yards for recreational use. Surrounding that is a Drying Ground to take the laundry from around the corner (see Ordnance Survey 1879 map on page 19). Girls were to be trained in the laundry so they could find jobs outside when of age and not to perpetuate pauperism in the family.

To the rear along the north boundary are the men's hospital and adjacent to that the women's hospital. The first infirmary was built in 1841 and remained largely unaltered until 1870 and again in 1885, when the Medical Officer condemned its condition and demanded that new wards and necessary improvements should be commenced without further delay.

Women's block (left). Women's infirmary (right)
© Assendon e-museum 2009.

The Matron's duty was performed by the Master's wife with a nurse appointed from outside, assisted by pauper inmates.

A building of note is the imposing Board Room (re-developed in 1895) for the Board of Guardians, since used

---

i   "The Trumpet Major", Thomas Hardy, Wordsworth, 1995.

for in-house meetings (see page 40). This building includes a water-closet for use by the Guardians and a room for the clerk, by far the best accommodation on the site; a weather-vane sits aloft. The Board of Guardians who meet in this Board Room keep down the cost to the ratepayers of providing for up to 250 inmates (ultimately 382) of the workhouse.

Weather vane on Boardroom roof.

Among the three dozen Guardians are Justices of the Peace (who serve ex officio) and Guardians who are subject to annual election by the ratepayers. They represent the individual parishes brought together to create the Henley Union under the New Poor Law of 1834. Thus, at their first meeting in June 1835 there were 10 local JPs, with Thomas Stonor in the chair and 27 elected Guardians, representing 21 parishes (later adding three Buckinghamshire parishes in 1847).

With the passing of the Education Act 1871, a new school has been erected, alongside the women's infirmary, for 100 children. On the ground floor are the boys' schoolroom and day room, separated from a similar girls' block by the school master's day room and school mistress's day room. Above we can see the dormitories, separated by the master's and mistress's bedrooms. Separate enclosed yards adjoin, which contain earth closets and a swing for the girls and a swing-post for the boys.

School.

By 1891, however, the number of schoolchildren fell, despite having taken in schoolchildren from Middlesex, and in 1894 it was decided to send the remaining ten children of school age to Henley National School. In 1906 the school building was converted into an infirmary and remained so until the 1980s.

The last building we come to, tucked away in the north east corner of the site, is the small mortuary, built in 1908. Whilst mortality rates were low within the workhouse, nevertheless provision of a mortuary was essential for the few deceased from the infirmary.

By then, with a children's home at Radnor House in New Street accommodating all the 18 remaining children, the workhouse, now reduced in size to 91 inmates, expanded the infirmary into the school building. This was to admit those who were on outdoor relief for nursing care as necessary, i.e. the sick and the elderly for long-stay care. Such care provision continued at Townlands Hospital until the Care in the Community Act of 1987, the workhouse concept having been overtaken meanwhile by the Public Assistance Act in 1929.

1. Introduction

The Story of Henley Union Workhouse and its People

Preface

My research over many years has taken me through the records of the Board of Guardians and Master at the Oxford Archives; those of the Poor Law Commissioners in London at the National Archives in Kew; and the census records and newspapers held in Henley Library. These all reveal what was going on in Henley Workhouse over the years and who was involved.

I have quoted fairly fully from these sources so that readers may gain an insight into circumstances both within the workhouse and outside in the community.

Paupers themselves kept no records, so it is only possible to discern what their lives in the workhouse were actually like by reference to official records written by administrators. This is what this book seeks to reflect.

So not only is building development covered in this book but also the local families whose lives were so dire that they had no choice other than to enter through the gates of the dreaded workhouse.

I have told their story chronologically and included names, where appropriate, which may be a source for family historians.

Introduction

The poor have always been with us: at one time the monasteries administered to the poor but after the Reformation it became necessary in 1601 to introduce a Poor Law for local government, in what was primarily a rural nation, to spend money on the poor by rating the land.

This Law spelled out where the responsibility lay for providing for those physically or mentally disabled citizens who could not earn their own living. Henceforth, each Parish was ordered to collect "competent sums of money for the necessary relief of the lame, impotent, old, blind and such among them being poor and not able to work." Thus the management of the poor was carried out locally by Parish overseers and administered by Justices of the Peace.

So the modern system of rating began with the Old (Parish) Poor Law of 1601 and it soon became established that rates would be based on ownership/use of landed property. The Overseers of the Poor were required to determine who would pay the amount in the pound (or "rate" to be levied), its collection and distribution within the Parish. This would be spent on benefits-in-kind such as food, shoes and on work schemes, e.g. in workhouses, but most of the income went on the dole paid to widows, the poor and the sick in their own homes.

These latter were classed as impotent poor who could not earn a living; on the other hand, where a problem was perceived for the able-bodied, work was organised for them by the Parish Vestry. In addition training and education was made available for the poor by way of pauper apprenticeships.

In July 1651, by deed of covenant of the Corporation of Henley, the Mayor of Henley and other persons had recently acquired from Richard Boult a parcel of land "for the use and benefit of the poor of Henley" lying upon the hill on the north side of the High Street. Annexed to this deed is a receipt by Richard Boult, the vendor, for £170, the amount of the purchase money. £70 of that sum appears to have come directly from the sum of £100 bequeathed by William Massam of Fawley Court in January 1602 "towards the setting of the poor of Henley on work that they might learn to live by their honest labour".

This three acres of land lying above Henley was not required at that time and was let out to farmers on a lease, e.g. in 1676, 1723 and 1773, by the Mayor, Aldermen and Burgesses, into whose care the land had been vested to administer. The rent and interest on the sum were paid to the Overseers of the Poor, and John Burn suspects them of applying this in aid of the poor rates rather than the poor![i]

Under the Old Poor Law, Parish Churchwardens and Overseers of the Poor were encouraged to erect houses of dwelling for the so-called impotent poor. So in 1727 Henley Council mortgaged the Town Lands in order to release money for the development of some houses in New Street in their ownership bequeathed by Robert Kenton, to convert them into a house for the maintenance of the poor in the town, under local control[ii] and providing organised work for the able-bodied.

However, an Act of 1782, known as the Gilbert Act, called for the better relief and employment of the poor, being a step up from the local poorhouse. Parishes were to unite and nominate Guardians of the Poor, with a Visitor to supervise them and appoint the Governor of the Poorhouse. Only the impotent poor were to go to the poorhouse; Guardians were to maintain and provide for the able-bodied poor elsewhere, hire them out to any labour and make up the deficiency in wages if farmers paid less than the going rate. Any JP could order the Guardians to provide housing and find employment for a complainant. In effect, this was a recognition retrospectively by Government of established practice in the localities.

Then an Act of Parliament was applied for by Henley Corporation in early 1790 to build a new workhouse, estimated to cost £1600. The need had been identified in 1786 as "the likeliest means of reducing the taxes." The existing house of maintenance was not sufficient to receive the poor and old pensioners, and rents paid were said to be a principal cause of the advancement of the rates! The town lands on the hill were

---

i   See Government Enquiry in 1820 into distribution of Henley Charities, Appendix A.

ii Oct 24, 1790. To be let on a building lease a piece of ground with considerable quantity of old buildings thereon in New Street. The front of the premises faces south; the extent of the frontage is 59'10" x 113' depth, exclusive of piece of ground adjoining to back part to be used as a garden and walled in 85' x 60'. Particulars from Mr Bradshaw, builder.[3]

thought to be a proper place.[i] Councillors noted, that in order to avoid the expense of £300 for the Act, if they and all the parishioners agreed to an extra 6d rate in the first year and 3d in the years to follow to pay back the interest on the borrowing and some of the principal each year, the expense to the Council of £300 in payment of the Act could be avoided. This resolution being adopted at the meeting, the Councillors all agreed with the property owners in the town that no property should be leased or sold in the town unless the lessee or new owner agreed to the extra rate charge. The rate then declared was to be 3s3d in the £ and 6d extra for the workhouse.

Between 1791 and 1801 the cost of British corn rose from 48s7d to 113s10d per Imperial quarter, so Henley's new workhouse was timely.

Henley's Poor House was erected at West Hill in 1790 to accommodate 150 poor persons of the town. At a Vestry meeting in April 1790 Barrett March, proprietor of the Red Lion Hotel, had agreed to lend £1200 as a mortgage on the three acres of Town Land demised for 500 years towards paying for the building of the workhouse (by 1836 this sum was said to be "long since paid"). Also a contribution of £80 was made by Henley Charities.

Construction was carried out by John Strange, bricklayer; the architect, surveyor and Inspector being William Bradshaw. Plans do not survive, but the building contract contains very full details of the specification[ii]. As built, it comprised two wings running north-south and a central range with an arcaded ground floor walk linking them at their northerly end (see cover). The building is of grey and red brick with a simple plaque at first floor level announcing, "This house was erected A.D.1790." Total cost was £1746.8s.7½d.

The system under the Old Poor Law continued into the 19th century, when it became clear from the 1801 census that the population of England was burgeoning. Unemployment became endemic and rising numbers of poor people needing financial support made calls upon the Parish for relief from poverty: such increases were proving unsustainable. So a rising poor rate nationally caused growing discontent among farmers, who brought increasing pressure on Government for a conclusive solution to the poor law problem during the years 1818-1831. Neither the influence of the Swing Riots in 1830, nor the Reform Bill about to be enacted in 1832 can be under-estimated. That year a long questionnaire was sent out by the Victorian administrator, Edwin Chadwick in London, posing questions to Parish Vestries throughout the country: such questions as to the number of labourers in receipt of allowances from the Parish; the wages paid in the neighbourhood and the scale of relief/subsidy given; the influence of hiring on establishing more "settlements" (under the Settlement Act) leading to possibly more relief for larger families than could be supported by their labour; and lastly, asking for any information on causes and consequences of the agricultural riots 1830/1.

The problem of poverty was overwhelming by 1832 and the Old Poor Law was seen as not conforming to proper and efficient public administration. Mr Chadwick's report in 1833 led to the prompt introduction of the New Poor Law in 1834. This

---

i   John Crocker papers deposited in archives of Henley Archaeological and Historical Group in Henley Town Hall, per Ox.Arch.MS/DD/Henley C.IV.11a.

ii   ORO BOR3/C.ICV/PW/11/2, 20 May 1790.

ended individual local initiative and instituted edicts from Somerset House in London on good practice to be introduced throughout the country. It required Parishes to combine into Unions to manage a workhouse in their area. Administration was to be under the direct control of three Poor Law Commissioners in London, thus doing away with local discretion and imposing uniformity. In addition to the central board, Assistant Commissioners would be appointed to issue regulations for each workhouse and for the labour to be made extreme.

The new attitude to the poor was embodied in the Poor Law Commissioners' insistence that the situation of the pauper "must cease to be really apparently so eligible (desirable) as the situation of the independent labourers of the lowest class" thus deterring applications for relief. Relieving Officers were required to undertake "due and efficient" administration of relief to the poor, and a punitive regime was introduced whereby, on reception at the workhouse and after examination by the Medical Officer, paupers were classified into the following categories:

1. Men infirm through age or any other cause;
2. Able-bodied men and youths above age 15;
3. Boys over seven and under 15;
4. Women infirm through age or any other cause;
5. Able-bodied women and girls over 15;
6. Girls over seven and under 15;
7. Children under seven years.

Thereafter, on admittance into the workhouse, husbands and wives, parents and children (having been searched and all articles taken away and home contents disposed of) were to be separated into quarters set apart from each other. In a nutshell, it was a policy of separation, segregation, classification and supervision.

Men's wing adjoining main block.

Women's wing.

Discipline was strictly imposed by way of regulations so that families were not allowed to converse with each other for fear of being deemed "disorderly" which was but one item in a list of punishable offences.

When the Poor Law Amendment Act was passed in 1834, Henley already had its workhouse. So Henley Corporation insisted that it was already dealing with its own problem. But, naturally, the Poor Law Commissioners (PLC) in Somerset House, London, decided that this should be taken over and expanded into a Henley Union of Parishes of the surrounding area, based on the Henley site known since 1650 as the "Town Lands", being in Corporation ownership.

However, a letter from the Assistant Poor Law Commissioner to the PLC dated 11th May 1835 records the concerns of Henley Vestry, "The Workhouse system has been acted upon in Henley for some time in degree and this policy is a strong instance of the good resulting from it. The rates are reduced to nearly one half and the Town is to be well satisfied to remain as they are – this I conceive to be impossible and Henley must be the centre of a considerable Union – considerable in extent, for the population is so difficult that I doubt I can bring more than 14-15,000 into it. This plan pleases the Henley people next to that of remaining where they are – and they are well content now that the detail of the Union is before them."[i]

So the merging of Parishes into a Union now required an agreed annual contribution to the running cost of the workhouse by each local Parish, as laid down by the Board of Guardians, who would administer the workhouse under the direct control of the Poor Law Commissioners at Somerset House.

In fact, after the later addition of Fawley, Hambleden and Medmenham, the population to be covered by Henley Union, according to the 1851 census, was 17,900. The Union of 21 parishes covered an area of some 90 square miles in South Oxfordshire, stretching as far north as Cuxham and Pyrton beyond Watlington, Oxon (see following map J Dils) and as far east as Medmenham in Buckinghamshire.

---

i   NB Matron's bay window overlooking Women's yards.

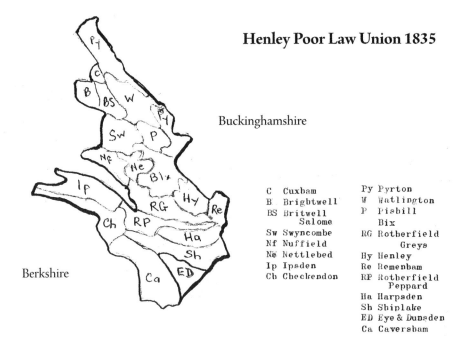

Henley Poor Law Union 1835

Buckinghamshire

Berkshire

C	Cuxham	Py	Pyrton
B	Brightwell	W	Watlington
BS	Britwell Salome	P	Pisbill
			Bix
Sw	Swyncombe	RG	Rotherfield Greys
Nf	Nuffield		
Ne	Nettlebed	Hy	Henley
Ip	Ipsden	Re	Remenham
Cb	Checkendon	RP	Rotherfield Peppard
		Ha	Harpsden
		Sh	Shiplake
		ED	Eye & Dunsden
		Ca	Caversham

Parishes of the Henley Union and their dues 1861[i]

PARISHES.	Area in Acres.	Population according to the Census of 1851.	Averages declared 1856. £
Bix	2826	367	330
Brightwell	1520	294	273
Britwell Prior	481	46	14
Britwell Salome	727	248	141
Caversham	4625	1752	668
Checkenden	2967	410	181
Cuxham	501	172	129
Eye and Dunsden ..	3108	829	388
Fawley	2681	254	217
Hambleden	6615	1365	717
Harpsden	1993	215	47
Henley	1737	3733	1197
Ipsden	2484	629	315
Medmenham	2298	401	118
Nettlebed	988	754	242
Nuffield	1645	251	143
Pishill	495	192	103
Pyrton	3963	692	530
Remenham	1591	486	100
Rotherfield Greys ..	2609	1518	273
Rotherfield Peppard ..	2159	406	229
Shiplake	2693	569	225
Swyncombe	3705	428	243
Watlington	3384	1884	959
	57795	17895	£7782

i   J.S. Burn.

2. Accommodation

IN JULY 1835 the Board of Guardians asked the Poor Law Commission for permission to continue to use the old poorhouse for 150 inmates pro tem. Improvements costing the modest sum of £119 were necessary in order to house the paupers according to the standard classifications during the forthcoming winter (separating men from women and boys from girls), otherwise paupers could not be separated into their "classes". The PLC quickly authorised this expenditure and a contract was placed with Mr Huggins of Henley accordingly.

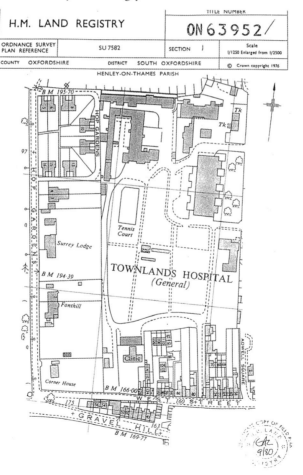

By November 1835 an advertisement appeared in the Reading Mercury that Henley Union were "desirous of obtaining plans for enlargement of the workhouse so as to contain 250 paupers, with rooms for the Board of Guardians, the Master and Mistress". The PLC sanctioned an estimate of £2,560 for the building work plus £1500 capital equipment. In July 1837 a major enlargement to the premises was the building of a block at the south end of the east wing to plans by Cooper and Sons of Henley, containing a waiting room, Board room and clerk's office on the ground floor, with additional accommodation for a girls' school and sleeping rooms on the floor above. The new building work was undertaken by C Strange, bricklayer; a certain Tyler, carpenter; J B Strange, stone mason; and Brown and Cook, painters and glaziers, and this building largely remains (2016).

However, this did not provide all that was needed and in December 1837 Richard Hall, Assistant Poor Law Commissioner, wrote to the Board of Guardians drawing attention to a lack of warmth and seclusion for the old, to the want of a nursery for very young children, and pointing out that "the condition of many of the wards is far less neat and clean than should be; many articles of clothing and of furniture and of utensils belonging to the paupers, as well as to the Union, are carelessly scattered about" while meals were "irregular and disorderly".[2] Much remained to be done.

One problem was the physical condition of the 50-year-old building itself and a feeling of the conditions prevailing can be obtained by the following. At the end of 1839 W H Parker, the Assistant Commissioner then responsible for Henley, asked for a report to be carried out by Dr Southwood Smith from PLC in London. After describing many of the principal rooms one by one: adult men's day room, adult men's dormitory, two girls' dormitories, "room for women with bastard children" and boys' dormitory, he reported:[1]

"The house is ill constructed throughout. The walls are thin, the ceilings low, the windows small, the rooms close, damp and dark, nor can the word clean be applied to a single room examined by me. It must be difficult if not impossible to warm them properly ... The general aspect of discomfort and the confined, damp and dirty condition of this whole establishment are the more striking from the singular openness and beauty of the situation, the dryness of the soil and the freshness of the external air. It is owing to these latter causes that the establishment has hitherto enjoyed an exemption from acute epidemic and contagious disease".[i]

However, there was already a severe outbreak among the workhouse children of 'itch' (scabies) – "the genuine offspring of filth, and in all the rooms the smell of brimstone (sulphur, burnt as a fumigant) is abominable".[2]

Nevertheless, the arrangements remained inadequate pending adoption of a number of schemes for improving them.

Minor alterations were carried out in February 1842 after it was ordered that chimneys be built to the Bastardy Ward (sic) and to the sleeping room above; Mr Strange's offer to do this work for £8 4s 0d was accepted.

---

i   For reference see page 6.

Prompted no doubt by the typhoid outbreak in 1841/2, a new infirmary was built by Robert Outhwaite to plans prepared by Richard Billing of Reading on the north-east boundary of the site (since demolished).[2] The following year the first school room with a boys' dormitory above it was built.

Until the end of the 19th century Henley Workhouse had a large percentage of children so that, in addition to the schoolrooms, there were covered play sheds in their yards and industrial workrooms for training purposes. Girls were also to be trained in the laundry attached to the general wash-house adjoining the kitchens.

Ventilation throughout the workhouse was of considerable importance as per Florence Nightingale's concepts. Various methods were suggested and best practice recommended, e.g. opaque glass was banned.

In 1844 the girls' sleeping dormitories over the Board Room were extended with a new block to the east.[2] All this allowed the numerous children of school age to be put to learning the 3 Rs while under supervision of the workhouse.

However, it was felt that the building was still unsatisfactory because in 1844 the Visiting Committee – the guardians sub-committee with special responsibility for the workhouse – reported that

Laundry. © Assendon e-museum 2009.

"the same yard (is) appropriated to the aged and the able-bodied and industrious and well-conducted poor (as to) those of bad character and those with bastard children. The same mixture of persons, though not to the same extent, exists with the sleeping apartments". Greville Piggott, the then current Assistant Commissioner PLC, agreed, "This is no doubt a great defect, entailing much discomfort and annoyance (on the aged and infirm)" but added that for the moment improvements at Henley were not a priority.[1] Nonetheless, in August 1844 an advertisement appeared for additions to the workhouse.[3]

Early in 1847 there was an explosion in the numbers received into the workhouse. Had this perhaps anything to do with the Poor Law Removal Bill of June 1846 or even the Corn Importation Bill of the same month? At the end of January there were 60 more inmates in the workhouse than the 276 approved by PLC. Old and infirm women were lodged in the Board Room and the clerk's office and their usual accommodation taken up by the able-bodied, and the Master was 'overwhelmed by the increased amount of duties imposed upon him'.[2]

This resulted in the so-called "deserving though unfortunate poor being exposed to be witnesses of the licentious conversation and the disgusting habits of the profligate"[3] and so classification was not simply a matter of deterrence and administrative convenience, but also of education and morality.

Therefore, in March 1847 the Guardians submitted to PLC fresh plans by Billing.[2] These provided for a new kitchen, laundry and receiving wards, increased accommodation for the old and infirm, new accommodation for the master and matron and – the most substantial part of the new works – for a dining hall and chapel, with sleeping accommodation on the floor above.

As regards Day Rooms for healthy inmates, these were to be large enough to receive all the respective classes of inmates, preferably on the ground floor. One general dining hall to be provided (but segregated so as to debar socialising). Suitable workrooms were to be provided in the yards plus suitable store rooms for linen, clothing, dry and other goods (see layout of Henley Union Workhouse on Ordnance Survey 1879 map below) where those buildings lying on the north-west side are still there (2010). Refractory wards were also to be provided.

Attention was paid to the need for a fire escape in each workhouse. (A mortuary, not shown on the 1879 map, was built in 1908 and located in the north-east corner of the site).

These additions entailed major alterations within the existing building (it is not known where, previously, the inmates had taken their meals). The revised laundry and kitchen were to be built on the northern boundary, the dining hall and chapel in a new range built along the west side of the east wing. By November 1847 the Visiting Committee reported that the work was nearly finished:

"The classification, both indoors and outdoors, in connection with the female side of the house has ... been effected whereby the abandoned and dissolute are separated from the rest. The dining room is finished and fitted up with benches conveniently

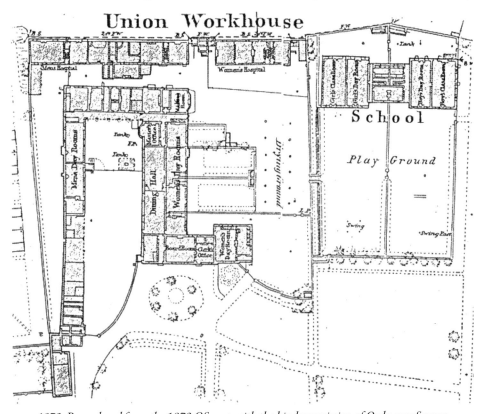

1879. Reproduced from the 1879 OS map with the kind permission of Ordnance Survey.

made for the accommodation of Paupers at meals, as well as divine service, a screen in the centre by the pulpit dividing the inmates into a male and female class. The new room for the master at the end of the dining room is also completed ..." [2]

They went on to describe the progress made with the other alterations and additions. Whereas in 1842 the workhouse could accommodate 276 inmates, when the work was finished it would be able to house 382. Furthermore, the house in the town which had been taken temporarily for boys during a measles outbreak would be retained for old and infirm men. [2]

The dining hall range remains today, fronting onto the workhouse courtyard to its west and with the bay window of the master's room at its northern end from which he could supervise the yard (see page 61). (The matron's room overlooked the women's yards on the east). Stylistically it is not dissimilar to the original building, and some effort has been made to create an attractive facade with burnt headers to the brickwork and windows with broad, rubbed brick lintels. [i]

There were few further alterations to the workhouse for another 20 years. In 1865 the Poor Law Board laid down new regulations for the design and layout of tramp wards. It is noteworthy that in 1862 John Hodges, a Guardian, sold to the Board of Guardians a portion of land adjoining the workhouse. This extended the site to West Hill and enabled a porter's lodge to be erected in 1867 by W C Strange, together with vagrant wards where tramps could be accommodated overnight. This new entrance replaced the one higher up West Hill where a path ran direct to the 1790 building and Board Room. Thereafter Mr Hodges purchased further land and two cottages thereabouts, which he donated to the Guardians. This offer was gladly received, "the acquirement and possession of the land being of very great importance to the Union". [1]

An Inspector's report of April 1866 states:

"Now that the Guardians are in possession of the land at the back of the workhouse, I suggest whether a window might not be opened on the convalescent room attached to the men's hospital. It strikes me that such an alteration would improve the ventilation of the room and render it more cheerful and agreeable, as well as more healthy." [1]

The Inspector visited again in September 1866 and reported [1]: "It is proposed when the porter's lodge and new vagrant wards are completed that the present vagrants wards at the workhouse shall be converted into infections wards. As regards the new vagrant wards, it will be seen that they will need bathrooms or workrooms provided, nor is any provision made for warming the beds. The floors of the wards are proposed to be formed of a concrete finish on the surface, with a key of Portland cement. This kind of floor cannot but I think, be soon cut to pieces by the rough nails of the vagrants' shoes; the floor ought properly to be boarded.

"The medical Wards are to be lighted by means of a same-sized lantern light in the roof of each. The four corners of each lantern to be glazed with louvre glass for ventilation. Further ventilation will be considered and provided. I would suggest a

---

i   Victorian County History for Oxford Vol. XVI.

further fanlight over the entrance door to each ward, glazed with self-perforated glass. Again, the men's ward, being 13 ft longer than the women's ward, will probably require that the lantern light should be made proportional or two ft longer.

"The proposed water closets open immediately into the wards instead of, which it is desirable on sanitary grounds, that there should be a small uncovered lobby to the closet. There is no provision for laying on the water to the flushing tank in connection with the water closets; this should, of course, be attended to and, lastly, in order to prevent damp from rising in the walls of the building, a slate course in cement should be built into this at 6 inches above ground level".[1]

This Inspector's report caused the PLB[i] to write accordingly to the Guardians in October 1866.[1] By March 1867 the Board of Guardians were in a position to inform the PLB of their plans, as follows: "The Board are proceeding with the execution of the Vagrants' Wards and Porter's Lodge, referred to in your letter of 1 October on the land recently acquired by the Guardians. I now beg to forward you the plans and specifications for the conversion of the present Tramp and Receiving Wards into Infections Wards for the inspection of PLB as requested. At the same time, I send the plans adopted in 1858 and referred to in your letter of 30 October 1858 on the conversion of the Tramp Wards at that time into the present Tramp Wards and Receiving Wards, conceiving they will be necessary for your better understanding of the present proposal." Sgd Nicholas Mercer, Clerk, 29 March 1867. So nine years later the plans were still a proposal!

The PLB quickly responded with detailed criticisms [1]: "It is proposed to convert the present Vagrant and Receiving Wards at this workhouse into Infections Wards for six male and six female patients and the proposal appears far from satisfactory. According to the accompanying plans, the building is two storeys high, consisting at present of two rooms on two floors. The ground floor rooms will be thrown into one for six male patients and the upper rooms into one for six female patients. The male ward will be 25¾ ft long, 15 ft broad and 8 ft high and, after deducting space occupied by the fireplace and chimney-stack in the middle of the room, will give about 62 ft of floor space and 497 cu ft average of six beds (similar details for female ward).

"The staircase steps to the Women's Ward would, if executed as proposed, be very steep and inconvenient, being ten in rise, and four of them winders, whereas they should all be fliers and not more than seven in rise.

"Dr Smith, on the occasion of his visit to the workhouse on 25 September last and again in the letter to them 1st October recommended that Infections Wards should be 12 ft high and give an allowance of 20 cu ft for each patient. Next, there is no accommodation provided for a nurse. Such provision was pointed out to the Guardians as necessary by Dr Smith."

The Inspector, Dr Edward Smith, visited Henley Union in May 1867 and submitted the following questionnaire: "Is the workhouse generally adequate to the wants of the Union? – Fairly so. Armchairs, benches with backs and other conveniences are required in the Old Men's Dayroom.

"Is provision for the sick and infectious cases sufficient? – No. See special report on the plan for proposed new fever wards." [1]

---

i   Poor Law Board replaced Poor Law Commission in 1847.

This prompted PLB to write again in June 1867 enquiring what steps the Guardians proposed to take to provide further accommodation for the inmates of the workhouse and to remedy the defects averted to by the Inspector.[1]

Alterations over a period of three years were suggested by the PLB, but again in 1867 the Inspector was calling for upgrading of the infirmary to accord with PLB rules on "fitness of wards and medical appliances".[1] This presumably was to accord with medical advances following a campaign in the late 1860s by the Lancet etc. for improvements in workhouse infirmaries. On a recent visit the infirmary had been full up as there were 13 girls with scarlet fever. He suggested to the Guardians the need for a number of improvements, particularly to the school and hospital.

This pressure from PLB forced the Guardians into resolving to build the Tramp Ward, as already approved by PLB, and to convert the building at present used as Tramp Wards into Infectious Wards, as originally suggested by Dr Smith and referred to in PLB letter of 6 May 1867: "and the Guardians think that for the very few infectious cases that have occurred in this Union, this alteration will be sufficient."[2]

So, at last, on 8 October 1867 the Guardians affixed their common seal to contract with Mr John Sadler for the erection of a porter's lodge and wards for vagrants (thus releasing the previous accommodation for development, as above).

However, in October 1868 all was still not right, with the Inspector reporting, "the women's Infirmary is a cheerless building with windows high from the floor. The arrangements of the Receiving Wards is unsatisfactory as they are used for infectious and fever cases as well" – contrary to regulations.[1]

So, at the instigation of the Chairman of the Board, Lord Camoys, the Clerk immediately wrote to PLB in October 1868 about such alterations in the workhouse and asked for "the requirements of the PLB with respect to the construction space for each occupant of the infirmaries and the children's day and sleeping rooms ...". Whereupon, Mr Henley, the Poor Law representative, attended the Board meeting in November and submitted to its consideration the extension of the school accommodation in the workhouse, the erection of receiving and infectious wards and other alterations.

According to a Directive dated October 1868 from the PLB, separate accommodation was to be provided relating to the following categories of inmate: aged, able-bodied, children and sick. Able-bodied women were to be subdivided into 2-3 classes with reference to "moral character or behaviour". A separate building was required for the sick, viz. ordinary sick, lying-in women; itch cases, "dirty and offensive cases", venereal disease, fever and smallpox in a detached building, plus a children's ward.

A minimum wall space per bed was outlined, and size and layout of wards and corridors was stipulated. Access to sunlight and fresh air was recommended. Day rooms for the sick were to be provided for a half of them. Arrangements were to be made for the distribution of hot and cold water to bathrooms and sick wards.[1]

Even so, by 1869 the Inspector reiterated that better accommodation was required for the aged, sick and children as well as better provision for fever cases. Also the Guardians' attention was called to the state of the general Receiving Wards.[1] It would appear that the building had remained much as it had been when set up 35 years previously at the time of the New Poor Law, having been built in 1790. In October

1868 the PLB Inspector had reported it as being an old building on leasehold ground and inconvenient in some respects.

The Guardians – mindful no doubt that any expenditure would be a charge on the rates – were again slow to act. When in February 1869 the Revd Dr Henry Almack, Rector of Fawley and Guardian for the Parish, produced plans for a new school and fever wards, these were defeated by 8 votes to 6, and the following month the Guardians found an excuse for procrastination, resolving that "as the further education of pauper children is now in an agitated and unsettled state, (they) refuse consent for any erection at the present of new building for schools." [2] (It is probable that the Guardians had in mind suggestions that were then current for the teaching of pauper children in large schools each serving a wide area). See the outcome in Chapter on Schools.

However, the Inspector was not to be thwarted as regards a new infirmary. In July 1869 he recalled a report from a recent predecessor, including the fact that the laundry with its large boiler lay underneath the men's infirmary "which nearly caused a most serious accident. (The heat was) quite improper in its relation to sick wards and no class of inmates should be subject to the possible effect of the bursting of a steam boiler." He reported to the Poor Law Board that "I am not without hope that if I receive strong support from the Board I shall be able to induce the Guardians to reconsider this decision" (i.e. their resolve to do nothing).[1]

The infirmary continued to come in for criticism so that in 1870 the four Medical Officers endorsed an initiative to set up a Henley Nursing Home for the reception of inpatients from the neighbourhood.[3] This was repudiated by an astute Ratepayer in an anonymous letter to the Henley Advertiser pointing out that such a facility was the duty of Henley Guardians to provide on site.

Henley workhouse accommodation in 1870 is listed below. From this it will be seen that **women** were in fact being classed according to their perceived moral standing! Men appear to have been dirtier in their habits requiring a "foul sleeping ward" in the Men's hospital.

First class women's day room, Second class women's day room, Third class women's day room, Infants' day room
Girls' school room, Girls' dormitory x 3
Infants' dormitory, Infants' nursery
Third class women's dormitory, First class women's dormitory, Second class women's dormitory x 2
Infants' dormitory
Old men's dormitory x 2
Young men's dormitory, Store room
Old men's day room, Young men's day room, Tailor's shop
Boys' dormitory x 2
Boys' school room, Men's hospital ward, Men's hospital day room, Foul sleeping ward, Men's hospital ward x 2
Nurse's room
Lying-in ward (for maternity cases), Laundry
Wash house, Bath room

Old women's day room
Old women's dormitory x 2
Women's hospital day room, Women's hospital ward x 2
Fever ward x 2 [i]

*This plan was submitted to PLB before new school for 100 children was built. It gives an indication of the extent of accommodation provided for inmates.

Early in 1870 PLB evidently heard through their Inspector that some fresh proposals were afoot. They responded with a frosty letter to the Guardians complaining of "the irregularity of the proceedings" and reminding them that any proposals, and any capital spending, must be approved by the Board [2]. The guardians prevaricated again, moving that consideration on any alterations be postponed *sine die*.

PLB persisted. In March 1870 they sent forms to be completed with the dimensions of each room and the numbers that it could accommodate. The resulting return revealed some interesting facts, not least that the PLB's own basis for calculations was at fault – not only for Henley but more generally [1]. In consultation with Mr Henley, Mr Sutton of PLB architectural department minuted that:

"The former method takes no account of width of rooms in relation to number of rows of beds nor of impediments to the placing of beds offered by doors, fireplaces and projections: in fact (at Henley) it assigns a number of beds which could not be placed in the several wards" and continued with the more general point that:

> "…it has often been represented to the Board that … the bed-holding capacity of workhouses having been greatly exaggerated, the Guardians have been misled and the Inspector as well as the Board have been, and are, placed in unnecessary antagonism with the Guardians." [1]

For Henley workhouse, the analysis of the figures showed that in some rooms the theoretical number of occupants greatly exceeded what was practical: Beds in the fever wards needed to be reduced from eight to four; in the old women's sick ward from five to two; in the third-class women's dormitory from 16 to 12. Other rooms were similarly affected. In December PLB wrote to the Guardians that "it clearly appears that the accommodation of the workhouse is insufficient for the requirements of the Union" and on the basis of these objective figures, the Guardians were bound to agree. [2]

Following the introduction of the Education Act, at the meeting in December 1870, the Revd Dr Almack, clearly the leading reformer among the Henley Guardians, again proposed that "immediate steps be taken towards erecting additional buildings", [2] and this time his motion was carried. He seems to have been already prepared with plans for a new school – possibly those that he had produced in February 1869 – so that on 3 January 1871, Frederick Haslam, architect (and borough surveyor) was ready to take these to London to show to PLB. Specifications and estimates were made the same month and in February 1871 all were approved. [2] In March a contract was signed with Charles Clements, Henley builder, for £1733. [3]

---

i   Extract from MH.12.9690.106479.

An interesting point had been raised in January when Nicholas Mercer, Clerk to the Guardians, asked PLB whether they would agree to building in concrete if that were cheaper. PLB replied that they preferred brick and that they had never as yet approved any building in concrete.[1]

PLB directed the Guardians in May 1871 to purchase land for sums not exceeding £700 5s 0d, and additional buildings to be erected for the accommodation of infant poor at a cost not to exceed the sum of £2000.[1]

Haslam's school building (see page 101) has a recessed centre between two wings. It provided separated new school rooms, day rooms and wash rooms for boys and girls, with dormitories above for each, and a sitting room and a bedroom each for the schoolmaster and schoolmistress.[2] By moving children out of the main body of the workhouse it must have considerably eased pressures on space and made conditions better for everyone (see page 29). And some modest provision was made to make the children's lives more pleasant: in the girls' playground was a swing and in the boys' a swing post (to be replaced in 1929 by a seesaw).[1]

Architectural notes: New Schools for 100 children to be erected on the east side of the workhouse near the north boundary of premises. On the first floor, Dormitory for 50 boys and 50 girls in four rows of beds and dwarf partitions down the centre; plus Master's bedroom and Mistress's bedroom. Bathrooms with six basins and two baths. On ground floor, boys' school room and day room plus Master's day room. Girls' side is the counterpart of the boys side. It will consist of the following rooms, offices, etc.

Boys' side	length(ft)	width(ft)
School room	39	18
Day room	39	18
Passage	4	29½
Master's day room	12	12
Staircase	12	7
In Lavatory, 6 basins, 2 baths	12	9
Dormitory for 50 boys in 4 rows of beds and dwarf partitions down the centre	39	36¾

	length(ft)	width(ft)
Master's bedroom	16¾	12
Staircase	16¾	7
Storerooms etc	16¾	9

The girls' side is the counterpart of the boys' side.

The boiler house and coal cellar are provided in the basement storey under the boys' schoolroom; outer earth closets are provided for the girls and a urinal for the boys, also earth closets for the use of the master and mistress in the boys and girls respective backyards. The architect, accompanied by the Master, conferred with Dr Smith and

Mr Henley on 29 December upon their plans which, except for one or two particulars, appeared generally satisfactory.

However it was noted that: The plans are not in accordance with the points to be attended to in the construction of workhouses. Airbrick ventilators are not proposed to be inserted at the floor levels of the dormitories, day and schoolrooms; both playgrounds are proposed to be fenced in on the south side, and the boys' playground on the east side with high walls. Doors should be provided in the walls of the backyards to allow the soil to be removed from the earth closets without being taken through the school building.[1]

Later in June 1872 the following major changes were made consequent on transfer of children out of the House into the new school buildings:[3]

Late boys' schoolroom	*became*	Day room for old infirm men x 20
Men's hospital day room		Bedroom for foul cases from Ward 28
Ward 28		Bathroom and lavatory to hospital
Storeroom adjoining		Storeroom for paupers' own clothing only
Ward 37/8 old women's dormitory		Hospital wards for sick
Ward 36		Day room for sick
Girls' schoolroom		Day ward for old infirm wards removed from 37/8
Schoolmaster's bedroom		Ward for peculiar complaints
Schoolmaster's day room		Bedroom for infirm old men
Old men's dormitory		Matron's storeroom for clothing, bedding etc
Young men's dormitory		Bedroom for old men removed from Ward 6
Boys' dormitory		Young men's bedroom
Ward 6		Ward for old women in no.5 bedroom ground floor

In July 1880 one of the Guardians, Richard Ovey, purchased five acres of land adjoining the workhouse. The following year the Clerk was asked to obtain from Mr Ovey the lowest price at which he would let that 2a meadow; this was quoted at £30 pa.

Later in 1883 the Infirmary accommodation again came in for criticism, with the Local Government Board (LGB) – successor to PLB – Inspector commenting on inadequacy of beds and difficulty of nursing in the Sick Wards.

"The female infirmary is a detached building with sufficient space around it and answers its purpose fairly well, with this exception, that the paid nurse occupies a room in the male infirmary and has not therefore access to the female ward without passing some distance through the outer area. A covered passage to connect the two buildings would be a great gain.

Women's Infirmary.

"With regard to the male sick wards, the two rooms, one on the ground floor and one on the first floor, at the end overlooking the Old Men's Ward, are airy and comfortable, but the three rooms on the first floor are, in my opinion, open to so many objections that they are now, and always have been, quite unsuitable for the treatment of the sick. The first room on the top of the stairs is a passage room and exposed to sudden draughts from the staircase, and all the three rooms are dark, badly ventilated, exposed to constant annoyance from smoke, steam, cooking, noise from inmates at work and the rattle of machinery. They are so close to the other buildings that it would be impossible to convert them into proper hospital wards, where ample ventilation is indispensable. They should therefore be used for some other purpose as it was never intended when the recent alterations were completed that they should be again classed as sick wards, but that a certain number of chronic cases should be moved across into wards then provided for the purpose. These rooms in the body of the House, in consequence of the difficulty of nursing, have hardly, if ever, been occupied.

"I am unable to suggest a thorough remedy, as to remove the machinery would only clear out a number of bad wards which could never be made suitable for the sick. And again, for the convenience and economy of nursing, it is most desirable that the male and female wards should not be too far apart. I should advise the Guardians to request the Medical Officer at once to clear out the three wards in question of sick cases, and to send over to the new wards such chronic cases as can be dealt with by wardsmen under paid supervision. It really amounts to a question of nursing, as the beds are at present generally inadequate." [1]

This letter was sent to the new committee of Guardians.

On 31 July 1883 Mr Wing, Borough Surveyor, attended the meeting and read the following report:

> In accordance with instructions received from the Visiting Committee, I have prepared a plan showing part of the present buildings at the Union Workhouse, with the ground plan of a proposed new block to contain boilerhouse, washeries and laundry. The new block will not interfere with any existing lights and I am given to understand that the space proposed to be taken from the women's exercise yards can be very well spared. The position of the new boilerhouse and its chimney is obviously a great improvement on the present arrangement. (1 new boiler instead of 2)[2]

Nothing appears to have happened because in February 1886 the Medical Officer, Dr Baines, condemned the condition of the Infirmary and demanded that new wards and necessary improvements should be commenced without further delay. He protested that "considering the number of acute cases we are constantly admitting, some of whom I believe have died from want of better accommodation, I should consider myself as Medical Officer of this workhouse morally guilty of manslaughter unless I make an official protest as to the want of suitable wards and improvements in the Infirmary." Dr Baines went on the say, "I must also ask the Board for suitable wards for idiots and persons suffering from mental disease, who, according to the new regulations for idiots, we cannot send to asylums. Last week an idiot boy was admitted into the Infirmary who it is impossible to retain there owing to his uncleanly habits."[1]

This seems to have had the desired effect because by May 1886 the LGB approved plans for upgrading the Infirmary accommodation. The Guardians proposed to defray the cost from current rates, and building was in progress by July. This development incorporated drains connected with sewers rather than the previous middens.[3]

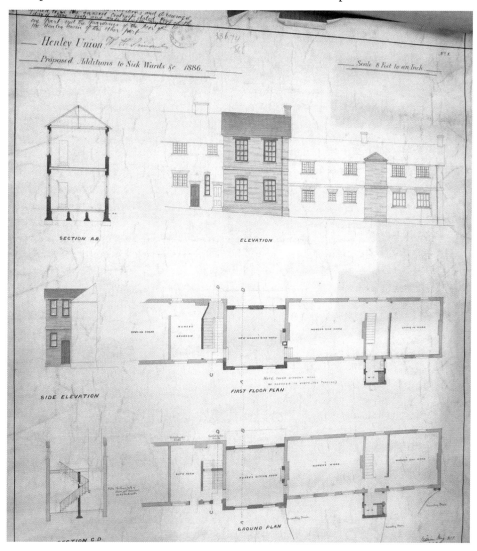

Proposed additions to Sick Wards 1886. With acknowledgement to Oxford History Centre.[i]

Water and Drainage. Meanwhile, the subject of water provision was at last exercising the Guardians, the Henley Water Company having been set up in 1881 viz.

---

i   OA PLU4/G/2YI/26.

14 August 1883 "the Directors of the Company have duly considered and fully gone into the matter of supplying the Henley Workhouse with water and I am now duly authorised both to enter into an undertaking on their behalf with the Board of Guardians to supply the whole of the workhouse as it is now constructed with water from the Company mains, either from West Hill or the Hop Gardens, at the annual rate or charge of £70. We have taken great care to ascertain as nearly as possible the quantity of water consumed, and the sum I have named is the lowest at which we could supply the quantity likely to be used."

The Guardians ordered the Clerk to write and request the price at which the Company would supply the water per thousand gallons per meter.[2]

On 28 August 1883, they replied:

"In answer to your letter on this subject, I have to inform you that the Directors of this Company have reconsidered the matter and they are now willing to enter into a contract to supply the workhouse at the annual charge of £60 or they will supply it by meter at 1/3d per 1,000 gallons. I may add that the rent of a meter suitable for this consumption would be £2 8s 0d per annum."

On 11 September 1883 they ordered that the Clerk write to the Secretary of the Henley Water Company that the Guardians were willing to contract for the supply of water at the rate of 1/- per 1,000 gallons per meter.[2] So the Guardians' negotiations ended favourably.

In 1886 plans were submitted for a new drainage scheme, together with the repairs to the Board Room, costing a total of £1574. The tender from Waldens and Cox for £1292 for the drainage was accepted but the Board Room work at £362 was referred back. This resulted in the following layout of the original site below.

Site Plan 1886

Wash House 1	Wash House 2	Staff Wash House	Folding Room Ironing	Boiler House & Pump Room	Nurses' Quarters	Old Women's Bedrooms Bathrooms, Lavatory Day Room
Men's Bathroom		Staff Bathroom	Kitchen	Heating Boiler	Matron's Kitchen	Master's Dining Room
			Bread Room		Cellars Underneath	
Men's Day Room					Master's Office	Master's Sitting Room
Washbasins						Women's Day Room
Men's Day Room						Wash Basins
Knife Room						Wash Basins
Tailor's Shop					LUNATIC	Women's Day Room
Vegetable Cleaning Room					BAYS	
Ambulance					DINING HALL	
Oakum			Courtyard			
Straw					Staff Quarters	
Coal					Waiting Room	Lavatory
Paint Shop						Strong Room
Paint Shop					Board Room	Clerk's Office
Men's Lavatory						Nursery Day Room & Scullery
Vegetable Store						
Gas Meter						

PLU4/G/2Y1/23-26, OA

The whole question of workhouse drainage and sewage disposal was considered further in May 1888 after a complaint was made by a neighbour to the Medical Officer of Health that the contents of earth closets had been placed near the piggeries adjoining his garden. (The combination of such smells must have been loathsome to him!)

However, by 1891 the LGB Inspector was calling for a thorough investigation to be made "as to the actual condition of the system of drainage."[1]

By 1894 the LGB Inspector was still concerned about the drains and called attention to "the most unsatisfactory and dangerous state of the drains of the House… I strongly advise the drains of the building should be rearranged and connected with the main drain of the town."[1]

On 15 May 1894 a plan of drainage works was presented which the Guardians desired to carry out at the schools of the Workhouse, following a report by Messrs Smith and Sons, architects, Reading, on the sanitary condition of the schools.

"As there has been an outbreak of diphtheria amongst the children affecting three boys and one girl, the Guardians wish to put the work in hand without delay; do away with the present earth closets and utilising the present building, so far as they will go for new water closets. We do not think it is necessary to have so many seats as at present and we propose to put four water closets for girls and three for boys, and a private water closet for the Master and Mistress respectively. The children's closets to be each separate closet with a partition between. The yard on the boys' side to serve for a urinal."[1]

LGB approved £150 outlay on 8 June and the contract was awarded to Messrs Waldens at £142. Later the Inspector reported:

"The drainage from the schools is about to be reconstructed according to the plans submitted to the Board. From the rest of the Workhouse the drains run, some to the public sewers, some to a tank in the middle of the large garden whence it is percolated into the soil. There are no WCs. The water from the chamber pots is poured on the dunghill by hand. Sinks are disconnected."[1]

Later in the year the Inspector reported:

"I visited the Workhouse on the 12th at night and again on 13th October 1894. The number of inmates was 99. In the infirmary there were 8M + 15F, of whom five are bedridden.

"I call attention to the most unsatisfactory and dangerous state of the drains of the House. During the last week the cookhouse, bathrooms and men's yard have been flooded with urine and other slops from the urinal in the hospital yard, proving the drains are in an imperfect condition and not properly trapped. I strongly advise the drains about the building should be re-arranged and connected with the main drain of the town. Nothing has yet been done except to clear the present drain."[1]

Constant complaints had been made by the LGB Inspector with regard to the sewerage. Charles Smith, Architect of Reading, had consulted with the Architect of LGB as to what he considered necessary, and nothing less would do as regards the proposed drainage works. A letter from LGB pronounced that the state of the drains at Henley Workhouse was not satisfactory and the Board were of the opinion that they should be set right and connected with the sewers of the town. Cost of the whole works and alterations to Board Room would amount to £1,000.[1]

However, the Board of Guardians was about to be re-formed so they prevaricated by giving a situation report on 12 November 1894. "The whole of the sewers at the Union schools have now been connected with the main sewers of the town and the drains to both Workhouse laundry and the Infirmary had been previously connected. There now remains only the drains of the Workhouse (itself) to be connected but there will be considerable outlay in the erection and fitting up of the closets."[1] It was left to the successor body under the new Local Government Act to take the necessary action and outlay.

In 1896 the workhouse had almost reached its final form. The only significant additions were made in 1895, when two-storey turrets to house water closets were added against the west and east faces of the east wing (see page 61), also against the west face of the west wing and against the north face of the Board Room wing. At the same time, the Board room was enlarged to the south with a new facade and improved heating, "as the present room is badly ventilated, too small for the proper seating of the Guardians and in the winter is inadequately warmed".[1] Architect for both schemes was Charles Smith of Reading. By now the dining hall appears to have lost its internal subdivision between the sexes.

The turrets are plain structures of brick; the new front to the Board room has three tall sash windows in a symmetrical arrangement with new entrance lobbies for Board room and for the adjacent clerk's office.[1]

A detailed plan of the workhouse, made in 1895 to show the new closet towers but showing also every other room in the building and indicating their use, is endorsed "generally correct" in 1928 (see page 36).[1]

Meanwhile in June 1895 a resolution was passed authorising the Visiting Committee to make arrangements for one of the disused Women's sleeping wards to be made suitable for a bedroom to be occupied by the Master and Matron in lieu of the apartment which those officers now had and which, in the opinion of the Medical Officer and the Board, was unfit for the Master and Matron to sleep in.

"Their present bedroom is immediately over the cookhouse and to obtain fresh air by means of the window is well nigh impossible, as the laundry is so near and the infirmary windows are close to, not only bringing in discharged air from there but the groans of sufferers are distinctly heard in the night in the Master's room. The Matron has not been in good health for some months and the Doctor attributes to some extent her indifferent health to the position of the bedroom and the circumstances as stated.

"There is very ample accommodation for women at the workhouse and for upwards of 10 years the sleeping ward proposed to be utilised has not been occupied".[1]

In January 1896 the Visiting Committee reported that: "The premises have the disadvantage of being old and this renders difficult the carrying out of the classification of inmates which is so much insisted upon by LGB. Still this has been arranged as far as possible.

The Board Room. Photo by permission of Henley Standard.

"When a system of drainage was adopted by the Town some few years ago it was considered by the Board that the sanitary arrangements of the House were, on the whole, in a fairly good condition and that as there was plenty of land it was not necessary to make a connection with the town sewers. However, opinion that this would have to be done has gained ground and on an outbreak of diphtheria in the Schools in April 1894, a thorough examination of the drains was made.

"It was then found that owing to the shifting nature of the soil, the pipes had, in many cases, given way and it was decided that the removal of the drainage, both of the schools and the house, should be carried out, and that the former should be proceeded with first. This was done at a cost of £193 and in January 1895 a contract for completing the whole scheme was made with Messrs Walden.

"Besides this it was decided to enlarge and improve the Board Room. To meet the cost of the new drainage scheme £1740 was, by consent of LGB, borrowed – to be repaid over 15 years, £75 half-yearly, equivalent to a rate of less than 1/6th of a penny, so that the demand on the ratepayers is an infinitesimal one and cannot be found a burden.

"The Schools, Tramp Wards and lodges are built on land which is the freehold of the Guardians and a scheme has been initiated for the purchase of the Workhouse and the rest of the land which is held in a lease from the Charitable Trustees."[1] But the Charity Trustees decided in October 1896 that they were not in favour of the sale of the freehold to the Guardians of the workhouse and so the Guardians took no further steps at that time.[2]

However, in 1905 there were long discussions in camera about the sale of Townlands from the Charity Trustees to the Board of Guardians. The price was settled at £4104. (Town not allowed to know about any of this).[i]

So hot and cold water was laid on throughout the infirmary at this time. Meanwhile, in late 1901 the schools were converted into infirmaries for 50 beds at a cost of £1000.[3] These wards remained in use until the 1980s.

And so the workhouse remained as such until 1929, when under a change of organisation it came under the aegis of the Public Assistance Institution. The following Table (over the page) gives a plan of how the workhouse was laid out on the ground floor in 1928 towards its demise. Other than the tailor's shop, very little activity now seems to be happening, apart from gardening presumably. Except for the nursery day room (infants now slept with mother?), inmates by now were mainly long-stay, aged, sick or lunatic.

The accommodation at Townlands Hospital was transferred to the National Health Service at its inception in 1948 and remains substantially intact though currently in poor condition.

Now, exciting building work is under way to redevelop the site as a health campus for the 21st century. The listed 1790 workhouse buildings and school will become assisted living accommodation for elderly people but continuing in part their original purpose (on a self-financing basis!).

---

i   John Crocker (ibid).

UNION HOUSE, PLAN OF GROUND FLOOR 1928

Washhouse No. 1	Master & Matron's Dining Room	Lunatics bedroom
No. 2	Men's Day Room No.1	Day room
Staff	Wash basins	Bathroom
Folding Room	Day Room No.2	Board Room
Ironing	Knife room	Waiting room
Boiler House	Tailor's shop	Women's Day Room 1
Nurse's quarters	Vegetable cleaning room	Wash basins
Old Women's Bedroom	Amb ulance	Day Room 2
Bathroom	Oakum	Master & Matron's sitting room
Day Room	Straw	Clerk's & Returning Officer's office
Lavatory	Coal	Lavatory
Pump Room	Paint shop No.1	Strong Room
Disinfection	No.2	Nursery day room
Men's bathroom	Men's Lavatory	scullery
Scullery	Vegetable store	Infirmary
Kitchen	Gas meter	Mortuary
Bread Room	Master's office	Hearse house
Matron's kitchen	Heating boiler	
	Dining Hall	
	Staff quarters	

Oxford Archives
PLU4/G/2M10/1-6 (FWC,2.1.1928)

Artist's impression of the new building.

3. Board of Guardians

GUARDIANS were appointed to oversee the organisation of the workhouse and the welfare of the inmates, according to the regulations laid down and strictly enforced by the Poor Law Commissioners in London under the Poor Law Act of 1834 and by Assistant Commissioners throughout the country to ensure that requirements were adhered to.

The new board of Guardians for Henley held its first meeting on 16 June 1835 having been convened to manage the business of the workhouse with the list of members above.[2] The chair was taken by Thomas Stonor, who became Lord Camoys a few years later, and remained as chairman until 1878. The names immediately beneath his are those of local JPs, who were decreed to be ex officio members of the board,[1] plus a representative of the Poor Law Commissioners in London. There follows the names of the Guardians elected annually by the ratepayers of the 21 parishes in the union, apparently on the basis of one guardian for every thousand of population. At the meeting James Dixon was elected vice-chairman, Mr C H Chapman was appointed clerk at £70 a year; Mr John Dodd Lyall and Mr Nicholas Mercer (a prominent Henley solicitor) became treasurer and auditor respectively, the latter later becoming a long serving clerk to the Board 1839-89[i]; but by 1886 of extreme age, Mr Mercer was criticised by the District Auditor for dilatoriness in making up the General Ledger.[2] Mr Bullock remained an absentee and had to be replaced after he was confined in a lunatic asylum in 1836. In 1847 three Buckinghamshire parishes were added to the union; Fawley, Hambleden and Medmenham (see page 18).

Thomas Stonor, 3rd Lord Camoys, 1797-1881.[ii]

Duties of the Board of Guardians included:

- being responsible to the Poor Law Commission for administration of the workhouse to accord with strict control exercised by them;
- establishing accommodation suitable for classifying the inmates into fixed categories and its maintenance/development.
- supervising the Master in his daily responsibility for ensuring the wellbeing and industry of the inmates and day-to-day finances;
- selecting a suitable diet for inmates from PLC dietary tables;
- financial control via tendering for annual contracts for necessaries;
- appointment of Workhouse officers, including Medical Officers and Relieving Officers;
- setting a Poor rate in £ for Henley Union ratepayers (see page 18);
- setting up committees to oversee workhouse admittances, activities, finances;
- responsibility for children's welfare and schooling;
- relationships with PLC Inspectors and responding to their suggestions/criticisms, etc.

---

i   His resignation in 1889 called for "a deep sense of his long and faithful service rendered during a period of 50 years".[2] He died the same year and is buried in Uxbridge (did he have a connection with Uxbridge Union – see page 105?).

ii By courtesy of the 7th Lord Camoys.

The Guardians began their task by advertising for two relieving officers, who would inspect and assess applicants for relief. They appointed Thomas Hester to cover a district based on Henley and Caversham and Thomas Barnes for one based on Watlington, at a salary of £75 and £80 a year respectively. Three medical officers were also appointed for a year in August 1835: Edward Young of Hart Street, Henley, at £100 a year plus 10s 6d for each birth attended; James Henry Brooks of Henley at £90 (plus midwifery) and Henry Barrett of Watlington at £80 (plus midwifery); they were to be appointed surgeons for Henley and the surrounding parishes of Caversham and Watlington and district respectively.[2]

In September 1834 an enquiry of the Poor Law Commissioners in London by the Watlington Parish Assistant Overseer of the Poor as to how to employ a superabundance of labourers aged 30 to 50 during the coming winter drew their standard reply: that it was "desirable to apply to able-bodied out of a workhouse the same consideration as would be applied within it. They should be employed on farm work only and be paid at a lower rate than the usual market rate of wages of a labourer, as the maintenance and due control of order and discipline is evidently more difficult when the paupers are at large than when in the House."[1] The commissioners were then asked to fix a table of wages or to say at what rate below the norm this large number of able-bodied labourers should be employed. They replied that they had no knowledge but suggested that paupers should be paid in proportion to the value or quantity of work that they did and **not** according to the time spent, nor to the number of their children[1] (as per the recent Speenhamland scheme).

Male	Female

| Waiting Room

Board Room reception | Retiring Closet | Board Room | Private Papers | Strong Closet |
| | | | Clerk's Office | |

To start with, the guardians met weekly but this was reduced to fortnightly in 1867, bearing in mind that some of the rural parish representatives had a journey of 10 miles or more to make by horse for meetings in Henley Union Workhouse. (A later example of the difficulties encountered involved the Revd H Coxe, a representative of Watlington on the Board, who "had a narrow escape in August 1909 when driving his carriage to Henley: near Crabtree Farm his horse stumbled and fell to the ground. Mr Coxe escaped injury and proceeded to the meeting".[3]

During all the years to the 1894 Local Government Act, the constituent members of the Board of Guardians were some 18 farmers and about 6 reverend gentlemen. Long service in addition to Lord Camoys included John Hodges of Bolney Court serving 25 years, of which 13 were in the chair; T N Watts, clothier, served 25 years, with 10 as Vice-chairman; W T Hews, auctioneer, served 21 years (1869-1890); and the Revd George Day, Rector of Brightwell Baldwin, served 17 years as Vice-chairman.

At its first meeting the Board of Guardians promptly appointed a committee of gentlemen to confer with the Henley Corporation on the appropriation of the existing workhouse. The question was whether it should be taken over from them or purchased by agreement. In November 1835 Henley Corporation expressed its willingness to sell the existing workhouse and land at a price to be fixed by two valuers; but subsequently the Corporation leased the building and site to the Guardians at a yearly rent of £80.[1]

After two years of dispute, the Guardians arranged that the existing workhouse be enlarged to accommodate at least 250 paupers and a tender of £2,560 was received for building work, to include a Board Room for meetings, plus a further £1,500 for capital equipment.[1] The new Guardians were fortunate to be able to lease such an appropriate and spacious site and buildings. The original building and later additions still stand as part of Townlands Hospital. "They are well built in red brick in Georgian style and are set in six acres of land".[i]

There was also the regular report by the PLB Inspector to consider. For instance in April 1866 he reported:

"I made the following entry in the Visitor's Book:

Boardroom.

i   "A History of Henley-on-Thames" J.S. Burn, Longman, 1861.

"I inspected this workhouse, which I found to be in its usual orderly and well-managed condition. The general state of the establishment in these respects reflects the highest credit upon those who manage and attend to it. I suggest that means should be provided of enabling the old men the more readily to communicate with the nurse at night in the case of emergency.

"I trust that the Guardians will soon resume the consideration of the question of a separate building for infections and contagious diseases, in which respect this establishment is most defective. The approach of, I am sure, the presence of cholera in this country renders this matter one that urgently calls for attention of the Guardians."[1]

Over the years the duty of the Board of Guardians included enabling the Master to undertake his responsibilities in running Henley Union Workhouse in accordance with the directions from the Poor Law Commission in London. So whereas the guardians were supervising the Master's activities, they in turn were under the eye of a PLC representative, who attended their meetings.

In 1868 this became Mr J J Henley (confusingly), who diligently served for 23 years and was knighted by Queen Victoria on his retirement. A letter of regret at the termination of his long official connections with them was sent by the Board of Guardians.[1] His influence may have tempered some of the directions emanating centrally from the Commissioners in London, to the benefit of local inmates and management.

The Guardians set up various standing committees, e.g. a Visiting Committee with special responsibility for the workhouse, a Finance Committee, an Assessment Committee, a School Committee and a School Attendance Committee. In 1901 a Special Committee was set up to consider re-organisation of the workhouse.

Guardians were responsible for the appointment of all the officers: Medical Officers, Relieving Officers, Clerk, Master and Matron, Schoolmaster/mistress, Gatekeeper and assistant, Nurse, laundress and eventually the industrial trainers (see lists for 1900/1 and 1909/10). Such appointments were under strict control by PLC, which became Poor Law Board in 1847 e.g.

"13 June 1864 PLB have received a report from Inspector Mr Cane from which it appears that persons had been appointed as Schoolmistress, Nurse and laundress at Henley Union who did not hold those offices on the occasion of his previous visit. No report of the resignation of the following officers:

Frances Mills, laundress
Mary Trist, schoolmistress
Mary Ann Hill, nurse"[1]

At each fortnightly meeting the Guardians inspected the Master's day book[i] and they reacted to any highlights and untoward incidents. The Master always presented himself to account for arisings. In particular in 1864 when the Secretary of the PLB in London took him to task over quantities of meat and bread ordered from day to day or 2-3 times per week, PLB quoted Article 200 No. 20 of the Government Consolidation Order: "the House Master is required to submit to the Guardians at every meeting an estimate for such provisions and to receive and execute the directions of the Guardians thereupon".[1]

---

i   Now only 1849-59 remain in Oxford Archives.

In September 1865 the Master reported to the Board of Guardians that five acres of land lately kept by Mr Taylor behind and immediately adjoining the workhouse is now vacant and that the Board had the opportunity of becoming tenants. The Board promptly resolved to take this on for a term of 14 years at an annual rent of £20.[2]

In accordance with their responsibilities, the Guardians continued to issue advertisements annually for local traders to tender for the supplies necessary for the feeding, clothing, cleaning and management of 250 paupers under their control. They also kept an eye on the actual weight delivered and challenged suppliers where necessary.

A detailed list of invoices under their scrutiny in September 1867 at Appendix C, gives an indication of the requirements and expenditure.

August 1867: Resolved that the following tenders for the supply of **Bread** be accepted. All are for a 4 lb loaf:

1. Henley District	6¾d	Mr Sparkes	
2. Caversham	7d	Mrs Leach	
3. Nettlebed	7¼d	Mr Saunders	
4. Shiplake	7¼d	Mr Reeves	
5. Hambleden	7d	Mr Sparkes	
6. Watlington	7d	Mr Norris	

6 August 1867: Invoices

Meat	6½d /lb	Mr Binfield
	5d /lb	(Mr Bullock wef Dec 68)
Baker	£42. 13. 10	
Grocer	£55. 7. 5	
Grocer	£14. 16. 5	
Grocer	£16. 0. 4	
Beer and spirits	£27. 10. 0	
Gas	£ 3. 6. 0	
Leatherseller	£15. 16. 10	
Drapers	£30. 11. 10	
Coal merchant	£13. 0. 0	
Brooms	£ 6. 8. 0	
Brushes (garden)	£ 1. 8. 10	
Butter print	£38. 0. 4	
Lunatic asylum, Littlemore	£206. 9. 6	
Margate Infirmary	£10. 8. 0	
Whitewashing	£24. 4. 9	
Bricklayer	£ 8. 3. 4	
Kinch adverts/stationery	£22. 11. 9	
Garden acct: chemist	3. 0	
Ironmonger	£51. 9. 1	
Ironmonger	£ 3. 13. 0	
Carpenter	£18. 5. 0	
Hairdresser	£ 5. 6. 5	
Sutton seeds	£ 9. 0. 0	

12 May 1868: Profit on Garden account = £44. 7. 7d passed to Common Fund.[i]
Coal contract: Toomer Bros to supply: 70 tons of Kelloe Wallsend coals at 22/3 per ton 50 tons of Aberdare steam coal at 19/4d per ton.

4 August 1868: Non-resident Henley Union Poor being supplied in:[ii]

St Mary Islington	£3. 5. 0
Holborn	£4. 13. 2
Eton	£3. 6. 2
Brentford	
Wycombe	
Greenwich	
Shoreditch	
Uxbridge	
Woolwich	
St Pancras	£ 11. 4. 8
Lunatic Asylum, Dayman, Littlemore	£166. 17. 5d

The Board of Guardians had to maintain vigilance. They had to tighten up the process in September 1867 by resolving "that all the works, repairs and accounts shall be referred by this Board to the Visiting Committee, such committee reporting from time to time to the Board, by whom alone orders for such works and payments shall be made." [2]

In 1868 a complaint was made to the Inspector, Mr Henley, by a pauper about his admission into the workhouse with his family. An order had been given by the Relieving Officer but he was placed in the Vagrant Ward for the night, although having already been examined by the Medical Officer. The PLB called the attention of the Guardians to the irregularity practised by the Workhouse Medical Officer who appeared to examine paupers at his private residence instead of at the workhouse. PLB requested the Guardians to issue directions to prevent this happening. Also to instruct the Master to abstain from placing in vagrant wards any persons not coming within the definition of vagrant or wandering poor.[1]

By March 1869 Mr Henley was calling for better accommodation for the aged, sick and children, as well as better provision for fever cases. The Guardians' attention was called to the state of the Receiving Wards in his previous report and this was now said to be under consideration. However, a year later the Visiting Committee was still drawing attention to "the great want of accommodation for the sick and infirm owing to the increase of the former". Many men and women were said to be keeping to their beds and the accommodation for the sick was unsatisfactory. Three months went by and they were still reporting that the men's infirmary was full.[1]

As outlined in the previous chapter on accommodation, plans for expansion of the workhouse were at last forced on the Guardians in May 1870.

In 1871 the Poor Law Board became the Local Government Board, which imposed new central guidance on Boards of Guardians. This did not alter the Guardians'

---

i It will be noted that here was income generation under way.

ii There were various cases of Henley Union paying for former residents now out of the area, under laws relating to the Settlement Act or those sent to the lunatic asylum.

regular agenda eg in May 1871,[2] routine examination of the Master's day book and his receipt and payment book and special books kept by the Master:

Examined Relieving Officers' outdoor relief lists and receipt and expenditure books.

Ordered payment of amount of invoices.

Cheques credited.

Parish contributions to poor rates.

Master's estimate of provisions etc.

Contracts for provisions accepted.

Payment for non-resident poor in other unions.

Occasional payments of Medical Officers, Vaccination Officers.

Revised balance sheet of the Master, Officers and miscellaneous account for the quarter, eg:

| in maintenance | £116. 9. 11¾d |
| rations | £ 21. 11. 1¾d |

Lord Camoys. Chairman of the Board. 1835-1878.[i]

Under the Public Health Act, in November 1872 the duties of the Board of Guardians had been further extended to encompass a new Rural Sanitary Authority. They decided to meet the statutory requirement to appoint a Sanitary Inspector by giving this title to existing Relieving Officers and paying them an extra £25 a year. However, the PLB wrote that the Board consider it objectionable as the duties of Inspectors of Nuisances (i.e. Sanitary Inspectors) had been very materially increased and it was of great importance that these duties should be discharged in a thoroughly satisfactory manner. PLB also thought that Relieving Officers should concentrate their efforts on efficient administration of relief to the poor. Therefore, the Authority decided to appoint a full-time Sanitary Inspector. On 1 July 1873 Mr George Mattick was appointed at a salary of £150 pa (much in excess of that paid above!) at age 36 and his appointment was renewed annually for more than 30 years.[2]

Cost Figures included in the annual listing in Board of Guardian minutes book for April 1872 are:

Outrelief	£2996 13s 5½d
In-maintenance	£918 9s 6½d
Lunatics	£388 16s 10d
Building repairs	£241 12s 2d
Clothing	£ 72 3s 2½d
Salaries	£571 14s 9d
Rations	£128 0s 0d

---

i   By courtesy of the 7th Lord Camoys.

This is an interesting reflection on the day-to-day expenditure incurred.

In December 1878 the Board of Guardians accepted an estimate from Mr Wilder of £1 10s 0d for the cost of heating the circular tank by means of exhaust from the engine. How green was that at this early date! Two months later the Board took out insurance on the boilers at a cost of £300.[2]

With so much laundry being done in house, the Guardians agreed to place a washing machine and ironing machine in the washhouse "worked by the steam engine used for the well".

The regularity of the work of the Board of Guardians continued as they scrutinised fortnightly the day-to-day working of the House and also reacted to the reports of the PLB Inspector when prevailed upon to do so. In the election of Guardians to the Board in April 1880 there were 8 farmers, 3 clergy in Holy Orders, a woollen draper, auctioneer, land agent, brewer, and 2 "gentlemen". John Fowden Hodges was re-elected Chairman. Attendance at Board meetings at around this time was spasmodic: of 32 members, only 11 attended in April; 9 in January. (See following chapter on Membership).

In May 1881 a long discussion by the Board of Guardians took place upon the letter received by the Clerk from Mr Henley in which he emphasised upon the Board the necessity of being provided with a hospital so that in case of any disease breaking out requiring isolation, the Board would be prepared. Cholera was dreaded as an epidemic. There was at present no case within or near the Town but it was thought wise to be in readiness. The Guardians noted that the difficulty of obtaining a piece of land prevented the Board from moving on the matter at that time.[3]

So in the absence of an infection ward, the Board of Guardians applied to the Local Board of Health in June 1881 for permission to use wards at the workhouse. It was resolved "not to allow the wards to be used as a permanent hospital for the town but that they might be used until such time that the Local Board provided a place of its own." This appears to be a precursor to the Smith isolation hospital which opened in 1892. However, the Local Board of Health did agree to allow them to use the wards at the workhouse in case of any infectious disease occurring.[3]

A new Vaccination Act required Vaccination Officers to be appointed in the communities. With LGB approval, the Guardians originally appointed the Medical Officers to incorporate the task of vaccinating all children against smallpox. In 1886, however, the Guardians' desire to appoint the Relieving Officers to register vaccinations was agreed to by LGB viz "18 October 1886 LGB stated no objection to appointment of Mr George Albert Stone to the office of Relieving Officer for Henley District at £100 pa", also stating that the Board assented to appointment of Mr Benjamin Glass Relieving officer as Vaccination officer for the Watlington Registration Sub-district for a fee of 1/- for each case of successful vaccination registered by him.

"That as regarding the proposed appointments of Messrs Bobin and Stone as Vaccination Officers, the Board will be prepared to consent to their holding that office upon being informed that each of them has entered into an undertaking in writing that he will resign said office if at any time it shall appear to the Board to be undesirable that the offices of Relieving Officer and Vaccination Officer should continue to be held by the same person." [1]

The LGB expressed their regret at the result of the inspection of vaccination in the Union by their Inspector in May. Dr Greswell's report showed that the work of the VOs was not under proper supervision and the Board suggested that the Guardians should appoint a Vaccination Committee who would be able to supervise its performance. The Board trusted that with the new arrangements in force the Vaccination Acts may be carried out satisfactorily and that steps might be taken to secure the vaccination of all unvaccinated children in the Union.

The Guardians ordered that the Clerk obtain from Messrs Bobin & Stone the required undertaking and inform the LGB that the Guardians believe that under the new arrangements the Vaccination Acts would be satisfactorily carried out.[1]

This arrangement seems to have worked satisfactorily because it was not until 1897 that the Inspector, Dr Bulstrode, called to task Joseph Bobin as Vaccination Officer in Caversham. He was said to perform his duties under the Vaccination Acts in a very unsatisfactory manner and, although Mr Bobin said he had made enquiries into cases of default, no such visits were recorded as having been made in 1897. Dr Bulstrode declared that birth sheets were in confusion and other papers were chaotic and he censured the officer very severely. LGB asked the Guardians to obtain a written explanation of the irregularities. Mr Bobin accepted that all charges made were true.

In response, the School Attendance Committee proposed not to re-appoint Mr Bobin as School Attendance Officer in order that he could give more time to vaccination.[1] But by 1899 his replacement, Joseph Painter, was also replaced under re-organisation, as was Benjamin Glass, Relieving Officer of Watlington:

Herbert Foster to cover Caversham, Kidmore End, Eye and Dunsden, Ipsden & Checkendon (aged 24, son of Clerk to the Clerk of Guardians at £75 pa). He promptly resigned in January 1900!
William Arthur Fredk Draper – Brightwell, Britwell Prior, Britwell Salome, Cuxham, Nettlebed, Nuffield, Pishill, Pyrton at £90 (aged 25, ex Schoolmaster).
D Burton – Stonor, Swyncombe & Watlington at £90.[2]

In July 1890 the Guardians had advertised in the Henley Advertiser that they were prepared to let the after-feed of the meadow at the rear of the Union Workhouse from 28 July to 1 January 1891, reserving the right for the workhouse children to use the meadow for an occasional half-holiday. It sounds as if, with far fewer inmates to be put to work (1891 census = 91 total number of all inmates), that the total land-holding was more than enough; and that the children could be let out to play "occasionally".

The reduction in number of inmates was probably due to most of the unemployed poor receiving outrelief by 1900, while mainly the "mentally deficient", the elderly, unmarried mothers and children and vagrants remained in the workhouses.

The Guardians were taken to task in 1891 by the Curator of Henley Cemetery. He asked the Board to give a direction for two handles to be put on each coffin "as it was unsafe without handles to lower a coffin into the graves". This was duly adhered to "at a cost not exceeding 6d"! [3]

In March 1891 the Guardians accepted tenders for the supply of bread, cheese, groceries, oil, meat, milk and coal. Contracts were let at 4¾d x 4 lb seconds loaf; Joints at 5½d per lb (+ 7d/lb for officers, who would get a better grade of meat). One of the

Guardians thought it "monstrous" that 5½d/lb was to be paid for joints, compared with 3¾d in Reading Union. The Master explained that the meat supplied consisted of clods and stickings but the bone was removed. They had sides of mutton for the infirmary. It was not what could be called "offal meat" it was very good meat. About 70lb was for the officers' table and 190lb for the inmates.[3]

Yet in December 1881 tenders had been accepted at 6 – 6½d for bread and 7½d for meat.[3] Mr Grove, Guardian, said he would prefer that **best** bread be supplied to the inmates if it was the chief thing upon which they were fed. This expensive suggestion was referred back.[3]

The coal tender at 21s and 25s was considered to be too high so it was decided to buy in small quantities.[3]

The following year showed the list of tenders being accepted as; bread at 4¼ – 4¾d; milk at 1s/gallon; meat at 5½d for inmates and 7½d for officers; grocery contract to Mr Neighbour (a Guardian); cheese, brooms, brushes and oils let to Mr Hodges (a Guardian); linen drapery etc to Atkinson Co.

By March 1904 sacks of flour were being purchased at 21s per sack in addition to the 4lb loaves at 4½d.[3]

The Guardians resolved in May 1890 to receive from Reading Union 30 males and 20 females at 6s 6d per week, provided that only a fair proportion of them were sick and infirm. Reading Union had about 70 people to place out for at least a year (not evident in the 1891 census return).

The last meeting of that Board of Guardians was held in April 1891 but there were very few changes in the elected new Board. These amounted to a reduction to only 1 member for Caversham and 1 for Greys.

The existing Guardians stated that they had been a happy family for many years. No qualification at all had been needed but now a £5 (rateable) qualification was being introduced.[3]

In August 1893 the new Board of Guardians petitioned Parliament and the Local Government Board regarding the Local Government Bill before Parliament affecting the position, constitution and duties of existing Boards of Guardians. They felt strongly that, while recognising in it a desire to deal in a liberal and comprehensive manner with the question of local government, they regretted to observe a general tendency throughout to subordinate Boards of Guardians to more recently created bodies to make the candidate's experience and qualifications for Poor Law administration of quite secondary importance [3] (see paragraph above "no qualifications at all had been needed").

The Guardians continued that while having regard to the recent considerable reduction in the rating qualifications for the office of Guardians or Petitioners, they did see some advantages in the entire abolition of a rating qualification but they were strongly of the opinion that it should be an important requisite for a candidate for election to be at least resident in the Parish or Union which he sought to represent.[3]

Nevertheless, the 1894 Act, in reducing the rating qualification, reflected the Liberal Government's attempt to take some of the administration of the countryside out of the hands of the landed gentry, who had always held a tight grip[i]. Emmeline

---

i   "Henley Rural" Brian Read, ELSP, 2003.

Pankhurst in 1895 condemned the old guard by saying that the Boards of Guardians had been made up of the kind of men known as "rate savers"; they were guardians not of the poor but of the rates! Even after the Board was reconstituted in 1895, the Henley Board of Guardians continued with property owners and relatively well-off farmers.[i] Brewer, George Brakspear, formerly Vice-chairman, became Chairman of the new body until his resignation in 1901 due to ill health.

Back to 1894, and in August the Board of Guardians were now concerned about the proposed transfer of Remenham to Wokingham Union (being on the Berkshire side of the River). This was opposed because it was felt that the ratepayers of Henley Union would be compelled to provide medical and Poor Law relief for the non-resident labouring classes of Remenham without receiving any contribution for the expenses incurred.[3] But a month later the LGB decided there were not sufficient grounds for refusing to confirm the Order of the Joint Committee to transfer Remenham to Wokingham Union.[3]

In 1893 Boards of Guardians were empowered to appoint a committee of ladies to visit parts of the workhouse where families were employed. However, the Henley Board did not consider the new Order was likely to affect **their** workhouse (my emphasis), although eventually in 1907 the Revd J W Nutt proposed that a committee of ladies be appointed.[3]

Tramps were a continual problem to the Guardians, see page 153, and in 1894 it was resolved that in view of the increase of tramps throughout the country and the unsatisfactory result arising from their different treatment in different Unions, the LGB be invited to hold a public inquiry, with a view to some General Tramps Order for universal adoption.[3]

Recruitment and retention of staff remained a problem for the Board. For instance, in 1896 Henley Guardians reported, "Subordinate officers have, on the whole, worked well, but several changes have taken place and the committee have found considerable difficulty in filling vacancies that have occurred." This appears to be the experience of nearly all Boards of Guardians. Possibly the confining and somewhat monotonous nature of the duties to be performed furnish the explanation.[3]

Some of the Guardians had demurred at the time of the appointment of their Clerk (Arthur Lloyds) to replace Nicholas Mercer in 1889, thinking that he was too young, but they now stated that he had not been found wanting in his duties. He went on to serve the Board until 1926.[ii] By 1901 he had extended his remit and amassed a salary of £400 pa, made up as follows:

Clerk to the Guardians	£ 160
Assessment Committee	£ 56
School Attendance Committee	£ 20
Henley Rural District Council	£ 110
Hambleden Rural District Council	£ 35
Smith Hospital Committee	£ 25

i   "Henley Rural", Brian Read, ELSP, 2003.

ii   Notably only two Clerks served between 1839-1926.

Union Year Book – Officers of the Board

1900-1901	Description	Residence	App.	1909-1910
A R Lloyds	Clerk	Henley	1889	A R Lloyds
	Treasurer	do	1874	John Simonds
Revd W Chapman	Chaplain	do	1906	Revd C Sadler
J A Riggs	Medical Officer	do	1901	A E Peake
W H Coates	do	Hambleden	1908	A S Wilson
W H Macpherson	do	Greys	1896	W H Macpherson
E Deane	do	Caversham	1907	G H Cheyney
E I Day	do	Nettlebed	1905	J M Pooley
W Winslow	do	Watlington	1904	T A Hawkesworth
G A Stone	Relieving Officer	Henley	1899	H Foster
W Draper	do	Watlington	1902	A S Stone
H Foster	do	Caversham	1907	J Raymond
G B Simmons	Master	Union Workhouse	1906	R Hodgkinson
Mrs M E Simmons	Matron	do	1906	K Hodgkinson
J Long	Gate Porter			
	& Labour Officer	do	1901	E N Knight
Mrs Long	Porteress	do	1901	Emily Knight
W Edgecombe	House Porter	do	1907	S Mason
Miss Webster	Nurse	do	1901	Mary Robb
D Bain	Stoker	do	1909	W Kirk
Mrs Edgecombe	Laundress	Henley		Day Officer
Miss Garlick	Girls' Trainer	Union Workhouse		
	Infirmary Attendant	do	1908	L Hemming
	do	Henley	1909	L Stockbridge
	Tailor	do	1908	George Badnell
	Foster Mother	Radnor House,		
		Henley	1906	Mary Jane Cleary

The census of 1901 shows that there were still only 91 inmates in the workhouse designed for 250, a continuing trend over the previous ten years. However, Mr R Ovey, now Chairman of the Board of Guardians, felt it undesirable to move the workhouse buildings from the present site. The lease for the land on which the workhouse stood had 35 years to run. Furthermore, the Board should adopt the "scattered homes" system for the children at present in the workhouse and the present schools should be converted into an infirmary, as the present one was now very unsuitable. Three houses would have to be taken, one for boys under 12; one for girls under 12 and one for infants. A sick room would have to be provided in each of these.[3]

Later that year, 1901, the purchase of the leasehold portion of the workhouse (i.e. not that part facing West Hill previously donated by Mr Hodges) was considered in camera by Henley Borough Corporation.[3]

Meanwhile, the inmates' needs still had to be met and tenders continued for meat and flour. In June 1901 these were required for "good seconds bread not more than 12 hours old to be delivered in loaves of 4lb each at the Workhouse and at such places in any or all of the Parishes at such time as the Master or Relieving Officer shall direct" (as out-relief).[3]

Whatever the changes decreed from LGB, long service by Guardians continued into the new century. For instance, in March 1904 Mr T Allnutt, a farmer, and Mr W Wiggins withdrew as Watlington representatives, Mr Allnutt having served 45 years (succeeding his father, Zachariah) and Mr Wiggins for 35 years. Mr W Hews, an auctioneer, had served 21 years when he died in 1890.[3] During his service Mr Allnutt had ridden 400 miles to and from meetings in Henley (including Henley Rural District Council).

Keeping down the rates continued to play a part in Guardians' agendas, such as the complaint made by the Board of Guardians in March 1904 about non-enforcement by the Police of their warrants issued against persons for non-payment of maintenance arrears towards the cost of inmates.[3]

The population of Reading was expanding and in February 1909 Reading Corporation made an application to LGB to extend their borough boundaries. Henley Guardians felt that the resultant LGB inquiry was of great importance to the ratepayers of Henley Union, seen as an attempt to take over Caversham, a valuable area for rating purposes. Oxfordshire County Council also strongly opposed this application.[3] But this eventually happened on 1 April 1914, with compensation payments by Reading Union of £500 p.a.

It is noteworthy to read a Henley Standard report in 1904 that "whatever is said of the Henley Board of Guardians and Rural District Council as public bodies, it cannot be argued against them that they do things rashly and in a hurry. On the contrary, they are prone to consider a question involving any considerable expenditure to themselves at unconscionable length".

This attitude appears to have continued. For example, in February 1923 the Guardians reported an enormous increase in the cost of public assistance against pre-war national figures: cuts were urged! [3]

The Local Government Act 1929 finally changed the old Poor Law administration of 1834, with its workhouses and relieving officers, and gave responsibility for what was now called "public assistance" to the County Councils. This change eventually culminated in the "welfare state" of 1948.

Meanwhile, The Board of Guardians continued to administer the workhouse until April 1930. At the penultimate annual meeting in 1929, Joshua Watts was re-elected as Chairman ("the last occasion on which to place him in the chair before the 'funeral' next year"). Mr Lett succeeded Lord Phillimore as Vice-chairman; and by now the Board included four women, Miss Cooper having been elected 24 years previously and still in place as chairman of the House Committee in 1931, (she was the daughter of the Town Clerk). At that time she said that some board members of the House had <u>not</u> been pleased at the introduction of a woman on the Board but since then her presence had been tolerated.

It was reported at this meeting that casuals again showed an increase: 997 males + 2 females + 10 children = 1,094 compared with 1,023 the previous month and 889 last year. By 1930 the figures were 1,105, made up of 1,022 men and (noticeably) 66 women and 17 children.[3]

Expressions of thanks and goodwill were given at the final meeting of the Henley Board of Guardians, which ceased to exist as from March 31st, 1930. An inventory, last taken 26 years ago, was necessary pending the handing over of the Institution under the new Public Assistance Act. Acting on the instructions of the County Council, an agreement was made to continue to rent Radnor House for children's accommodation for one year at £75.[3]

Mr and Mrs F W Cave were to continue as Master and Matron, having completed 20 years' service. The extraordinary kindness of the Matron was noted and "the Master, although his duties were arduous and required a firm hand, had carried out his duties in a most satisfactory manner", according to the Vice-chairman.[3]

Mr Watts, the Chairman, gave a valedictory statement, saying they had now come to the parting of the ways, the old order changeth and they had to give place to the new. Personally, he had 35 years' experience

Joshua Watts.

of Boards of Guardians and still felt himself a child in the administration of the Poor Law. On the new committee would be members who had had no previous experience, while there would be many old members who he hoped would be proper colleagues in the work they had to carry out.[3]

At the conclusion of business, the Union Jack which always floated from the flag pole on Board days, was lowered to half mast.[3]

4. Membership of Henley Union Board of Guardians

THE FIRST list of guardians in June 1835 is shown on page 37. Guardians from the Parishes were elected annually but there was little competition over the years to be elected a guardian. As an example, election results in April 1857 for Guardians showed four elected from five in Henley: William Dobson 199; Thomas Riggs 205; Richard Taylor 163; Thomas Watts 177; and not Henry Green 108. In Rotherfield Greys the Revd James Smith and Thomas Horner were elected in preference to William Reeves of Highmoor. Ex officio members consisted of Justices of the Peace, local landowners until 1894 and included a representative from the Poor Law Commission.

As will be seen from the listing for 1868, of the 32 elected members there were 17 farmers and six reverend gentlemen representing what had now become 24 parishes.

Board of Guardians of Henley Union April 21, 1868

At the first meeting of the new Board of Guardians, the Clerk laid before them the following list of elected Guardians for the ensuing year:

Bix	Farmer, Rocky Lane Farm	Mr Edmund Whitefield A'Bear
Brightwell	Clerk	Revd George Day
Britwell Prior	Farmer	Mr Thomas William Hicks
Britwell Salome	Clerk	Revd James Thomas Jackson
Caversham	Clerk	Revd Joshua Bennett
	Kidmore End, Farmer	Mr Thomas Green
Checkendon	Bottom Farm, Farmer	Mr George Collett
Cuxham	Manor Farm, Farmer	Mr Robert Palmer
Eye and Dunsden	Bishopslands, Farmer	Mr William Pottinger
Fawley	Clerk	Revd Henry Almack DD
Hambleden	Huttons Farm, Farmer	Mr T Deane
	Clerk	Revd William Henry Ridley
Harpsden	Clerk	Revd Frederic Bagot DCL
Henley	Bell Street Clothier	Messrs Thos Nathanial Watts,
	Bell Street Tailor	Henry Toovey,
	Solicitor	John Southerden Burn
	Surrey Lodge, Gentleman	Charles Lucey
Ipsden	Hall Place, Farmer	Mr James Richens
Medmenham	States Farm, Farmer	Mr William Hobbs

Nettlebed	Soundess House, Esquire	Mr William Gardner Cornwall
Nuffield	Mays Farm, Farmer	Mr Alfred Speck
Pishill	Pishill Farm, Farmer	Mr Silas Lovegrove Pyrton
Pyrton	Pyrton Farm, Farmer	Mr Alfred Cooper and
	Stonor Farm, Farmer	Mr James Thomas Wells
Remenham	Remenham Hill, Gentleman	Mr Charles Plumbe
Rotherfield Greys	Coldharbour, Farmer	Mr Alfred Piercy and
		Mr Edward John Plummer
Rotherfield Peppard	Cowfields Farm, Farmer	Mr Charles Langford
Shiplake	The Mills, Paper-maker	Mr William Edward Saker
Swyncombe	Park Corner, Farmer	Mr George Griffiths Dixon
Watlington	Watlington Farm, Farmer	Thomas Alexander Alnutt
		and Mr Moses Wiggins

There was no change of membership in 1869 (See Appendix D). In fact, annual election of parish guardians usually resulted in few changes (some guardians even being replaced by their sons, e.g. Moses Wiggins 1835-1869 by William, still there in 1893, and the Deane family, Hambleden farmers 1868-1890).

However the election in 1871 resulted in 10 changes, with 3 sons of farmers replacing their fathers. Lord Camoys continued in the chair but the Revd George Day of Britwell retired as Vice-chairman because of illness and was replaced by Thomas Watts of Henley.

The Election of Guardians in April 1874 resulted in some changes: [2]

Britwell Prior	John Stevens replaced H Cooper
Caversham	Stevenson Saunders replaced Fred Oslam
Checkendon	H Moase replaced Revd C Abbey
Nettlebed	H Cook replaced L Glasspool
Nuffield	John Marshall replaced Alfred Wells
Pyrton	Edward Hammersley replaced Alfred Cooper
Rotherfield Peppard	Revd Williams replaced Charles Langford

Many guardians put in years of long service as guardians. Charles Lucey Esq served at least from 1868-1884 and farmer Charles Langford 1861-1874. Henley clothier Thomas Watts served from 1858 until his death after 25 years "as a zealous and active member", with 10 years as Vice-chairman.

The Reading Mercury reported that "The public should think about things and act on their convictions rather than leaving the whole thing to take its chance and making the election of our Guardians a sham and a mockery ... and see the great danger of Local Government that is not constantly reinforced and reinvigorated by public opinion and criticism."

Following the formation of a new Local Government Board in 1884, the Henley Union then consisted of the members and officers as listed in Appendix D.

Once again in 1886 there was no contest as such the four guardians for the town of Henley were Messrs G E Brakspear, C Lucey, W Plumbe and W Hews. The only changes in representation were:

Bix   Mr Henry Lillywhite in place of Mr Gutteridge
Fawley   Rev A H Fairbairn in place of Dr Almack (deceased)
Rotherfield Greys   Mr G T Ingram
Swyncombe   Mr E Sarney instead of Mr G Dixon (deceased)

At the first meeting of the new Board, J F Hodges was elected Chairman and G E Brakspear Vice-Chairman; nominations were made to the Finance Committee, Garden Committee, Assessment Committee and School Attendance Committee.

Attendance in 1888

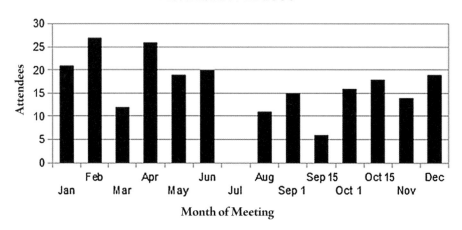

Attendance in 1889

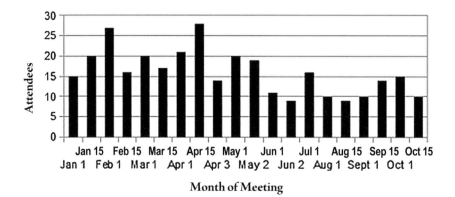

Note the effect of (a) nominations for a new Board of Guardians in February; (b) first meeting of the re-elected Board in April; (c) the absence of farmer Guardians in August at harvest time and also in early September.

No contest in 1888 but in 1889 there were elections in Henley (4 elected from 8 nominated) and also in Rotherfield Greys where a grocer and a builder replaced the Revd North Pindar temporarily.

Nominations for election were made at February meetings of the Board, which was always well attended! Otherwise, attendance fluctuated after high attendance at the initial April meeting (see attendance record for 1888-1889).

By 1890 a whole new set of Guardians appeared, with only seven of the originals retained.

Note the following four deaths occurring while in office 1891-2. In 1892 a gentleman of Caxton Terrace, Henley, George Walton Turner "refused to serve". In that year William Moffatt, a farmer, was appointed to fill the vacancy for Cuxham.

1890

Bix	Middle Assendon	Farmer	Henry Lillywhite
Brightwell	Pyrton Vicarage	Clerk	Revd Hillgrove Coxe
Britwell Prior/		Farmer	James Prowse Franklin
Britwell cum Sotwell			
Caversham	Vicarage	Clerk	Revd Arthur Molineux
	Dean Farm	Farmer	Walter James Henman
	Kidmore Farm	Farmer	Richard Hall d Mar 91
Checkendon Cuxham	Little Stoke	Farmer	Wm Charles Dodd
Eye and Dunsden	Rowe Lane Farm	Farmer	Thomas Wm Armstrong d Dec 91
Fawley	Rectory	Clerk	Revd William Afric Tanner
Hambleden	Mill End	Miller	Charles James Barnett
	Hayden Farm	Farmer	Louis Wm Francis Deane
Harpsden	Rectory	Clerk	Revd Frederic Bagot d Dec 91
Henley	Hart Street	Auctioneer	Wm Thos Hews d Oct 92 after 21 years
	Copse Hill, Greys	Brewer	Geo Edward Brakspear
	West Hill House	Brewer	Fredk Herbert Holmes
	Hart Street	Grocer	Alexander Groves
	Reading Road	Gent	Edmund Chamberlain jnr
Ipsden			
Medmenham	Bockmer Farm	Farmer	Philip Hobbs
Nettlebed	Vicarage	Clerk	Revd Henry Algernon Baumgartner
Nuffield	Haydon Farm	Farmer	John Willis
Pishill			John Grove
Pyrton	Stonor Farm	Farmer	James Thomas Wells
	Clare Farm	Farmer	William Rost
	Tetsworth		
Remenham	Willminster Cottage	Estate Agent	William Simonds
Rotherfield Greys	Reading Rd	Gent	Edmund Chamberlain

Rotherfield Peppard	Clacks Farm Kingwood	Farmer	J Hampton
Shiplake	Shiplake Mills	Paper Mfr	Theophilis Neighbour
Swyncombe	Park Corner	Retd Farmer	Elijah Sarney
Watlington		Farmer	Thos Alexander Allnutt
		Farmer	William Wiggins

In April 1893 five candidates were nominated to the Board, viz. G Brakspear, Vice-chairman; F H Holmes; A Groves; H Crocker (shoe-repairer); E Rawlins. Parish representatives now included:

Britwell Salome/Britwell Prior	Revd J Willis
Kidmore End	Revd J Smith Masters
Hambleden	Edwin West of Frieth in place of J Deane
Harpsden	Revd J Nutt
Ipsden	Mr Hatt for Mr Ramsbottom Rotherfield
Peppard	E Williams

The following members retired in December 1894 after many years' service: J Wells, Canon Pindar, E Sarney.

In 1896 Pyrton Parish was divided into two parishes, Pyrton, Pyrton and Stonor, thereby resulting in two Guardians being elected.

With the poor rate being levied at so much in the £, there was doubtless an incentive for the landed guardians to keep down the costs of running the institution except for the minimum conditions set by the Poor Law Board. However, Henley Union was considered to be largely benign rather than venal, although H Crocker (elected 1893) did resign in protest at one stage.

In August 1897 QC's opinion had to be sought on the Board of Guardians' disqualification of Mr D Lidderdale. They wished to make void any proceedings in which he may take part based on his not making his declaration within one month of election.

By 1900 Kelly's Directory gave the listing of elected guardians for Henley Rural District shown in Appendix D.

Then in 1913 the Henley Standard reported that the Henley Guardians election was not, apparently, arousing much interest, except in the case of Swyncombe, where there may be a contest, no opposition being offered to the retiring members, all of whom sought re-election.

"Only in Swyncombe was there likely to be a contest, the Revd C A K Irwin having been nominated in addition to the retiring member. If the election were to take place, it would only indicate the feelings of admiration which each candidate's fitness for the position had inspired, for each had proposed the other!"

During WW1 it was business as usual on a fortnightly basis. Mr Neighbour had become Chairman and there were nine in attendance in January 1916. (106 persons in the House).

However by 1931, after establishment of Public Assistance institutions, Henley Town Council reported that members were unwilling to serve on the Guardians Committee (five members). The Deputy Mayor said it seemed by this that people elected to the old body had now no desire to serve, not being publicly elected, as the whole thing lacked interest from every point of view. There was difficulty up and down the country to get people to serve as the status of members was so diametrically opposed to what it used to be and the principle was wrong. A Councillor said the difficulty was that they did not know the needs of the poor people in Wallingford District and the people who came from that District did not know the needs of people living in Henley. It was felt that the Guardians Committee was not invested with any powers and could only make recommendations.[3]

Nevertheless, after the formation of Henley area Guardians Committee in 1931 comprising the former Union area of Henley, the Oxfordshire parishes and also Wallingford, members were nominated by Borough and District Councils.

In 1938 these consisted of:
Henley Borough Council 5
Henley Rural District Council 9
Oxfordshire County Council 7 (representing "County electoral divisions")
OCC, not being elected members of Council 11 (including Miss J Cooper since 1905)

The Committee continued to meet monthly until re-organisation in 1948.

5. The Master

WHEN HENLEY'S Poor House was placed in New Street in 1727, 20 rules of procedure and responsibilities for the Master and Mistress were laid down.[i]

These were presumably brought forward when the New Poor Law was enacted in 1834, coinciding with most of the new rules for guidance of Master & Mistress laid down by PLC in September 1834, viz.

> To Keep a book containing alphabetical list of all paupers and their families removed to/from the Parish, together with Orders for Removal;
>
> Keep a book of accounts with cost of labour, showing profit and loss; Keep a book of accounts with cost/sale/weight of Pigs
>
> See the Roots are properly stacked and measured and shall superintend splitting thereof;
>
> Stock-check half-yearly;
>
> See all workmen on/off premises and be workmanlike; etc.

Early on in 1776 there were complaints from Churchwardens and Overseers that the incumbent warden had broken his Articles in many instances and particularly: not keeping clean the poor in the workhouse; and in not teaching the poor any letters and accounts; and in not saying grace before meals; and in not reading prayers or attending church with them:

"We found that Bawtree is a very improper person to continue" and he was discharged. It was agreed that Richard Grey and his wife look after the Poor. But by 1789 Thomas Hornsby was appointed "to farm the Poor" at the same wage.

He had come from Surrey and was contracted for three years at a public meeting in Henley by the Overseers of the Poor for the following: "at his own proper costs and charges in the Workhouse in New Street, and elsewhere if so ordered by the Overseers and/or Churchwardens, to provide such poor people as shall be lawfully entitled to receive relief and maintenance from the Parish, sufficient lodging, meat, drink, medicines and employment etc; also at his own costs pay, bear and defray such expenses incurred in taking examination of paupers, orders of removal, orders of bastardy etc except for trials and litigations at Quarter Sessions". So, for offloading their duties to the poor of the Parish, the Select Vestry would pay Thos Hornsby the

---

i   John Crocker's papers lodged in Henley Archaeological and Historical Group archives, Henley Town Hall.

sum of £800 a year. For this commitment, Thomas Hornsby would have the proceeds of the Poor House work, labour and services.[i]

However, the 3-year term was not completed because upon the opening of the workhouse at the Town lands in May 1790, Thomas Windows and his wife were confirmed as Master and Mistress of the Poor House at £25 a quarter and allowed to keep 10% of the inmates' earnings.[i]

Thereafter, life in the workhouse continued according to the rules laid down for Masters and Mistresses as amended in 1799 (see table below), and those adopted for controlling the poor in the Poorhouse (see page 70). Thus, in September 1795 an inmate, William Young, was turned out for disorderly behaviour and not conforming to the rules of the House.[i]

By early 1797 Mr Windows himself was ordered to leave the House. Perhaps this was on account of allowing the children to work for Mr Orme & Son (a previous Vestry Committee member) and for Mr Matthews: they were ordered in January 1797 that the children do leave their work at 7 o'clock in the evening. There followed a complete ban on boys and girls being let out to hire from the House without the consent of the Committee and that no boy or girl under 8 years of age be let out at less than 18d per week each and when turned of 8 years not less than 20d per week.[i] (Child labour laws not yet introduced).

Rules for Masters and Mistresses 1727

To summon the Poor by bell half an hour before divine service and to conduct them thither.

To ring a bell half an hour before the hour of work and before meals.

To always be at meals and to say grace.

To keep exact account of all earnings in the House;

To receive the money and to pay the encouragement money, and they shall employ any number of the Poor to work in the garden, to clean the house, to prepare victuals and to bake and brew or any other work about the house.

To attend to Rule 9 for the Poor as to spirituous liquor or smoking;

To keep front gates locked and not to let the Poor out except on necessary occasions; and to see they return.

To keep account to all who are admitted and by whose order, to take account of clothes and property and to ticket the same; also to those who are discharged from the House.

Not to admit any visitor without a written order.

To keep the provision book entered up every day, specifying quantities used and stock in hand. Never to receive any article with a bill of parcels and to examine and weigh all goods sent to the House.

---

i   John Crocker (ibid).

Be particular about cleanliness, see the children combed and washed each day, cause all beds to be made before noon, and all useful rooms to be swept every day and washed twice a week in summer and once in winter, and to see that bedrooms are kept open at all proper times.

To see all Poor in bed by 9 o'clock and all fires and candles are put out.

To read the rules to the Poor each Sunday after dinner.

A minute book to be kept of all offences against the rules.

No repairs to be done except on order of the Select Vestry, nor must any perquisites or gratuities be accepted from any source of the poor, or from any visitor on pain of being discharged.

To attend appropriately any sick or infirm to see that they are attended by an apothecary or surgeon, and that they conform to his directions, and to keep the new admittances from the rest until they have been examined by the surgeon.

That the Mistress shall have two girls constantly in the kitchen to learn household employment, the eldest to have preference until they are ready to take outside work.

To have all linen marked with permanent ink.

To cause all children to attend school each day. To be employed in no other business.

To adhere to the dietary table.

So in 1798 John Whiteacre (or "Whidiker") and his wife were appointed to act as Master and Mistress of the Workhouse at 22 guineas a quarter, to which was added one shilling per week for beer.[3]

In November 1799 the Vestry considered the current difficulty of the poor and decided to afford them some extraordinary relief, even if resulting in an increase of the poor rates. At the same time a committee was formed to plan for the better and more economical regulation of the House. For a start, it appeared that the method of supplying the House with necessaries by contracts had been given up, much to the disadvantage of the parish. They therefore ordered that, in future, contracts be made for flour, meat, cheese, butter, soap, candles etc as formerly and that the Master of the House deliver to the Committee every Wednesday night a list of all the articles wanted the succeeding week.

Only three weeks later the conduct of John Whidiker, the Master, was brought into question by the Committee for having "ordered from Mr Bullock a leg of veal at 7d per lb without order of leave from any of the officers. The same being charged to and paid by the Overseers was extremely unbecoming, knowing of falsehood, endeavoured to deceive the Committee". The Committee resolved unanimously that John Whidiker and his wife be immediately discharged.[i]

As an interim measure, it was agreed to employ a Committee Member, John Ilton, as Master of the Workhouse. A new Master and Mistress of the Poor House were appointed in 1821 and considerable saving arose from the system where everyone in the Poor House had to do such work as their respective age and ability would permit. Encouragement money was paid to every man who earned 4s 6d per week and to every woman earning 3s per week.

---

i   Henley Borough Records C111 Select Vestry Book BOR 3/C/V/PW/12b.

When the New Poor Law was instituted in 1834, William Jackson was in office as Master, having previously been a member of Henley Select Vestry. His wife, Martha, acted as Matron and, in the 1841 census they were both recorded as 55 years of age.

That same year they were authorised by the Board of Guardians not only to supply the person who cleaned the tramps a little beer and tobacco as extra allowance but also to take into consideration the washerwoman in the House. The Board considered the difficulty of the washing done in the winter months and ordered that each person so engaged "be allowed such quantity of beer not exceeding a pint per head per day as the Master at his discretion shall think necessary." (Nowadays we should bear in mind that beer was more potable than well water).

The next incumbent was Samuel Mortlock, an important, long-serving Master. Those who came under his jurisdiction can be considered fortunate in having such a largely benign administrator in place. For 36 years he was the kingpin in the operation of the workhouse. He must have worked 24 hours a day and 365 days a year (24/7 in modern parlance), being responsible for feeding, clothing and keeping occupied as many as 350 inmates in his care, ranging from orphaned infants to old and sick. He was in charge when Henley Workhouse was at its peak in numbers. His service is dealt with in detail in the next chapter.

After Samuel's death in 1884 the Matron, Mrs Eliza Mortlock, asked if she could continue as Matron.[1] This was most unusual as it meant that the new Master had to be single. Steward of Infirmary, Mr Henry Dominy aged 30, fitted the bill and took over in 1885. But this arrangement did not work out and by October 1885 Eliza Mortlock resigned, after 19 years' service. Much respected, she died from English cholera in Twyford in October 1891 aged 64.[3] Mr Dominy was replaced in December 1885 by Mr and Mrs John Martin. One can imagine the changes that were to take place after 36 years under Mr Mortlock.

The Master's accommodation alongside the dining room to the right.

John Martin seems to have been "a new broom" and oversaw a dramatic reduction in the number of inmates, particularly schoolchildren. Mr Mortlock's death also seems to have precipitated the departure of some members of staff, eg Mr and Mrs White, school teachers after 9 years service and, perhaps coincidentally, the Relieving Officer for Caversham, William Leach, after 20 years (replaced by Joseph Bobin). In November 1885 The Relieving Officer for Henley, W S Harding, also resigned.

Problems ensued: for instance, by May 1887 the Master wrote about an alleged assault by him on an inmate, Edward Wiltshire.[3] "In reply to a summons issued against me by Edward Wiltshire, said to have been committed on 17 January last, I attended before the Henley Bench of Magistrates on 25th ult. After hearing the evidence of Wiltshire, Jerome (an inmate), Dr Baines, the Gate-porter and a statement from myself, the magistrates proceeded to lecture me with reference to rumour and idle gossip they had heard. I was told I should be very careful in dealing with old men of Wiltshire's description; they had heard I was very harsh in dealing with old people.

"If such was the case, I was informed that I was not required to offer any explanation or statement in reference to the accusation. I informed the Bench that so far as I was concerned any ratepayer was at perfect liberty to visit the House and see the inmates separately with a view to find where the harshness was.

"The Mayor stated that a complaint had been made to him that I had hustled a young woman out of the House who had come to visit her sister. I informed him that the person he referred to refused to have her bag searched and had prohibited articles in it and that it was competent for me to write to the Board of Guardians on the subject. I was further told that old man Jerome knew more than he had told them but he was afraid to speak. I had five witnesses present: two only were called. The case was then dismissed.

"I would respectfully draw attention to the fact that I was summoned to answer a charge of assault. This having failed, I was taunted in open court with reference to matters foreign to the case, and reflections were made as to the manner in which I performed my duties as Master of the House. The old man Jerome, called by Wiltshire, corroborated the evidence given by the porter but has since said that he knew nothing about the matter and did not know that Wiltshire was going to call upon him. He has also pointed where he was standing and it is quite impossible for him to have seen anything that took place."

The Master continued,

"As this is a matter which not only concerns me but, in my opinion affects the Board also, I feel bound to report the magistrates' observations to me, especially as the charge was reported in my Journal on 8 February last and was then investigated by the Board."

Sgd J Martin, Master.

There was condemnation by the Board of Guardians who expressed in the strongest manner the action of those local magistrates who had taken upon themselves to publicly charge the Master of this Union with cruelty to its inmates and administer to him an unwarrantable rebuke, and it further expressed its entire approval of the manner in which the Master's duties were performed.[3]

So the Guardians stood by him borne out by the Inspector's report in January 1896 that the general condition and discipline of the House has been satisfactory and to acknowledge that this state of things was due to the faithful and excellent way in which the Master and Matron have carried out their duties.

However, in due course, unfortunately for John Martin, his wife, Sarah had to resign as Matron in February 1900 due to ill health ("nervous prostration due to overwork"). Mr Martin was obliged to cease to hold the office of master under provisions of the 1879 General Order appointing Master **plus** Matron. It was recorded that "the Master and Matron have been good officers" during their 19 years of service.[1]

Two months later George Simmonds was appointed Master, aged 31 and ex Master of Bingham Workhouse, Notts. His wife, Mary, accompanied him as Matron.[1]

In October 1901 one of the Guardians, Mr Watts, proposed that salaries of Master and Matron be increased from £65 to £75 pa and from £35 to £45 pa respectively. He said that in Mr and Mrs Simmonds they had good, kind and efficient officers with whom he would be very sorry to part. Their work had greatly increased owing to the new dietary table and, currently, the Matron received no higher salary than the Nurse. At the present time there were no able-bodied paupers in the house and this gave the officers more to attend to. The Guardians had paid Mr and Mrs Martin £130 pa and the salaries of their present Master and Matron only came to £100.

Opposing, Mr Brakspear said that in 1886 the salaries of the entire staff amounted to £391 and there were then 116 inmates; in 1901 the salaries amounted to £442 and there were now 91 inmates; in 1886 the children were taught at the workhouse and now they attended the National schools. The Chairman said it was contemplated shortly to board the children out of the workhouse. The resolution was lost.[3]

Subsequently, after Mr and Mrs Simmonds transferred to Reading Union Workhouse, they were removed from there in 1907, although the Poor Law Journal reported it as a resignation.[3]

By 1906 Mr and Mrs R Hodgkinson were in place, followed in 1910 by Mr and Mrs Cave (Mr Cave was applying for exemption from war service in May 1918).[3]

Mr and Mrs Cave served meritoriously for 20 years or more. Indeed, in January 1920 the Chaplain, the Revd Penyston, wrote in the report book that great harmony existed between the officers and the inmates and he was much indebted to the Master and Matron for their assistance at all times.[3]

Plaudits were again recorded in a letter of appreciation received by the Master, Mr Cave, in January 1931 thanking him and the Matron for their kindness in the treatment of the writer's mother: "No-one could possibly have been treated better during her trying illness." [3]

Later in the 1930s Henley Workhouse was known locally as "The Grubber" and was managed by Mr Fred Shirley and his wife. An illustration from this period can be found on page 170 showing a boat outing. Henley does appear to have been well served down the years by just a few long-serving benign Masters and Matrons of the Workhouse.

Samuel Mortlock

In 1848 there arrived to become Master of Henley Union Workhouse Samuel Mortlock, who had been Master of Aldersgate Workhouse in East London. He brought his wife, Ann, to act as Matron, and his son aged 19, a clerk. All three must have been delighted to escape the winter fogs and summer cholera of London.

He had been an active Chartist, whose petition to Parliament had sought voting reforms. It would appear that his character was not of the usual harsh order like Dickens' Mr Bumble. Samuel Mortlock was clearly humane and was particularly concerned for the children. He even took them on a day trip in 1851 to the Great Exhibition. Also he set up an annual charitable appeal in Henley to provide a special Christmas dinner for the inmates. Mr Bumble would hardly have bothered with any of that.

Samuel was a regular major prize winner at the summer and winter Henley Horticultural society shows, both for flowers and for vegetables, with a great input no doubt, from the inmates cultivating the acres within the workhouse. Glimpses of his private life show him chairing an elocution class presentation for the local Reading, Chess and Music Society in 1864.[i] Then, in 1869, he was enthusiastically supporting the resurrection of the Henley Cricket Club (recently rebuilt in 2010).

However, life for Samuel Mortlock certainly had its difficulties. In 1865 his wife, Ann, died. This was exacerbated by the departure of his niece, who had acted as assistant Matron. In order for Mr Mortlock to continue in what was a two-handed appointment, it was agreed to appoint a local woman, Eliza Pearman, as Matron in September 1866 and Samuel Mortlock was then re-appointed as Master.[1] Later, in 1868, he married her. A child was born the following summer but lived not long enough to be named.

In accordance with Poor Law Board regulations to enforce industry, order, punctuality and cleanliness of the inmates, Samuel Mortlock's duties also included keeping accounts for both the running expenses of the workhouse and for the profits or losses from the work done by the inmates.[1] For instance, in March 1881 the Henley Advertiser gave notice of firewood from Henley Union to be sold at 3s 6d per 100 bundle – surely an income-generating initiative?

With few paid staff (only five in the 1841 census), he depended in large measure on the unpaid and unwilling work of some of the inmates for tasks in the kitchen, laundry, cleaning and gardening etc. Initially the Master was responsible for the baking of bread and the brewing of beer, not only for the workhouse itself but also what was required for outdoor relief.

It is hard to credit that, on top of all these cares, his laid-down duties included that of maintenance in good order of the town fire-engine and, in the case of fire in the parish, "he shall have the engine taken to it with haste and superintend its working."[1] In 2008 a summoning bell could still be seen above the entrance to the infirmary, later to perform the function of a school bell.

The picture of these duties emerges clearly from the correspondence between the Guardians and the Commissioners in London, who supervised everything down to the last detail. It is to be hoped that the Board of Guardians was always ready with sympathetic and understanding support for the master but above them stood the formidable Secretary to the Poor Law Commission in Somerset House, London, Edwin Chadwick, who was not even answerable to Parliament and who required that the workhouse should be regarded as the very last option of the able-bodied poor.

Nevertheless, by March of 1849, Assistant Poor Law Commissioner, Greville Piggott, reported "very important improvements in the internal arrangements of the workhouse since the Mortlocks' appointment."(the previous year)[1]

Samuel Mortlock was pretty astute in his dealings as manager of the workhouse. For instance, in 1851 he was concerned to make a great saving in fuel in the men's day wards by installing two Arnott stoves similar to those in the dining room. In 1859 he made arrangements for the heating of the boilers to be by coal costing 15s 6d per ton bought direct from London wharves, making a saving of 1s 6d per ton on the local tender even after barge costs to Henley wharf.[2] In April of that year, Greville Piggott visited and expressed his entire satisfaction with the present state of management in response to the Master's suggested savings in personnel of £35 per

---

i   R J A Griffiths, Mortlock Encyclopedia.

annum.[2] Later that year the proceeds for roots, oakum, gypsum produced £19 10s 10d income generation.[2]

The Master had successive problems with some of the staff, particularly the chaplain. After the resignation in 1842 of the Revd J Maynard, a trawl was made to find a successor but the salary of £35 pa was unattractive and had to be raised to £50 pa. In May 1842 the Henley Rector, the Revd James King, complained about the Union's bad treatment of and interference with the previous chaplain, especially the poor pay. He reluctantly agreed to come in and minister to the sick and dying "so long as they were not infectious" but exhorted the Master to bring the inmates into church. The Revd J K Chittendon was then appointed and served until 1847, when he was called upon by the Guardians to resign because of neglect of duty.[2]

By 1849 the then chaplain was keeping a report book[i] on his attendances at the workhouse and the examination and progress of the children therein and on the moral and religious state of the inmates in general. He records, in April 1849, "a decided improvement in the deportment of the boys, a mood of greater subordination and obedience – a most satisfactory change since the last Schoolmaster left". As to the girls' school, he expressed his entire satisfaction with the manner in which the schoolmistress (Miss Dumbledon) conducted their education, moral and instructional. In his opinion, she was deserving of the Guardians' highest confidence. However, in December 1850 the Master was reporting the schoolmistress for using insulting language to him in the presence of children and for general misconduct including beating and otherwise ill-treating the children under her care. Furthermore, according to the Master's day book[ii] in May 1851, Miss Dumbledon was very insolent when he complained about her sending the girls from the school into the town at night without his knowledge. He said he would report her to the Guardians, whereupon she became very sullen and remained so. She even refused to attend the children to their meals in the hall.[1]

In October 1849 the Master took the dispute with the chaplain, the Revd James Arrowsmith, to the Guardians. It had been the custom for the children of both schools to attend prayers at the parish church every Wednesday and Friday morning and, by the wish of the past chaplain, the Revd Edmund Gooch, the girls continued to go to church on Fridays. However, "alterations in the diet" were found to interfere with the dinner hour, so the practice was discontinued. On Friday, 19 October the chaplain came to the house and, without consulting the Master, ordered the schoolmistress and girls to the parish church. The chaplain had since informed the Master that he considered the schools to be under his own entire charge and control. The Master thereupon quoted Article 125 of the Commissioners' General Order, authorising himself to maintain order and discipline.[2]

Another staff problem arose in October 1850 when the Master reported that, for want of hands to do the work in the house, he was obliged to employ women with bastard children and known bad character as nurses and to assist in the laundry, the cookhouse and elsewhere. This was completely contrary to the orders of the Poor Law Board, as it was quite impossible to prevent the women communicating

---

i   Chaplin's Report Book PLU 4/W/A1/2.

ii Master's Day Book PLU 4/W/AI/I.

with the other classes of inmates. The Master suggested having some temporary assistance "rather than break up all classification and discipline". An example of this concern occurred the following month when Ann Sadler gave birth to her fourth bastard child.[2]

Fluctuations in the number of inmates caused this request to be repeated in May 1851, in consequence of several women leaving the house, and again in August when total numbers had fallen to 160 (harvest time).[1]

Again, the Master was in dispute with the chaplain in December 1850 about his interference in discipline and management of the house and the hospital. One Sunday morning the chaplain, having conducted divine service at the workhouse, protested at the Master following his usual custom of hearing reading by the children of both schools and catechising them. The chaplain wished the children to be taken to the parish church but the Master had applied several times to the church authorities to have the necessary accommodation made for the children while at church because, at present, the schoolmaster and schoolmistress had no control over them during their attendance there "with the result that they were morally injured."[2]

That was not the end of the Master's problems: the same month, all the able-bodied men refused to attend prayers after supper so the following were locked up – Thomas Jones, Stephen Lovejoy, William Perrin, George Hobbs, Thomas Harris, James Thrupp, – Alloway, William Bell, John Martin, Edward King and William Bloomfield. They were all sent before the Town Magistrates, who sentenced the first five to serve 21 days in Oxford Prison. For his assault on the Master, William Bloomfield was sentenced to two months in prison.[2]

That was not all. On the 23 December Richard Stephenson was sentenced to serve three months in Oxford Prison for running away with Union clothing on 10 April (presumably re-appearing in Henley in December).[2]

Worst of all, on New Year's Eve there were 18 cases of disorderly conduct for which three inmates were sent to prison and 15 punished by the Master and discharged.[2]

Presumably order was restored for normal working in 1851. That was a census year and it will be seen from the Table on page 93 that this saw a peak in numbers within the workhouse, so perhaps there had been an element of overcrowding affecting the atmosphere.

Staff in place at the time of the 1851 census on 30 March in addition to Master and Mistress were the schoolmaster, Joseph Wood, aged 43 from Derby and Miss Susannah Dumbledon, aged 22 from Oxford, the schoolmistress; Joseph Wood's wife, Ann, aged 46 from Farnborough, was acting as nurse. Two other staff members were Thomas Livingstone and his wife, working as house porter and assistant.

Ten years later in June 1861 the Master's performance was brought into question by the Board of Guardians:

1. Whether he allowed a pauper named Bowden to work for Mr Pennington on land in Mr Mortlock's private occupation? Reply - Mr Bowden being an aged pauper of nearly 90 was permitted, at Mr Pennington's request, to go out for a little relaxation, and that the Master had not employed him but that paupers had attended his cows.

2. Whether the horse for pumping had been discontinued and for how long? The horse has not been used since last Summer. The old men pump.
3. Whether any relation of the Master resides with him in the House? Reply - His niece had done so for three years and assists Matron in her duties.
4. Whether the coals of the Union are employed in heating the pit and greenhouse? Reply - Cinders are used for this purpose.
5. Whether the fowls kept at the House are fed at the cost of the Union? Reply - Fowls are fed on scraps and Union barley sometimes with the Master's oats and that eggs and poultry are used in the House.

The Master was reproved by the Board of Guardians who resolved that Mr Mortlock had exceeded the rules of the House in allowing an inmate to work out of its premises and that Mr Mortlock discontinue the employment of pauper inmates upon his own land and cattle without the sanction of the Board. Furthermore,

That the Master's horse be employed for the pumping according to previous Minutes July 1857.

That the Board disapproved of the Master's niece residing permanently without some specific arrangement. She needs to be paid a salary of £1 pa.

The Board had not objected to the employment of the cinders for the greenhouse and pit but to the use of coals.

The Board think it desirable that the purchase of fowls kept at the cost of the Union should be taken into account.[2]

The Master was taken to task in March 1864 in a Statement of the Auditor, viz:

…perfect except for quarterly balance of provisions kept imperfectly; in several instances the calculations were erroneous – ask for explanation of quantities of meat and bread ordered/not ordered (surcharge of 12/7d was subsequently paid).

A letter of explanation from N Mercer, Clerk, 13 July 1864 stated: "These were as ordered by the Master from day to day or 2-3 times per week." (PLB annotated: "Mr Mercer is a highly respectable solicitor and, very careful to the best of his ability. Nevertheless, it is not seldom necessary to impress upon his mind the importance of regularity." sgd R B Cane.)

Samuel Mortlock letter dd 17 July 1864: "I beg to say that I am sorry that the mistakes should have had any trouble about them. They arose from an accidental miskeeping of figures and I will endeavour in future to avoid the recurrence of similar errors. I am, Sir, your obedient servant, S Mortlock."

Secretary PLB London replied: "By Article 200 No 20 of the Government Consolidation Order, the House Master is required to submit to the Guardians at every meeting an estimate for such provisions – and to receive and execute the directions of the Guardians thereupon." So what in the 21st century could be called micro-management was indeed being exercised by the local Government Board in London in 1864.

As stated previously, the job was 24/7, which meant being on site full-time. What was it that caused Mr and Mrs Mortlock to absent themselves simultaneously from the workhouse in June 1873 "without consent" causing the Master to be censured by the Board of Governors? [3] He was certainly in compliance when applying for a fortnight's leave of absence in August that year.

So all was not harmonious with the Guardians. In April 1875 the Master experienced more trouble in the form of an anonymous letter to LGB: [1]

> I beg to call your attention to certain things that have been going on at the Henley Union for some time past and ought to be put a stop to. The Master there seems to have all the power in his own hands and it is quite against the rules.
>
> I read the other day of an inquiry by an Inspector from your Board and, among other things, it was stated that the Master kept a pony and he was ordered to send it away. This was, I think, at the Amersham Union. Well, if one master of a Workhouse is not allowed to keep a pony, how is it that the Master of HU is allowed to keep his hunter and feed it on provender grown on the Union grounds? And besides, I am told he keeps an able-bodied man in the House to groom and exercise his horse. It is high time a stop was put to such things. I should like to know what becomes of all the hay grown on the meadow belonging to the Union?
>
> And another thing I am told is that the Master keeps a conservator and keeps another able-bodied man in the House to look after it who is quite able to get his own living.
>
> And besides I am told that the Master let a woman go out of the House to nurse a servant of the Chairman of the Board who was ill, for a favour. This woman, whose name I hear was Caterer, was so engaged for some months and left a child in the House while she was away, and when she was done with she was sent back to the Union. This happened during the late winter. I also hear that the Officers at this Union live in daily fear and they put up with anything sooner than find fault as they are afraid to be turned out of their places. This ought not to be and I hope you will see into it and alter it.
>
> And I am also told that the Matron keeps 4-5 able-bodied women to wait on herself. She has a parlour maid, kitchen maid, chamber maid, ladies maid, and these maids have their maids. I hope your Board will see into these things and take a little of the power out of the hands of the Master, for he seems to pay the Board little attention, so I hear.
>
> I am, gentlemen, one who likes to see justice done to all, and must sign myself An Inhabitant of HoT.

Mr Henley, the local LGB Inspector, responded that the horse had been kept for some time, with the sanction of the Guardians, for the ostensible purpose of pumping water for the use of the House. The other matters may be allowed and as for the last three paragraphs, the Finance Committee had closely investigated the Master's expenditure. Mr Henley stated that the Chairman of that Committee was on bad terms with the Master and had on two occasions endeavoured to find justice. The Guardians were against him so that any abuse in the House would have been brought to light.[1]

In June 1875 the Master reported that there was not sufficient labour in the House to work the pump. Had it not been in the winter, it would have been impossible to get a sufficient supply of water. The horse pump which was put up many years ago was never adapted to the use it was intended, being much too hard work than one horse can do.

Therefore, George Clark was hired for adapting well machinery for steam power, for £75 minus £7 10s taken for the old horse gear wheels etc = £67 10s (there was a value in metal even then!). This was accepted by the Board because manual labour from the House did not now exist.

Unusually, Mr Mortlock was found guilty of neglect of duty in January 1877. A complaint had been made against him for not using a hearse to carry the body of George Barney who died in the workhouse and was sent to Watlington for burial in a small cart drawn by a pony unequal to the task so that the body did not arrive at the church until an hour after dark. Consequently, the clergyman was kept waiting for an hour.[3]

Samuel Mortlock died in office in 1884 at the age of 76. He had suffered a serious accident the previous year when his horse shied at an unattended steam engine.

Whatever transpired before, the Reading Mercury (9th December 1884) published a warm tribute to him by the Guardians and stated that he had always considered the interests of the public and the comfort of the deserving poor; and no one had done more in checking pauperism than he. His able manner in conducting the mastership had won for the house a reputation as one of the best conducted houses in the country, an opinion which had been endorsed by Guardian Mr J S Burn in 1858 in his book.[i]

The Guardians gave credit for his zeal, energy and fidelity in performing his duties. No Benthamite he, Mr Mortlock was said to be anxious to do all that the law would permit him to do for the comfort and welfare of the inmates, particularly the children, whose welfare and amusement were the objective of his day. Furthermore, he took pride in the children who subsequently did well in the outside world. He could point to men and women now filling honourable positions in life who had left his care 10-30 years ago. Indeed, in 1869 the Inspector had reported the great interest taken by the Master in the children's welfare; having previously reported favourably "the usual highest credit upon those who manage and attend to it."

He lies buried in an unmarked grave in Henley Cemetery, where I paid tribute to him.

Unfortunately, despite searching in Oxfordshire for a photograph of Samuel, none has been forthcoming.

---

i   J. S. Burns (ibid).

6. The Inmates

THIS CHAPTER gives an outline of the workhouse regime and glimpses of the individuals inside. The workhouse was primarily intended to cater for the poor, the sick, the mentally infirm, pregnant women and children, some of whom had been orphaned or abandoned. The 1834 legislation was intended (notwithstanding the low level of wages amounting to only about 7s per week) to deter the able-bodied poor from relying on public assistance. The following notice appeared in the press in September 1834:

"Henley-upon-Thames"

"The parish Authorities have determined, in order to prevent the Abuse of Parochial Charity, that whenever any individual receiving Parish Relief, shall be found expending any Part thereof in a Public House, his Pay shall be immediately stopped. They also caution all Innkeepers not to endanger the Renewal of their Licences, by serving such Persons with Liquor. And in order that any Imposition may be speedily detected, they have determined that a list of the Persons receiving Parochial Assistance shall be left at the Poorhouse, that information may be given them of any instance which may have occurred of misapplied relief".[1]

Rules which were adopted for the poor in the Henley poorhouse[i]

These were presumably brought forward in 1835, viz:

All who are able to attend morning and evening service in the church are to go and return with the master in regular order. Those refusing to attend or behaving improperly shall lose their next meal.

All in health shall be employed in such labour as age and ability admit, and for those that work about the house, the hours of labour shall be from 7 o'clock to 7 o'clock from Lady Day to Michaelmas and from 8 am to 6 pm between Michaelmas and Lady Day.

Anyone who refuse or neglect their work shall be fed bread and water for 1, 2 or 3 days, as the Vestry shall direct.

Must be punctual at meals. Anyone 10 minutes late shall forfeit the meal.

All meals to be taken in hall and none taken away.

---

i   John Crocker (ibid).

They cannot leave hall after supper til prayers are read and they are to repair in a quiet manner.

Every man who earns 4/6d a week shall receive 2d a week (in the shilling) encouragement money, every woman earning 3/- a week shall get 2d in the shilling encouragement money and every child earning 2/- shall get 1d in the shilling. N.B. Poor House finances were different in that "encouragement money" was allowed. No such payment was allowed under the 1834 Poor Law.

Those employed out of the house must give account of daily earnings and hours worked. They shall not be allowed on any account to take their own earnings. They will get their dinner allowance at supper-time.

Any person not rendering a true account of their earnings shall forfeit their encouragement money for one month.

No-one to bring spirituous liquor into the house or to smoke in a bedroom. They shall lose their next meal as punishment.

Any person found guilty of stealing or selling their provisions or clothing or in breach of trust shall be punished with the utmost severity of the law.

Swearing, quarrelling or fighting will be punished by being fed on bread and water for 1, 2 or 3 days, as directed.

Not to go out without permission of Master or Mistress. Those not returning in good order at correct time or found begging shall not go out again for a month.

All poor persons admitted to the house must give up their clothing and property as per Act of Parliament and they shall wear no other clothes except those provided by the Select Vestry.

Speaking disrespectfully to the officers or the Select Vestry, using improper language respecting their provisions or treatment shall be occupied in hard labour and fed on bread and water.

As from 1835 each category of inmate was assigned their own day-room, dormitory and exercise yard in the workhouse (see p16). Members of families in the House were permitted to meet together only at very infrequent intervals and were not allowed to talk during meals in the communal dining room or chapel where a dividing partition separated them. Noteworthy is the resolution by the Board of Guardians in April 1836 that girls should be separated from the women "some of whom may be considered to be immoral".[2]

Reference is made to a "Bastardy Ward" in the minutes of February 1842, which suggests that those children were almost certainly sleeping separately from their mothers.

The cruelty of the workhouse lay in its psychological harshness. This involved depersonalising the individual, e.g. by the issue of pauper uniforms and a regime of monotony and regimentation. Workhouse rules laid down that the inmate should rise at 5am in the summer, and 7am in winter and should be set to work from

7am (8am in winter) to noon and then from 1pm to 6pm – and should go to bed at 8pm. The master of the workhouse was instructed to enforce "industry, order, punctuality and cleanliness" on the inmates.[i] "Victorian virtues of the discipline of hard work and repression when invoked in the workhouse led to a regime of institutionalisation, regimentation and the imposition of conformity. Able-bodied men were expected to work but nevertheless male inmates were prone to suffer the tedium of underemployment." [ii]

The Board of Guardians felt strongly that workhouse employment "should be of such as can be done by task or piece work, that it should be of such character to be instantly available on every emergency which may arise and that it should, if practicable, be such as can be carried out beneficially or with as little loss to the Union as possible and moreover that it should be of such a description as to induce the pauper to endeavour to obtain independent labour" (outside the workhouse)[1]. However, when someone entered the workhouse they had to part with everything, every stick of furniture, even the bed must go. How on earth could they begin life again on their own account?

With these objectives in mind, the tasks considered were root-splitting, grinding of corn by hand mill, digging gravel for roads and farmers' work. Also included was garden work in the grounds of the workhouse (see below), under the eyes of the bowler-hatted Superintendent of Labour; as can be seen, workhouse uniform was being worn. A dilapidated greenhouse is still there, which must have provided seedlings

Inmates working in the Workhouse garden with the Superintendent of Labour in the background.

---

i "The Poor Law in 19th Century, England and Wales" Ann Digby, The Historical Association.

ii Pamela Horn "Labouring Life in the Victorian Countryside" Sutton Publishing 1970.

The Greenhouse.

for male inmates to plant out in the three acres of vegetable garden on site. And Mr Jones, seedsman, sent in a bill for fruit trees and fancy shrubs ordered by the Master.

Later on, Mr Clements, the local builder, was re-erecting a shed to become a fowl house for the supply of fresh eggs. An additional task resulted from pig sties being erected in 1840 at a cost of £10 and there was cow-keeping to be done: two more cows were purchased in 1881 and milling was made part of industrial training in the schools. Throughout 1849-50 the Master was reporting in his Journal the killing of a fattened pig or two, weighing up to 350lb, but in 1873 the Guardians resolved that no more pigs be fattened up to be sold at Henley Market without their authority. Those now fattening to be sold at Henley Market [2] (more income generation!).

The less able and more aged would be expected to collect, sort and break pebbles. A pin manufactory was to be introduced for the employment of children, also straw-plaiting, as a means of maintaining order and regularity in the juvenile department. Boys would be taught shoe-making and tailoring prior to apprenticeship. No person was to be left without employment, carried out regularly and systematically – for example knitting stockings, needlework, spinning and the like. Older girls were to be taught housework prior to employment outside in domestic service. Able-bodied women were set the task of cleaning, sewing, cooking, laundering and nursing care within the workhouse.

On a visit to the Henley workhouse in April 1835, Richard Hall, assistant poor law commissioner, spoke to many of the inmates. "As an exception to the general expression of satisfaction on the part of the Paupers, one *lady* in *earings* (sic) (original emphasis), who was employed in starching some caps, told me that she had been in the house eleven years, and did not like it nearly so well as formerly, for that "now the Society was so *very* uncultivated."[1]

Kitchens.

Drying Grounds.

On admission into the workhouse, personal clothing was locked away. Uniform clothing for females was made by able-bodied women inmates within the workhouse from bulk purchase of material. For males, however, it was announced in 1840 in the local newspaper that tenders were required by Henley Union for men's fustian jackets, waistcoats and trousers – full size, and for boys 13-15 and boys 9-12.

Laundry.

But by October 1850 the Master reported want of clothing for the old men and he proposed a strong cloth coat and waistcoat instead of fustian jacket, suggesting that the former would be much warmer and more economical.

In later years, the uniform for able-bodied women was generally a shapeless, waistless frock reaching to the ankles, with a smock over.

Standards of accommodation within the workhouse complied with strict regulations laid down by the law. In July 1835, immediately prior to the poorhouse's transformation into a workhouse, the local newspaper, Reading Mercury, carried requests for tender for the following items for the dormitories:

> 50 strong iron bedsteads (painted) each 2'6" wide, 6' long with elastic 1" wide hooping iron for bottoms. 1" sq legs, frame 1½ x ⅝"m braces 1 x ⅝" and a 5" plate at head.

Inmate uniform.

25 strong double bedsteads (painted) 3'9" wide, the substance and the length the same as single bedsteads.

50 single flock beds, with superior strong hessian ticks.

25 bolsters with same cases.

50 9-quarter blankets. 25 coloured coverlids. 10 quarters.

300 yards of good strong sheeting.

From this list it may be discerned that in addition to the extra 50 single beds and flock mattresses being provided, each with one blanket, there were also to be 25 double beds with covers. Were these for mothers with babies, as these beds were only 3'9" wide although bed-sharing by young adults was then quite normal? Sheets would undoubtedly be made by hand by the women inmates from the 300 yards of "good strong sheeting" bought in.

Later on, reference is made to the bedding provided in 1869: "the beds are of straw, some are of flock and in the hospital there are a few feather beds." The vagrant wards being quite new then, the men were sleeping on coconut matting hammocks, slung on free stanchions. "It is cheap, simple and clean."[1]

In August 1835 the shopping list was greatly expanded when tendering for: "Coal, salt, black pepper, brooms per dozen, mustard, best blue starch, vinegar, candles, bacon, soap, oatmeal, dry peas, sugar, tea, cheese, butter, flour, malt, hops, thread, worsted, tape, linsey/wolsey, calico, flannel, Dowlas, men's/boys' cloth and caps, shoes, blue handkerchiefs, stockings, smock frocks, foul weather jackets, bread, mutton, beef, suet and ox-cheek. Coffins: 3-5 ft and over 5 ft + shrouds."[2] A motley list indeed of items needed to set up an expanded workhouse.

In March 1836 the Poor Law Commissioners in London were asked retrospectively whether men, boys and girls should be allowed out of the workhouse to labour, but the Commissioners ruled that this would interfere with the labour market and compel independent labourers to compete.[1]

At this early stage, the Board of Guardians resolved that girls should be separated from the women. Perhaps this was on the grounds of morality, particularly after Ann Harris and James Wheeler had been committed to Oxford prison in April 1836 for improper conduct; Ann took her infant with her.[2]

Inmates were admitted to the workhouse at times of great penury for them, after assessment by the Relieving Officer. Winter was a time of particular hardship, after the work available in the fields at harvesting and then threshing the corn was completed. But by the middle of November, work was hard to find and recourse might have to be made to the food available only in the workhouse for the man and his family. Come the spring, however, agricultural labourers were more in demand, so the family was free to seek another roof over their heads. For instance, in July

Workhouse entrance porch.
© Assendon e-museum 2009.

1837 the Guardians reported that James Bartlett and two children, having recovered of his illness, is desirous of leaving the workhouse, having found employment; a loan to him of 15s was granted, his master having agreed to allow 1s per week out of his wages.

Under "Labour in the House", the Visiting Committee reported in December 1841 that there were now in the House 17 or 18 men who were quite able-bodied and should be systematically and regularly employed. It was therefore recommended that some respectable and intelligent man should be employed, at a sum not exceeding 15s per week, to set out work for such paupers under the direction of the Master. This was the first Superintendent of Labour (combined with the duties of Gatekeeper in due course).[2]

In October 1849 root stocks costing £30 10s and then split had fetched only £23 14s, a loss of £6 16s, so other kinds of labour for able-bodied men had to be tried. The Master later reported that 22 cwt of old rope costing £14 8s 6d had been turned into oakum and doormats and sold for £22 2s 4d.[1] (an example of the Master's account-keeping).

Occupancy Showing "Ins & Outs" Variations by month, 1849-1851[i]

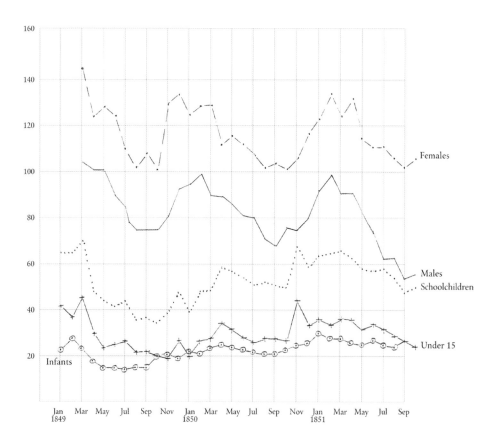

In August 1835 details of the following paupers were entered into the Board of Guardians Minute Book:

---

i   According to figures reported fortnightly in "Kinch's Advertiser".

William Richardson (50), consumptive;

Widow Simmonds and 3 children (one a bastard). "No relief for bastard";

Ann Richardson and 3 children. Husband transported. 2 youngest (children) "bastards" – into Workhouse.

John Holland family ill with typhus fever. 5s burial fee;

Sarah Wilson dead with typhus, leaving idiot brother. 5s burial fee;

Ann Harris has had 2 bastards (1 recently burnt to death) is now pregnant with child – into Workhouse;

Mary Crutchfield, widow. Suspected case of "imposition" – into Workhouse;

Sarah Ward (23), widow with 1 child. From best information from Relieving Officer it is supposed this woman is a Prostitute in Reading. Relief discontinued.

And in May 1836 Phoebe Hawkins, a single woman pregnant with her fourth bastard child, was allowed to be admitted into the House along with her two children.[2]

In 1837 Sarah King's husband, James, absconded, leaving his wife on the Parish. She was admitted into the Workhouse by the Relieving Officer and the Clerk offered a reward of 2 guineas for the apprehension of her husband.[2]

Likewise, John Wiggins' wife and 3 children were ordered into the workhouse, "the pauper having absconded". Proceedings were in train.[2]

According to the census returns, the numbers of inmates in the workhouse fluctuated somewhat. These totals are analysed in detail in Census analysis (page 8).

It will be seen that broadly similar total numbers of male and female inmates were recorded at each census. The exception is the over-65 group in which, at each census, men outnumbered women by more that two to one, the discrepancy being especially marked in 1851. These men were mostly widowers (19 of 25 in 1851) who were probably not coping with living alone (see p.80).

Among the intake of inmates following the new Poor Law act in 1834 were Alice Champ, a deserted wife with four children; also Sarah George, dubbed "insane", from Rotherfield Greys.[2] In September of that year the Relieving Officer reported on James King, who was then apprehended for leaving his family of five children to become chargeable on the Parish. He was given one month to pay the expenses incurred. How sad must have been the situation of Mary Ann Cowling when in April 1842 the Master reported he had delivered up the pauper's child to the mother at Reading upon her being discharged from gaol.

In August 1849 the Master reported that William Stonell absented himself without the Master's knowledge and returned drunk and refractory. He was locked up but immediately commenced breaking the door. The Town Magistrate ordered him six hours in the stocks for being drunk and he was to be brought up again for the damage done to the door.

According to the Master's Journal, a dramatic scene took place in May 1850. William Knight aged 61 of Pyrton was taken into custody about noon for breaking into the Store Room and stealing a quantity of clothes belonging to the Union. Knight had discharged himself from the workhouse on the Monday and it appeared he must have got over the walls from the front of the House into the young men's yard and

Number of inmates according to Poor Law categories

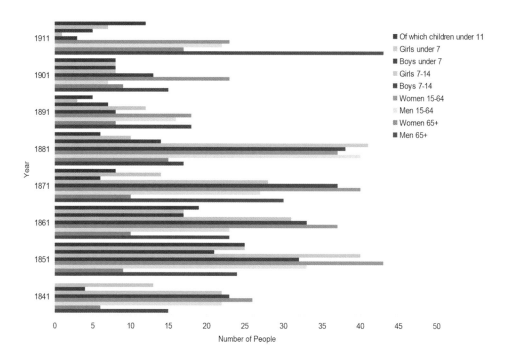

had taken a 30-rung ladder from its place and must have then got over the walls in the women's yards to the back of the men's infirmary. Here he was discovered by one of the patients named Wood, who was in the lower hospital. Wood rang the alarm bell for the Master and removed the ladder from the wall, thereby preventing Knight from making his escape. Knight was committed to Oxford for trial and sentenced to seven years transportation.

Also of interest are three large families (revealed by the census of 1851) all members of which were in the Workhouse: a 40 year old agricultural labourer with a wife and five children plus his widowed father; a 51 year old agricultural labourer with his wife and six children; and a 25 year old unmarried servant with four children and her agricultural labouring mother.

Increasingly, according to the census figures (see above), during the period 1841-71 women of working age outnumbered the men (by 2:1 in 1861) and, in particular, unmarried people outnumbered those who were or who had been married. Into this category come the female servants who were unmarried mothers and who found themselves in the workhouse as paupers. For example, in Summer 1851 there was Eliza Smith who was given leave of absence in June in order to make arrangements to go to a place of service which was provided for her. She left the house wearing Union clothing. "On Saturday last her bastard child was brought to the workhouse, she having deserted it." [2]

On 16 August 1851 the Master reported that Ann Caterer of Watlington, (who became long stay until her death), was delivered with a male bastard child. Another child was born in 1862 and remained in the House until 1920. Five days later Ellen Wise of Brightwell gave birth to a female bastard child.[2]

In 1861 there was a total of 13 unmarried servants in the House with 26 children. Under the Old Poor Law, the putative father would have been sought out by the Parish Overseers and forced to contribute to the child's upbringing. The PLC had ordered that no allowance was to be paid to mothers of bastards outside the House. Therefore, young domestic servants who became pregnant, either by downstairs staff or even by the master of the household or his son, found their only recourse was to give birth in the workhouse: "great-bellied women with nowhere to go"[i]. In those Victorian years, they were categorised as "fallen women with bastard children" and once admitted into the workhouse, they found it difficult to find situations outside which would take a child. So their situation and prospects remained dire and they continued to be inmates, together with their infants. From the schedule of accommodation (see page 26), it would appear that these infants were separated from their mothers and placed in the infants' dormitory.

Children up to the age of three could stay with their mother, being placed in the nursery while she was working in the house. Ordinarily, Poor Law Orders allowed mothers access to children under seven 'at all reasonable times'. Beyond that age, parents could request a daily 'interview' with their children, though more often such meetings generally took place for an hour on Sunday afternoons.

As listed previously, there was one woman who had "two bastards" (one recently burned to death) and was now pregnant again and another woman from Brightwell, near Watlington, with 3 children (the two younger being bastards) whose husband

Inmates – Some Occupations

1851	1861	1871	1881	1891	1901	1911
Female servant x 37	Female servant x 9	Housemaid/domestic servant x 9	Domestic serv x 17	F servant x 1	Domestic cook	Farm labourer/ field worker x 20
Ag. labourer x 28	Ag. labs x 25	Ag. labs x 48	Ag labs x 31	Ag labs x 14	Farm labourer	Laundress x 13
Lace-maker x 5	Shoemaker	Cook	Field worker x 9	Sawyer	Farm carter	Domestic general x 8
Strawplait maker	Gardener	Seamstress	Painter	Wheelwright	Gen.labourer	General labourer x 13
Basket maker	Blacksmith	Tailor	Baker	Bricklayer	Shepherd	Chair/wood turner x 3
Baker	Groom	Commercial clerk	Gardener	Bargeman	Nursemaid	Sawyer x 3
Woodman	Carpenter	Laundress	Tailor	Garden lab.	Bricklayer	Maltster x 2
Shepherd	Brickmaker	Milkwoman	Laundress	General dealer	Boatman's lab.	Coachmen x 2
Shoemaker	Shepherd	Hostler	Needleworker	Cork cutter	Laundress	Brickmaker/layer
Painter/glazier	Painter	Gilder	Nurse	Shoemaker	Sawyer	Iron moulder
Bargeman	Bricklayer	Sailor	Fisherman	Watchmaker	Maltster	Stableman/horseman
Cabiner-maker	Charwoman	Carpenter	Blacksmith	**Vagrants**	**Vagrants**	Chimney sweep
Hemp dresser	Stableman	Butcher	General labourer	Draper's asst	Gen. labourer x 2	Cowman
Blacksmith	Sawyer	Shoemaker	Shoemaker	Lock gas fitter	House painter	Butcher
Cooper	Maltster	Nursemaid	Charwoman	Carpenter, retd.	Plasterer's lab.	Seaman
Carpenter	Miller	Blacksmith	Post boy (age 73)	Gen. labourers 3		Rag & bone dealer
Sawyer	Iron founder	**Vagrants**	Wood sawyer			Whitesmith
Boiler-maker		Bricklayer's lab x 2				
Gardener		Baker				**Traveller**
Vagrants		Rivetter engine works				Cutler
Ag. labourer x 2		Carpenter				
Miller		Stonemason				
		Ag. lab x 2				

i   Pamela Horn "Labouring Life in the Victorian Countryside" Sutton Publishing 1970.

had been transported, presumably some time since. In Henley in 1851 this group constituted 21% of the inmates. In 1858 the Inspector listed seven able-bodied women six with bastards and one deserted with four children. Furthermore, there were three married servants with five children and four unmarried lace-makers or straw-plait makers (from Buckinghamshire) with 6 children (in 1861).

Main occupations are listed on the previous page from the censuses between 1851-1901 (occupations were not recorded in 1841). From this it will be seen that, as expected hereabouts, the primary and low-paid work was in agricultural labouring for men and domestic service for (mainly young) women. As far as agricultural labourers were concerned, available work fluctuated according to season, and reflected the great agricultural depression 1871-81.

Nevertheless, even with the censuses being taken in April, the numbers of agricultural labourers in the house were substantial (see List of Occupations), reflecting the nature of the rural economy in the locality. Also listed are other unskilled workers and some skilled artisans. Of particular note are the boilermaker who was from Birmingham in 1851; the brickmaker and bricklayers, maltsters and ironfounder in 1861; the commercial clerk and the gilder, both from London, in 1871; and in 1891 there was a cork-cutter and a watchmaker. It is said that tramps preferred to stay outside the workhouses on census night. In those years when recorded it is interesting to note the variety of occupations as well as place of birth.

So where did the inmates come from? Surprisingly, some came from a widespread area, possibly after being in service, by marriage to local people.

Inmates – Marital Status

(All ages)		1851	1861	1871	1881	1891	1901	1911
Married	M	9	5	7	5	3	2	8
	F	12	3	5	6	1	6	6
Unmarried	M	20	18	21	16	11	8	34
	F	31	29	12	18	10	7	19
Widowed	M	17	21	21	16	14	8	22
	F	5	10	12	18	10	7	13

Married Inmates

Unmarried Inmates

Widowed Inmates

Those married, with or without children, survived better out of the workhouse.

1871   two thirds of widowers were aged 70-80 without a pension (N/A until 1909). 50% of widows were younger, aged 32-69.

1881   More than 50% of these widows were aged under 70-80 and finding it hard to survive without a breadwinner at a time of agricultural depression.

1901   One wonders why the significant dip?

For example:

1841   Andover
1851   Warwickshire, Birmingham, Taunton
1861   Cork, Ireland; Gloucestershire; Lambeth
1871   St Marylebone; St George's Hanover Square, London (gilder)
1881   Lambeth; West Bromwich; Stratfield Saye and Alton, Hants. Bath
1891   Somerset, Barnet, Yorkshire, Northants, Liverpool, Anglesey,
       Staffordshire, Barking, St Pancras.
1901   Notts, Birmingham, Stratford-on-Avon, Somerset, Hants, Wilts,
       London, Chesterfield, Sheffield, Norfolk.[i]

Vagrants came from Kilburn in Middx, Scotland etc.

As far as the inmates were concerned, offences against the rules of the workhouse were regarded as a breach of criminal law, even extending to a charge of theft of workhouse clothing when not returning from temporary leave of absence. When inmates ran away from the workhouse, the automatic charge on apprehension was that they had absconded wearing union clothing – all inmates being required to wear a uniform (see p.74) and their own clothing locked away on their admission. On 12 October 1841 an inmate, Henry Costar, returned to the House, having run away in union clothing on 20 March and was brought before the Board and admonished "and it appearing to be his second offence it was ordered that he be deprived of one meat dinner per week for a month and to have water and gruel instead, and be placed in solitary confinement on each day that he is so deprived of his meat dinner".[2]

Trouble broke out in the workhouse in January 1847. The Reading Mercury reported that:

> 30 inmates of the workhouse on Wednesday morning were brought before Magistrates having refused to perform their accustomed employment. On examination they allowed that the labour was very moderate, they had no complaint to make of their rations or against the Master of the house, but a man having recently been appointed to overlook them they had chosen to take umbrage at it or as they expressed themselves, "they warn't a-going to work under a ganger."
>
> After being lectured on the impropriety of their conduct by the Magistrates, seven of them still refusing to return to their work, they were committed to the gaols of the counties in which the parishes were situated to which they respectively belonged, viz Aylesbury and Oxford gaols for 21 days.

In March 1842 a 16 year-old girl, Elizabeth Eady, from Bix, absconded together with two unmarried mothers who left their four children behind.[2] All three were apprehended and committed to Oxford gaol for three months for running away with union clothing. In April 1849 Elizabeth absconded from the House again, taking with her the Union clothing for herself and illegitimate child. In February 1851 the Master reported Elizabeth Eady giving birth to her third bastard child. Fourteen

---

i   See also pp198-212.

years later, in June 1856, the same Elizabeth Eady was an unmarried servant with three children, living with a blind man in Reading; and that summer she abandoned her five-year-old son "in the water meadow by the waterside" [3]. So perhaps "keeping bad company" was indeed to be guarded against.

A few more entries of note in the extant Master's Journal,[i] are:

> George Holloway was reported in February 1851 as having absconded with Union clothing, leaving his wife and 3 children chargeable to the Parish of Caversham. He was apprehended at the end of March and taken before the Town Magistrates. In consequence of the past conduct of this man, the Master considered it his duty to press for punishment for each case. He was therefore committed to gaol for 3 months for each offence.

On the other hand, William Bond was brought into custody from Guildford earlier that month by a constable of the Town upon a charge of deserting his two children. He was sentenced to 6 weeks imprisonment.

Elizabeth Foster must have come to the end of her tether in April 1851. She was taken into custody for deserting her six children. She was told that if she came into the workhouse to join her family, or take them out and support them, that no further punishment would be inflicted. This, however, she refused to do. The Magistrate then sentenced her to 3 months with hard labour.

The Master had other problems in the House. He reported in April that several of the old men had become so imbecile and unmanageable, as well as dirty in their habits, it has been necessary to put them under temporary restraint. Hopefully, this situation was resolved at the end of May when the Master reported that Mrs Farling, the person recommended as a nurse "came down last night by the coach and has entered upon her duties conditionally. She is 34 years of age and I should think will make a good officer."

Meanwhile, in March, four inmates were sent to prison for breaking windows and two for refusing work: five were punished by the Master. Furthermore, in May Thomas Neighbour was sentenced to 21 days for refractory conduct.[3]

In January 1862 there arose the case of Lucy Major, a pauper inmate of the house being reported to be in the family way (already with two illegitimate children). The Guardians ordered that the matter be referred to the Medical Officer for his view. Dr Jeston informed the Guardians two weeks later that, having examined Lucy Major, he considered her to be about five months gone. Thereupon the Guardians resolved to investigate the circumstances connected with this case and whether it may have arisen from any want of discipline in the house. Two weeks later the committee appointed were of the opinion that due caution was not exercised in preventing the access of male inmates to the cooking and engine house and that there had been a want of security against communication between the infirmary and kitchen at night. It appeared that the "office" of unlocking the female inmates' wards was for a long period deputed to the kitchen maid and that no muster roll of the inmates was ever called.[2]

---

i   PLU4/W/1A1/1

In January 1869, a strict sentence was passed on a woman, Elizabeth Rockall, for disorderly conduct in the House. Such behaviour was not tolerated and she served 21 days in Oxford Gaol, with hard labour (which was unusual for a woman).[2]

That same month George Cox and James Grainger were charged with having stolen one pair of boots valued at 9s, property of the Guardians. They were sentenced to two months hard labour.[3]

PLB Inspectors made regular inspections of premises and reported their findings to HQ in London as to how well the regulations were being complied with. These reveal conditions for inmates in Henley Union, e.g. in May 1867 the Inspector's questionnaire was completed as follows:

Are Receiving Wards in a proper state? There are none.

Is the Workhouse School well managed? I believe so. But nearly 30 children are sick in bed with skin disease, and the Sick Wards are greatly over-crowded.

... I think it reasonable that the Poor Law Board should forward the following suggestions to the Guardians:

1. Some of the yard urgently needs re-tarring;

2. Two adults, whether idiots or otherwise, should not sleep in 1 bed;

3. Iron enamelled wash basins are required for personal washing;

4. Arm chairs, benches with backs and other similar comforts are needed in the Old Men's Dayroom. Waterproof sheets with funnels are required for the dirty cases.

5. Call attention to the great prevalence of skin disease (affecting the children) and the present overcrowded state of the Sick Wards.

Number of people in the Workhouse 1871 showing seasonal variations for inmates

(see also pp85-86)

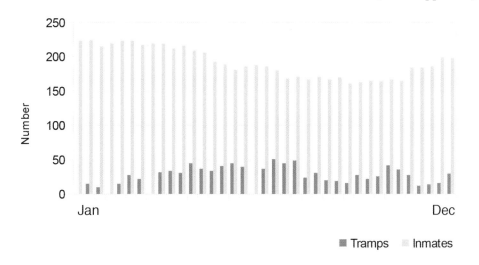

In July 1870 a 35-year-old widow, Sarah Brewer, was brought before the Town Bench charged with unlawfully running away from Henley, having discharged herself from the workhouse with her four children and subsequently leaving three of her children (twin sons and a two-year-old daughter) abandoned and sitting on the door step of the Porter's Lodge. They were taken back into the House and became chargeable to the Common Fund. Sarah was sentenced to 21 days hard labour in Oxford gaol.[3] Afterwards, in September, she was charged with neglecting to maintain her four children, not having returned to see them and they therefore remained chargeable to Common Fund; sentenced to 21 days.

In August 1870 there were four more recalcitrant paupers appearing before the Bench:

> Richard Tomlin of Henley, a woodman, was charged with neglecting to maintain his wife and three children whereby they became chargeable to the Common Fund of the Henley Union on 2 August. Mr Harding, Relieving Officer, said that the defendant was earning 13s a week and that he gave his wife and children nothing. The wife and children were relieved by him on the 2nd instant. Convicted and sentenced to 21 days hard labour.
>
> Thomas Norris, tramp, was charged with refusing to perform a certain task of work as to his age, strength and capacity in return for food and lodging afforded him at the workhouse. Prisoner pleaded guilty and was sentenced to 21 days hard labour (see also chapter on vagrants).
>
> William Neil, tramp, was charged with tearing up and destroying his own clothes at the Tramp Ward of Henley Union on 22nd inst. Convicted and sentenced to 21 days hard labour.
>
> Ann Heath, an inmate of Henley Workhouse, was charged by Mr Mortlock with being refractory and guilty of misconduct in the Workhouse on 16 December by fighting with other inmates and using abusive language. Defendant was convicted and, being "an old offender", was sentenced to 42 days hard labour.[3] Nevertheless, on Christmas Eve she was again charged with being "refractory".

Another recalcitrant parent was Thomas Coke, rope spinner of Henley, charged again in March 1871 with neglecting to maintain his wife and three children, chargeable to Henley Union. He was sentenced to 6 weeks hard labour, on account of previous conviction.[3]

At the end of 1871 Thomas Stone was sentenced for absconding from the workhouse on 19 December, taking with him a suit of clothes, the property of the Guardians. James Spickernell, the Porter, said that the defendant had been admitted on the 5th.[3]

On a more serious note, at Watlington Petty Sessions in 1872 it was reported that on Jan 3 Thomas Stacey, an inmate at Henley Union Workhouse, was charged with assaulting Samuel Mortlock, the Master of the workhouse on 2nd inst. Prisoner pleaded not guilty. The Master deposed that on the 2nd a complaint was made to him of the prisoner having misconducted himself and, upon enquiry, he found that the prisoner had been playing tricks with his gruel and he accused him of doing so and remonstrated with him, upon which the prisoner kicked him and then struck him in the back of the neck with his fist. The prisoner was then taken charge of by Henry Stevens, who corroborated the evidence. Convicted and sentenced to 21 days hard labour.[3]

The prisoner was then charged with wilfully breaking and damaging the door post of the cell at the workhouse. Henry Stevens deposed that the prisoner was placed in the cell after committing the assault above mentioned and shortly afterwards, upon visiting the cell, he found the doorpost broken and the cell otherwise damaged. He then took off the prisoner's shoes and left him ... The damage done amounted to 5s. Convicted and sentenced to 14 days hard labour, to commence at expiration of the above term.[3]

More trouble occurred in the House in March 1873.

> Jane Simmonds, inmate of Henley Workhouse was charged with disorderly conduct in the House by fighting with another inmate on 23 March. Rose Hannah Hopkins deposed that she was in the kitchen and prisoner came to her and inquired if a man named John Pain was there, that one word brought on another and prisoner ran after her and struck her in the face with a roll of linen ... that she returned the blow and prisoner, who had a baby in her arms, then threw the baby down on the mat and came at her and struck her in the face with her hand and she (witness) then knocked prisoner down. Prisoner had no right to be in the kitchen.
>
> Evidence was corroborated by another witness named Sophia Atkins and the prisoner, an old offender, was sentenced to 42 days hard labour.[3]

Then, in September 1873 the same Jane Simmonds was charged with running away from the Town of Henley and leaving her two bastard children, whereby they became chargeable to the Common Fund. She was convicted and sentenced to one month hard labour.[3]

Likewise, the following month, John Jemmett, a labourer, was brought up charged with unlawfully running away from Henley, leaving his two children chargeable. Having pleaded guilty, he was sentenced to 21 days hard labour.[3]

By 1874, like all other workhouses, Henley Union was suffering from the dearth of female labour. On an inspection visit in August, Mr Henley remarked that the beds in the female sick wards were too crowded, which was evidently done to save the labour of cleaning and nursing as some wards were empty. Also, the receiving wards were not very clean, which should be remedied.

The following table shows the seasonal variation of incumbents Winter-Summer, when work was more available in this agricultural area. Tramps in particular were on the roads during June, whereas inmate numbers dropped during the harvest months of July/August.

Inmates 1881

	Inmates	Tramps
January	195	
February	194	29
March	178	66
April	169	69
May	167	53

June	161	102
July	148	62
August	147	48
September	152	40
October	166	70
November	179	46
December	N/A	

On Sept 6, 1883, the Clerk read the following letter:

> Gentlemen, May I call your attention to Mary Anne Lovejoy, who has been admitted into the infirmary suffering from mental excitement, which I believe has been caused by abusive language used towards her in the laundry by the Superintendent. Yours faithfully, Egerton Baines, Medical Officer.

The Guardians resolved,

> Appearing from the foregoing report, and others on various occasions, the Board came to the conclusion that it was undesirable to continue the services of Jonathan Miles, the attendant to the steam boilers, and Elizabeth Miles, his wife, industrial trainer in laundry work. Ordered that their services be forthwith discontinued.[1]

In 1884 John Wilkins, an inmate of the Union Workhouse, was charged with assaulting David Seward, the Assistant Master, on October 14. The complainant said that on the day in question he was examining the wards when he found the defendant in the House instead of being at work in the garden, and told him if he did no work then he should pick oakum. Some time after he found the defendant still indoors and was about to take him to pick oakum when he struck at him, falling down himself with the complainant beside him. After some wrestling, the complainant, who was scratched and marked, made his escape.

Wilkins, in defence, said he was subject to epileptic fits and on the Monday previous to the day in question he had had a fit of this kind and was so very bad thereafter that he could not work. After careful consideration of the case, the Magistrates assured the defendant that if he was well enough to assault the Master, who still had the marks on his face, he was well enough to work. Sentenced to 21 days hard labour.[3]

In 1886 there was a dispute put to the Henley Borough Bench about who should pay for the removal of Eliza Elliott to the workhouse. She was 84 years old, living at Greys and had received outdoor relief from the Henley Guardians. The application to the Bench was to determine chargeability, the Guardians having refused to pay in the light of the following background.

The Clerk produced certificates of the marriage of the woman with Henry Elliott and of his death. He knew that Mrs Elliott had lived in Remenham Parish (now within the Wokingham Union) for many years previous before coming to live in Barlows Yard in Henley. She was not chargeable to any Parish in the Henley Union. Mrs Elliott had said that she lived for many years at Remenham near the "Horse-shoes" (the Two Horseshoes being a pub). Her husband, who was working for Mr Noble of Park Place, met with an accident while on a horse and shortly afterwards received relief. The Bench granted the application.[3]

Perhaps an understandable situation arose in January 1887 when George Pavey of Reading was charged with leaving his father chargeable to Henley Parish. The Relieving Officer said that the defendant had offered to give his father a home but he refused to have his stepmother too! The Guardians would not agree to that arrangement and he was ordered to pay two shillings a week towards his father's maintenance.[3]

On 5 July 1887 LGB wrote, having received a report from their Inspector, who visited the Henley Union Workhouse on the 9th, from which they learnt that the Medical Officer called attention in his Workhouse Medical Report Book to the case of an inmate, Edward Wiltshire, who on several occasions had refused to take food, and asked whether, if necessary, he would be justified in administering nourishment by force, as he should in the case of a lunatic whose life was in danger. "The Board direct me to state that it seems to them to be a matter which must be left to the MO himself to determine ... The Board understand from their Inspector that EW is not at present classed as a lunatic and they think it desirable that the MO should be requested forthwith to write to the Guardians upon the man's sanity in order that, if necessary, he may be removed to an asylum."

The Clerk ordered to inform LGB that EW is not now an inmate of the workhouse, neither is he chargeable to the Union.[1]

Later, Edward Wiltshire, now being an inmate of the workhouse, it was ordered that the MO be requested to write to the Board upon the man's sanity which he did on 9 Aug 1887; "EW has been under daily observation since July 19. I find he is of 'sound mind' and his conduct is entirely due to his bad temper. He refuses medical treatment, stating nothing but brandy and beer will cure him."

The Inspector in July 1887 was probably unaware that previously Edward Wiltshire had taken out a summons against the Master alleging an assault, which was dismissed by the magistrates. Dr Baines had commented that he was a very troublesome old man and unruly in his conduct.[3] One can imagine the disruption in the workhouse caused by him or perhaps it gave the other inmates some distraction from their boredom!

An application from Roebuck Smith of Greys Green to receive into the workhouse the illegitimate child of Mary Taylor was made. Ordered that the application be adjourned till the next Board day and that the Clerk make enquiries as to the whereabouts of the mother of the child.

26 July 1887 Child be received into the workhouse. Advice to be obtained from LGB. Letter from the Master of Marylebone Workhouse that Mary Taylor had discharged herself and was at present residing at No 6 St Edmunds Terrace, Regent's Park. Ordered that the Master see her and induce her to remove her child from the workhouse here. Complied 20 Sep.

The Guardians had to take care when placing girls in service. For instance, in September 1887 the Guardians received an application from the wife of C Talbot of East Greenwich for permission to take Florence Cranfield out of the House. Permission was only given subject to enquiries as to Mr Talbot's respectability.[2] (Perhaps the Guardians were mindful that they did not want her returning with an illegitimate child!)

Indeed, the arrangement did not last very long because in 1890 poor Florence was being removed from her uncle, John Cranfield.

Whenever possible maintenance payments were obtained. For example, in 1890 the Hiscock brothers, George, Henry and Arthur were summoned to show why they should not provide for the maintenance of their father, who was chargeable to Henley Union. They were ordered to pay 1s each per week.

In December 1891, a letter was sent from LGB, regarding Mary Ann Lovejoy,[i] who met her death through falling into a copper of boiling water in the laundry at the Workhouse of Henley Union.

... It is the duty of the Medical Officer to report to the Board the case of every sudden and every accidental death which may occur in the workhouse. No such report has been received ... sent to Dr Baines, who replied:

> On Dec 31, 1891 I was called to this workhouse about 1pm to see Mary Ann Lovejoy, aged 42 years, who had slipped on a low stool and fallen into a copper containing boiling water and linen. She was very badly scalded and died 14 hours afterwards.
>
> An inquest was held on Jan 1st 1892 and a verdict of accidental death was returned. No blame being attached to anyone.
>
> This woman has been employed in the laundry over 20 years. (E Baines).

The Guardians considered no blame could be attached to any officer, nor to the arrangement of supervision in the laundry but that the accident arose through the unfortunate woman disregarding the rules.[1]

In August 1893 the Inspector reported that there was a large amount of spare space:

> Is there a workhouse infection hospital detached from the main building? Yes, but serious cases are now sent to the Smith Infection Hospital. Several such cases are there now.
>
> Is the workhouse school well managed? I think so.
>
> Are the children regularly taken out for exercise? Yes.
>
> No. of children in school: boys – 18; girls – 16.
>
> No. of children under industrial instruction: boys – 0; girls – 4.
>
> There are 2 non-conformists who would be allowed to attend chapel outside if they desire.
>
> No. of insane paupers on the day of visit: 2.
>
> What is the provision for the drainage and is it sufficient? There are no WCs. sinks to the laundry; water runs into the town sewers. I think on the whole the drainage may pass.[1]

---

i   No immediate relation to Lovejoys on p.91.

In August 1888 the Local Government Inspector had reported:

Parishes: 23 Population: mainly agricultural (22,550)

	No of Beds	*Number of Occupants*		
		1887	*1886*	*1885*
Able-bodied men	22	0	3	3
Old men	41	10	13	13
Boys	43	20	26	24
Male Infirmary	24	13	10	10
Infectious	0	0	0	0
Receiving	4	0	1	1
Able-bodied women	34	11	14	13
Old women	8	5	5	7
Girls	30	16	21	27
Female Infirmary	29	17	13	13
Infectious	0		3	1
Receiving	2	0	0	0
Lying-in	4	0	0	0
Nursery	12	0	0	0
Totals	253	92	109	115
Vagrants, male	13	9	5	4
Vagrants, female	9	2	0	0

Children attend National School in the town at 3d pw.

> 1-2 non-conformists, who would be allowed to attend chapels outside if they applied for leave.
>
> No. of insane paupers – 1 female
>
> Medical Officer + Nurse
>
> The number of bed-ridden patients is small.
>
> Smith Infections Hospital is available. The Master has authority to engage a night nurse whenever needed.
>
> Water supplied from the public supply.

Such reports do serve to give some indication of the conditions prevailing within Henley Union Workhouse through the years.

But individual hardship continued. For example, William Moore was a farm labourer aged 36 earning 13s per week. He was stone deaf and had just lost his wife who had died leaving an infant three days old. There were four other children in the family: William aged 12, John 8, Lucy 5 and Elsie 3. Moore had applied to the Guardians to admit his family into the Workhouse. Application was made to LGB for consent to receive the two girls and infant into the Workhouse, leaving the two boys to be maintained by their father. It was pointed out that owing to the small earnings of the man and of the absence of accommodation at the cottage, Moore was unable to make arrangements for any woman to attend to his family.

On 2 December 1896 Ellen Florence Maskell, a pregnant inmate, was removed to Bradfield Union as she was born in Reading. Her father, a ballast man, lived in Tilehurst then in Smethwick, Birmingham, now in Bradfield Union. So Henley Union soon offloaded the cost of keeping her plus child.

Later, it was reported that on 2 Jan 1901 Harriet Brooks, widow of Watlington, who lately discharged herself from Henley Union, was charged with wandering abroad and lodging in an outhouse without having any visible means of subsistence. The Police Constable found the accused in an outhouse where she had been for 4 hours during the night of Tuesday last. A penny was found upon her. She was sentenced to 7 days imprisonment without hard labour.

Long Stay: A widowed agricultural labourer, John Green, born in Thame, appears to have spent the last ten years of his life (1841-51) as an inmate. Likewise, single retirees, having no pension, often saw out their lives in the workhouse, e.g. R Hutton, an unmarried agricultural labourer from Rotherfield Greys spent 10 years inside the Workhouse, as did T Hoarey, a Henley widower and agricultural labourer. If ill health made it impossible to work for a living, the only recourse was to the workhouse.

Likewise, a laundress from Bath Susan Smith (presumably the widow of a local man) spent 1881-91 in the workhouse, as did Elizabeth Martin, a seamstress from Watlington, listed in the censuses 1871-81.

Long stay cases also included those labelled "imbeciles", e.g. Ann Caterer with a late-born daughter Mary Ann ("bastard") both for more than 40 years; George Allaway and his sister for 30 years; Susan Taylor for 30 years; and Elsie Cresswell, reassessed in 1891 as an epileptic from childhood, who had been admitted 10 years earlier at age 26 as an "imbecile".

At least two orphan children lived in the workhouse for more than 10 years from age 2–12: Jo Mungay was admitted with his sister and 10 years later he was labelled as "of weak mind".

The following deaths were reported in the Henley Advertiser in 1884:

Jan 6 at Union House, Henley   George Evans, aged 82
Jan 8   Wm Stallwood, aged 64
Jan 16   Joan Hellaman, aged 79

This appears to be a bad month – perhaps influenza at this time of year? Normally the death rate was spasmodic.

Such deaths were recorded as occurring at 78 West Hill, i.e. the address of the porter's lodge. Was this mandatory or empathetic? A mortuary was built in 1908, later turned into a chapel of rest.

Impropriety was still being borne in mind as per the example of a letter received by the

Mortuary.

Board of Guardians in 1895 from the "Friendless and Fallen Female Preventive and Reformatory Institution" [1] established in 1857, 200 Euston Road, London, which quoted "Open all night refuge. Outdoor no. of inmates to maintain: 240. Sustains the following Homes:

Established for 102 friendly girls in their teens	50	Parsons Green
	26	Holloway Road
Total 102	26	Holloway Road
Reformatory Homes for 117	24	Euston Road
	33	Holloway Road
	30	Brompton Road Brompton
Total 117	30	Parsons Green"

Now take the case of the Lovejoy family. Frederick and Mary Ann are photographed, perhaps on their wedding day, dressed for an occasion. Frederick was in work as a labourer and by 1896 there were seven sons. Then he died of TB so Mary Ann and the three younger sons went into the workhouse. Tragically, six weeks later Mary Ann also died, orphaning Henry aged 11, John aged 7 and Hughie aged 4. Five years later John and Hugh were still in the workhouse.

At age 16 the boys would have been found a job, apprenticed out or sent to HMS Exmouth for training – not so much "escaped" from the workhouse, more like "put out from"… Happier times came for Henry, who became a well known Henley postman pictured over the page, aged 75.[i]

But in August 1898 Henley Guardians selected a more benign-sounding institution in which to place Mary Ann Haynes, aged 13 years; The Society for the Rescue of Young Women and Children, whose offices were at 79 Finsbury Pavement, London. Mary Ann's father had deserted her and the rest of the family with the mother a few years previously.

"The girl was up till a short time since with an aunt but in consequence of her

Frederick and Mary Ann Lovejoy.

---

i   Hugh's descendants are in Australia, grandson Terry Lovejoy being an astronomer with the Lovejoy comet named after him (information supplied by Susan Phillips).

unruly conduct has again become an inmate of this workhouse. The girl is generally of a depraved and immoral behaviour, and the Guardians cannot allow her to mix with other girls in the workhouse."

The cost of maintaining the girl in the above institution was 4s per week, payable by the Guardians, who had constituted themselves guardians of this girl. It was proposed that she remain there until reaching the age of 16. LGB duly sanctioned this procedure, and Mary Ann was sent to the care of Miss Hopton, Knighton Girls Home, Widsford Wells, Essex.[1]

A quandary arose when, in 1901, the brother of an inmate of the Workhouse had sent £1 to his sister which she wished to have for the benefit of her two children. The Clerk said that legally the money belonged to the Guardians.

Henry James Lovejoy.

Several of the Board were averse to taking the money from the man, who was a soldier in India, and the matter was referred to the Visiting Committee for consideration.

Hardship continued for the populace. In January 1904 a farm labourer was quoted as saying of the Corn Laws then pertaining: "I be protected and I be starving".[1]

By February 1904 there were 97 inmates in the workhouse: 28 children and 69 adults (24 under age 60, of which 13 were temporarily disabled and 11 in ill health, i.e. none able-bodied). Of 45 over age 60, 30 were men, with an age range 63-93 and 15 women 66-86.[3]

Single mothers still made their way to the workhouse. In January 1904 a maintenance order was issued against Frederick Jemmett, 24, labourer of Friday Street after Anna Hussey entered the workhouse pregnant on November 13. In court, Jemmett admitted paternity and agreed to pay 2s 6d per week for 13 years plus costs, payable to the Guardians.[1]

In November 1907 at Henley Borough Bench, an elderly man named John Honey, a war veteran who had lost an arm in the Crimean war, appeared at the instance of the Henley Guardians for neglecting to maintain himself on his war pension.[3]

In November 1908 at a meeting of the Board of Guardians, reports showed a big increase in the number of able-bodied men in the workhouse. The Revd Coxe feared that the increase would continue owing to the prevailing distress from unemployment. He mentioned that on a certain day he went into a village in the Union and saw 17 young fellows who told him they were out of work and would have to go to the workhouse.[3] (No social security payments were available at that time.)

On 1st January 1909 the first payment of old age pensions of 5s per week was payable to persons over 70 years of age. 102 were eligible at Henley Post Office and on receipt of this benefit they were then made guests of the Liberal Club at tea provided at the Town Hall.[3] Did this result in the reduction in numbers reported by the Master in June 1911: 104 inmates compared with 117 for the corresponding week in 1910.[3]

The number of Inmates in the Henley Workhouse at time of census

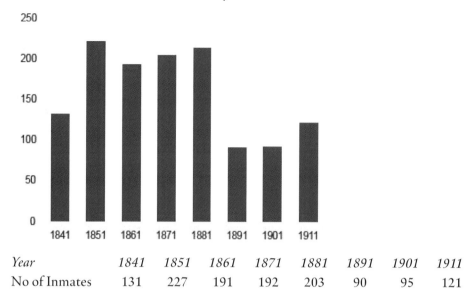

Year	1841	1851	1861	1871	1881	1891	1901	1911
No of Inmates	131	227	191	192	203	90	95	121

The drop in numbers between 1881 and 1891 is mainly of children not being contracted in from Middlesex.

In 1912 there was a report of a fire breaking out in the stone yard through the boiling over of tar in a large copper used for treating wood blocks for kerbs.

World War I and 1916 saw a shortage of labour for the garden so the Master would have to hire workers. Miss Cooper, Guardian, asked whether employment could be offered to women willing to undertake such work? In reply, the Master said that the labour required was primarily for potato planting: "If they can do that, all well and good." A month later the newspaper reported that during the past fortnight a party of lady gardeners of Henley were working in the gardens of Henley Union.[3] (no mention of potatoes!)

In the 20th century John Crocker, who died aged 99 in 2004, recalled as a boy in Henley seeing the inmates of the workhouse returning from church, the women in long striped dresses from neck to ankle (see page 74) and the men in grey suits. He also noted that his grandfather, H Crocker, resigned from the Town Council in protest at what he considered to be inhuman conditions at the workhouse.

By 1920 the Master reported 92 inmates in the House: 64 had been recently admitted, 1 child being born; 46 had been discharged;[i] 17 had died and the present number in the house was 94. Of these, there were 15 belonging to Henley Union aged between 70-78; 6 aged 80-89 and 1 over 90. Of those belonging to Wycombe, there were 6 aged 70-80; 4 aged 80-89 and 1 over 90. So 28% of the inmates were by now elderly. Visiting hours were to be extended on Sundays from 11-12 noon and 1-3pm for relatives.[3]

---

i   Note the increase in turnover between admissions and discharges (social security being paid?).

It is noteworthy that the hours of the tailor were to be reduced from 44 to 22 hrs per week and wages reduced from £2 to £1 pw consequent on the facilities afforded by ready-made clothes.

A decade later under the new Public Institution regime in 1931 the Master, still Mr Cave, reported six deaths during the month of those aged 81, 76, 78, 70, 72 and 71. Inmates had numbered 92: 77 admitted during the half year and four births with 59 discharges and nine deaths, this left a total of 105 inmates. Of these 88 were from Oxfordshire and 17 from Buckinghamshire. 40 of them were over 79 years and two over 90, so 40% of inmates were elderly long-stay now.

So the Institution continued as a place of last resort, mainly for the aged and sick. (Elderly long-stay care continued at Townlands Hospital until the 1987 Care in the Community Act decreed discharge into residential care homes).

Towards the end of the 19th century, a daughter of Henley's Town Clerk, Miss Lucy Cooper, painted the following picture of the Workhouse. It has a very benign atmosphere and one can but hope that not too much artistic licence has been taken in this representation of the life of the inmates at that time.[i]

The Union as it was up to 1930.

---

i   Painting by Lucy Cooper as permitted by Town Clerk, Henley-on-Thames Council.

7. Children

FROM THE TABLE analysing census returns[i], it will be seen that between 1841-1881, about 50% of inmates were children under 14 years of age (not counting the scholars from Middlesex – see next section). These children were mostly orphans, abandoned[ii] or illegitimate, often inside the workhouse with their unmarried mothers. Indeed, in 1871 the census labels the children as either "legitimate" or "bastards".

Before the 1870 Education Act it was a parent's duty to clothe, feed, educate and discipline their children. Pauper children, however, were seen as the responsibility of the Parish, who should provide orphanages, and then apprenticeships for boys and training in domestic service for girls.

For instance, in July 1860 George Carthew, a tailor in Marylebone, was asked to take on an apprentice Eliah Cane, aged 14, fatherless and deserted by his mother.[2]

Examples of the type of children in the workhouse are shown by three families in the 1861 census: 2 widows each with 4 children and aged 42 and 27 were obviously destitute without a bread-winner; also there were 6 children called Smith from Bix aged between 13 years and 8 months, presumably orphaned. Similarly in 1891 there were 3 orphans sent back from London to Henley by relatives, who reputedly stole the accompanying money and put them into the workhouse.

Nevertheless, Mr Mortlock was directed by the Guardians in 1869 "to receive from the parents the sums due for children in the House (presumably 'bastards') and to report from time to time the defaulters, with a view to saving the expense of their maintenance".[2]

In July 1869 there were 42 boys and 45 girls in residence prior to the building of the new school for 100 children (see next chapter on the School). This followed on from the Poor Law Inspector's concern in October 1868: "The boys do not look well and both their school room and dormitory are unsatisfactory."[1] He therefore suggested to the Guardians the need for a number of improvements.

As referred to in a previous chapter on The Master, Mr Mortlock took a great interest in the children's welfare, according to the Inspector, and tried to mitigate their plight as far as possible. After Mr Mortlock's death, a new Guardian elected in 1887 took on a special concern for the children. It was said that Mr Barnett could not have been more sympathetic in the treatment of them. He launched the idea, in due course, of scattered homes and was credited with being most devoted in everything to do with the welfare of the children.[3]

---

i   See page 5.

ii   1851 census lists 13 orphans and 3 deserted.

It was deemed that the children were to be trained to be employable on leaving school so as not to be a further burden on the rates. The PLB principle was that "all children in the workhouse shall be trained to habits of usefulness, industry and virtue". There is reference to payments made by the Master for outfits of clothing provided for children leaving the House to go into domestic service. Hours of work were laid down and, indeed, in November 1868 the Board of Guardians stated that they were of the opinion that the Factory Acts should be applied to this Union insofar as the children shall not be employed under 10 years of age.[2] (See also the chapter on The Master in 1785.)

The employment of girls from the school to do washing in the general laundry under the superintendence of the Industrial Mistress required the use of great care and vigilance in order to prevent undue intercourse between the girls and the women employed in the laundry, averred the Inspector in 1874.

Dr Barnado opened his homes for children in 1870, believing that "the ordinary workhouse was and is too much of an institution and too little of a home. The hapless inmates are indeed rescued from want and active criminality but are in no real sense trained for life outside the walls. Their moral fibre is unequal to the strain of temptation." Nevertheless, the Guardians went ahead and built a new school in 1870. The Revd Bennett even suggested providing in the playgrounds "The means of amusement for the children."

Poor little orphans Isabella aged 9, Emma aged 8, Ann aged 6 and Alice aged 4, the four orphan children of Samuel Hinton Pearce and wife Jane, had to be resettled from Woolwich Union to Henley in August 1873.[2]

Suffering also were deprived children from the locality: George Legge was prosecuted for neglecting to maintain his ten children under the age of 16. He was convicted and fined £5 plus 16s 6d costs or 2 months hard labour. As the sentence was to be suspended if he removed his children from the Workhouse forthwith, he took his children out on the same day.[3]

Welfare of sick children was promoted by placing a contract with the Metropolitan Infirmary at Margate, a 36 bed unit set up in the beneficial sea air in 1791 for scrofulous children. TB cases were sent for a cure until age 16. For instance in 1873 Eliza Brookland was sent there from Henley. In 1885, following a visit by the Master at the behest of the Guardians he reported in respect of three boys (W Newport, G Clements still there until 1889 and K Payne). "All of these cases were said to be of so severe a character and disease in each so markedly constitutional that the removal of either child at present could not be recommended. Further stay at Margate was likely in each case to effect a cure." However, W Nightingale was reported to be fairly convalescent and there was not reason for him not to return.[1]

In 1889 there were still five children including Frederick Soundy and Harriet Fox, being paid for at Margate Infirmary at 10s 6d each per week. Emily Clements was sent there that year in place of Gertrude Vernon and Ethel Cranfield was sent there in June 1891. A report on Ada Ambrose at Dane Hill Infirmary, Margate was requested in January 1896.[2]

Earlier, in 1887, the Board of Guardians agreed to pay £10 per annum for 3 years to the Cripples Home and Industrial School for Girls at 17a Marylebone Road, London for the maintenance and education of a cripple girl, Amy Hobbs, belonging to the Parish of Hambleden.[2]

There was a resolution passed by the Board of Guardians with the Relieving Officers in June 1888 "for all young persons under age 16 years residing within their district and who have been placed out of the Union Workhouse (presumably into domestic service or apprenticeships) to report thereon to the Guardians at least twice in each year ..."[1]

The children's welfare came to the fore when in March 1889 an LGB Inspector visited Henley Union and recommended that the children go out for a walk at least two days a week, having previously discovered that they were only occasionally taken out for exercise.[1]

Mrs Baines, the doctor's wife, had a kind thought in 1889 when she supplied hoops for the children because, with few toys provided, there was little scope for play, apart from tag and the swing provided in the school playgrounds.

In August 1894 an outbreak of diphtheria was reported due to the insanitary condition of closets and defective drains. During the week commencing 15 April three boys and a girl were affected.[1]

Flora Thompson referred to the obedience and shame engendered by the workhouse, which the children of Henley Union would certainly have felt when sent to the local National School after 1894. The number of children overall was diminishing. However, in 1896, the Visiting Committee considered that the increase of illegitimate children in the House warranted taking proceedings against putative fathers for maintenance.[1]

In 1895 the LGB were asked for their "authority to pay a sum of £5 pa to mistresses (ie employers) who take girls from the workhouse for whom it may be difficult to obtain situations" (ie a subsidy), "this amount to be expended by the mistresses for providing clothing and pocket money to the girls." However, the LGB responded that they were not aware of any legal authority for payments of this kind, being termed relief in aid of wages, and going on to say that there were training houses and other institutions in which such girls as those referred to could be trained for service.[1] Back in 1889 private subscription was obtained so £3 could be granted for an outfit for the son of Ambrose Haines, a deaf and dumb boy about to be apprenticed.[2] But in September 1895 the Board consented to outfits being provided to Robert Dill and Alfred Bromsdale on leaving the workhouse to be employed by Mr Watts of Henley and Mr Norcott of Rotherfield Greys.

A report on the Industrial Trainer, Esther Holmes, was made in 1895 viz;

> No. of children in the school = 26 girls – engaged in housework and needlework.
> No. of children under instruction = 6 – aged 13-15.
> Hours of instruction: 0645 – 0715, 0900 – 1200, 1400 – 1630
> Those who have left school have 5½ hours work.[1]

The next month Miss Holmes resigned and the following advertisement was inserted for her replacement:

> Female Industrial Trainer: Candidates must be single or widows, between 25 – 40 years of age. Duties are to take charge of the girls maintained in the workhouse out of school hours and see that they are kept clean and tidy; be responsible for the cleanliness of that part of the workhouse occupied by them, and instruct them in needlework, cutting out, sewing and to train

them generally in domestic work; also to assist the Matron when required in such manner as the Guardians may from time to time direct. Salary £20 pa, with board and lodging and washing in the workhouse and an allowance of £3 10s 0d pa in lieu of beer.[3]

Nevertheless, 9 months later when the Inspector made another visit, he reported that of 28 boys and girls then in the workhouse, 10 girls aged 10 – 14 were under instruction in laundrywork and domestic service from 0745 to 0845 and from 1pm to 5 – 6pm and from 6.30 – 7.00pm and he stated that children under 11 years attending school should not be receiving industrial training in addition for more than an hour daily.[1]

In 1896 the Visiting Committee recommended that two boys, Charles Haines and John Brunsden, be supplied with outfits at the cost of £1 each to enable them to go on board a fishing smack for 2 months on trials [3] (see page 99).

At about this time the Chairman of the Board of Guardians, Mr George Brakspear, made a generous gift of 15 guineas to be placed in the Post Office Savings Bank at a rate of 10s per child over 10 years and 5s each under 10 years so as to encourage them in thrift.[2]

This contrasted with the niggardly request by Henley National Schools for fees to be paid for the attendance of workhouse school children at 3d per week. The Guardians replied that they had no legal authority to pay.[2]

A special case was raised with LGB in July 1897 by Guardian Edmond Chamberlain. He asked about the legality of admitting children into Henley Union Workhouse under the following circumstances: A man is left a widower with three children under the age of 3½ years. His weekly earnings are 13s, his rent is 3s weekly, his work is 3 miles distant from home, which necessitates his leaving before 0500, returning home about 8pm. The children are, under the circumstances, left to themselves all day, "naturally with bad results." The man would pay a small contribution weekly to the Guardians.

In reply, LGB stated that it rested with the Guardians to decide whether to grant relief to a widower by bringing the children into the workhouse. If the widower were able-bodied, the Board's approval should be obtained to any proposal to grant relief in this manner.[1] So no concern with the children's welfare; just comply with the rules!

In the following two years the reports sent from London by the Inspectors were as follows:

14 July 1897 Re Lily Minns, Industrial Trainer in Housework at the Workhouse.

The average daily number of children under her instruction is five. The Board direct me to state that this number is insufficient to admit of an award being made in respect of the salary of this trainer for the year ended 25 March 1897.

And in 1898: "I visited this workhouse on May 23 and found that the Industrial Trainer had left and was told by the Master that there were so few children that it was not intended that another Industrial Trainer should be appointed. [1]

Censuses of 1891 and 1901 show the percentage of children in the workhouse had fallen to 25-35%. (In fact, in 1898 the LGB Inspector reported that in the nursery for 12 infants there were "none there".)

Guardian Revd J W Nutt had inspected the schools and said that children from the workhouse had given the greatest satisfaction to teachers. Therefore, in June 1899 Mr Neighbour of the Henley Board of Guardians proposed a resolution to the effect that children be sent to the national schools and that fees be paid for them for the ensuing year.[3]

In January 1901 the Clerk reported that he had received an application from the Lewisham Guardians for the maintenance of two lads named Gardner and Hales on board the training ship Exmouth, moored at Greys, Essex. These lads were already chargeable to Henley Union but had been placed on board the training ship. The Captain of the ship had reported that the lads were performing their duties very well and would in time make efficient seamen. The Guardians expressed their great pleasure in hearing of the conduct of the lads and said the Board were quite willing for them to remain on the ship and that they would accept the chargeability for them.[3]

George Rawlins also had the benefit of training on the Exmouth. His letter to the Clerk in 1906 reported that he was now on HMS High Flier; he was rated ordinary seaman seven weeks before time and "only the best boys are rated before age 18", he proudly wrote. Even better was a pay increase from 4s 1d to 8s 9d per week. Mr A'Bear, who corresponded with several boys sent from the cottage homes promised to write to Rawlins.

A month later, the Clerk received another letter from the Metropolitan Asylum Board in respect of the lad Gardner stating that the cost of maintenance would be 9 s per week until the boy was 18 years of age. As it was not clear whether the lad would be a private in the Royal Navy or the Merchant Service, the Clerk was directed to request that at the expiration of his term on the Exmouth, the lad would be bound to enter the Royal Navy.[3]

By then the Guardians were considering alternative accommodation for the children. They visited Wallingford Cottage Home and reported in April 1901, Mr Barnett now suggested adopting the "scattered homes" principle. "As regards the Cottage Homes question: three houses in or near Henley to be secured for accommodation of the children in the workhouse (Nov 1901). Although, children might be better looked after in private homes, only orphans or deserted children should be boarded out. Architect to prepare plans for re-arrangements of the school into an infirmary."

Therefore, at their meeting in December 1902 the Guardians had a shock when informed that the property at Binfield Heath which they "had proposed to take for the purposes of establishing Cottage Homes, could not be made answerable except at such an expense as would make it too expensive."[3]

They had to think again, at length. Just over a year later in February 1904 they were considering the subject in committee as to the possibility of cottage homes for children. By April there was being constructed a children's home at Radnor House, since demolished, in New Street with accommodation for 18 children.[3] The workhouse matron was given the additional duty of superintendent at a salary of £10 pa. Thereafter, the 1913 Act on cottage homes decreed that no children over 3 years

Belmont House.

of age should be inside a workhouse but were to be fostered out. Belmont House at 23 New Street was later brought into use.

The stigma of illegitimacy destroyed the lives of millions of unfortunate young women and blighted those of their children. If a girl's lover deserted her and her parents could not or would not support her and the child, recourse to the workhouse was usually the only option. The baby would be born in the infirmary and the girl would be encouraged to give the baby up for adoption. Otherwise, after weaning, the girl would be urged to leave the workhouse with her baby to seek employment but this was usually impossible to find with the baby in tow. There are therefore examples of girls abandoning their infants and leaving the immediate area. If she could not find work, she would have to return to the women's section of the workhouse, segregated as being considered to be "morally degenerate".

But it should be recognised that, although confined within the workhouse and its strict regime, hundreds of children over the years were fed and clothed (perhaps better than might have been affordable by their family). Especially, they were educated, as mass illiteracy became history. Signing the marriage register with a cross was no longer happening. And in May 1920 the Guardians were agreeing to the **adoption** of one of the children in their care in the children's home.[3]

Also by this time, dental treatment was being provided and would continue.[3]

It should be acknowledged that over the years thousands of children who would have been deprived of a future were reared in the workhouse and were schooled in the 3Rs, making them employable outside in the community.

8. School

THE EDUCATION of children was addressed at an early stage in Henley Workhouse by the establishment of separate school rooms for boys and for girls. A schoolmaster and a schoolmistress were appointed to regulate the discipline and organisation of the school and to check on the cleanliness of the children. The objective was to give pauper children 'superior eligibility' so that their better education would permit them to compete in the labour market and not become a burden on the rates that their parents had been.

The schoolteacher's lot was an unenviable one and there was a considerable turnover of teaching staff. The work was badly paid and of low status but reasonable standards were expected by school inspectors. It was a live-in job that entailed supervising the children throughout the 24 hour day as well as instructing them in the classroom.

In February 1837, the schoolmaster, Edward Edwards, was suspended by the Board of Guardians for impregnating a pauper in the house. An order for his dismissal was then issued, against which he appealed to the PLC in London. He maintained that it was not he and that his wife had been present; in any case, he said, paupers ought not to be allowed out into the grounds! He asked if he might resign rather than be dismissed, but this the PLC refused.[1]

The PLC were then asked, in February 1837, whether the children might attend the National Schools a quarter of a mile away. The PLC had no objection provided that the children were escorted there **and back**[1] (my emphasis).

An additional schoolroom was added to the workhouse in April 1840, together with a washroom and boys' sleeping wards. Also a new school building was built after 1847 because, under the Poor Law Amendment Act of 1844, school districts under elected boards were required to provide special services for the destitute homeless poor and poor children, and the Act placed responsibility for the supervision of such boards upon the Poor Law Commission.[1]

In January 1847, Greville Piggott reported that the school was not well managed and that the chaplain had failed to record his weekly visits. He said that the children were insufficiently instructed in reading and writing but the girls did have instruction in laundry work.[1]

Later, in January 1849, the schoolmaster, Mr Fisher, was reported for drunkenness and improper behaviour in the dining hall and afterwards for using threatening language to the master and the porter. In the following March, the master was reporting the schoolmistress for misconduct in beating and otherwise ill-using children in her care.[1] Was this the same mistress who was extolled by the chaplain in April? (see page 65).

Further staff employed in the workhouse were instructors in shoemaking (at £15 12s 0d per annum); tailoring (ditto) and laundry work (£10 per annum). Thus it was intended to give the children a skill to make their own living outside the workhouse and to break the cycle of dependency.

For example, in May 1865 the Inspector reported that 70 (sic) children were in the school (38 boys and 31 girls), 29 of them being industrially trained, being of an appropriate age.

The PLB sent Inspectors annually to report on the state of the school and its staffing. In October 1865 the Inspector reported on his examination of:

	James Saunders	Lizzie Way
	Schoolmaster	Schoolmistress
	38 boys, (43 average)	36 girls (36 average)
Salary	£55 16s 0d pa	£23 4s 0d (probation)
Skill as a teacher	good	fair
(resigned)	Sept 1866	Dec 1866

In November 1867 the Inspector reported as follows:
boys – 45; girls – 38. Total 83 pupils.

Whether school is improved or otherwise since last visit: Boys' school retrograded from the neglect of the last Master; Girls' school improved.

New appointment of William Woodward, shoemaker at 12s pw – 6 children under instruction.

Henry Wheeler, Instructor in Agriculture – 12 children under instruction.

Deborah Cook, Laundrywork – new appointment at £15 per annum.

Comment: Four industrial instructors with training for a school having 79 (sic) scholars is a larger number than usual – or than is proper in the Board's circular. Do you recommend that it should be allowed in this case and, if not, which for the four should be dispensed with? Four have, I believe, been allowed.

In October 1868 Mr Henley, the Poor Law Inspector, reported on the inadequacy of some of the arrangements in the House. On a recent visit the women's infirmary "a cheerless building" had been full up as there were 13 girls with scarlet fever. The boys "do not look well, and both their schoolroom and dormitory are unsatisfactory". He suggested to the Guardians the need for a number of improvements, particularly to the school and hospital.[2]

"As Henry Wheeler, the Agricultural Instructor, is also Porter and Superintendent of Adult Labour, the grant in respect of his salary will be discontinued. But the Board (PLB) will be prepared to make a grant in respect of the salaries of the instructors in shoemaking, tailoring and laundrywork…."

By 1869 the Inspector, H Bowyer, found the boys' school "much fallen off in general instruction though on the whole fair. The girls, on the contrary, had improved and were now superior to the boys." Some new reading books for the boys were recommended. (Does this ring bells in 2016?!)

The Inspector examined the workhouse again in January 1870 and reported:

David Coy, Schoolmaster very fair
Mary Bradfield, Schoolmistress very fair
Boys: 40; girls 33/40
Ellen Heather, laundry at £12 pa (resigned May 70)
Jo Dyke tailor at £15 12s 0d pa (aged 35, m 5 children)
Jesse Cornish shoemaking
William Woodward had left owing to his family being ill with scarlet fever and it being unsafe for him to come amongst the boys.[1]

By July the Inspector, J J Henley, was complaining that there had been constant changes in the staff of the school which was prejudicial to the children, Miss Bradfield having resigned.

Between 1865 and 1873 there were five schoolmasters, paid at £30 pa, who came and went. Of the four schoolmistresses, paid at £25 pa, during the same period, one unfortunate 28-year-old died in service. Advertisements for a married couple resulted in the appointment of Mr and Mrs White in 1876, who served for 9 years until the Schoolmaster refused to cane two boys at the behest of the new master.

In the Inspector's report of his examination of David Coy and Alice Dickson, Schoolmaster and Schoolmistress, dated 2 January 1871 (pre-dating the impending school building), he stated that Mr Coy resigned last May in consequence of the dissatisfaction expressed by the Guardians at his conduct. The Inspector was informed that he left the House the same day without leave. Coy subsequently expressed regret at his conduct, however, and promised amendment and he was re-appointed in August 1870. In November he appeared to have again given cause for dissatisfaction and a Committee of Guardians was appointed to inquire into his conduct. They reported on 23 November that he did not visit the dormitories in the morning and seldom in the evening, leaving the children in the charge of the eldest boy in the school; that two beds were dirty, four not clean and neat, and that "Mr Coy, by his answers and admissions, showed a general want of interest and of responsibility about the boys".

On 1st December the Committee reported that Mr Coy kept a boy up all night without reason and they concluded, "It is clear to us that Mr Coy has been guilty of great neglect, that he has shown a wrong spirit and that he is not a person to be depended upon".[1]

However, the Inspector was concerned that the certificate of conduct given by the Clerk to the Guardians on 24 May 1870 at the time of Coy's resignation had stated, "This is to testify that during the time Mr David Coy held the office of Schoolmaster at the Henley Union Workhouse his general character and conduct were very good and that he resigned his appointment voluntarily." The Inspector insisted that this was at variance with the above report by the Clerk and asked them to state which of the two documents "expressed their deliberate opinion".[1]

Furthermore, the Committee of the Guardians also reported on 27 November that Miss Dickson was guilty of carelessness in the general superintendence and industrial training: but there had been no complaint against her since and the Clerk believed that she was misled by the Schoolmaster.

At their meeting the day after the Inspector's report, the Guardians referred to the item in the report book by the Visiting Committee of the Guardians on 8 December: "Mr Mortlock reports that Mr Coy and Miss Dickson are attending to their duties in a satisfactory manner." The Guardians felt that the Schoolmaster had already been reprimanded by the Visiting Committee but the PLB requested a special report from the Guardians after three months.[1]

Meanwhile, the Guardians had met in October 1868 to approve PLB proposals to remedy complaints made by the Inspector which highlighted the need for a new school for boys and girls to be built, with a day room to each and dormitories above, including a room for the Schoolmaster and one for the Schoolmistress, with lavatories, water closets etc and an apparatus for warming the building by means of hot water. Nevertheless, the Guardians voted against this proposal[3], presumably on account of cost. However, by December 1870 (first Education Act under way) there were architectural plans for the erection of new schools for 100 children and these were forthwith sent to PLB for their approval.[1]

The new school was fitted out in December 1871 with 20 additional single iron bedsteads for boys plus desks, forms and cupboards for both schoolrooms; with store rooms, cupboards and racks for children's clothing; also gas fittings costing £20. This considerably eased pressure on space and made the conditions better for everyone (see page 29 for consequent layout of accommodation). By December 1872 the Inspector was reporting on "the schools which have recently been built" and were now open.[1]

He found 44 boys and 42 girls under a new schoolmistress. Children in the school appeared to be healthy and well looked after, though it appeared that the late schoolmaster, David Cleary, could not have exerted himself as much as he ought to have done. Many children had been ill with whooping cough and, regrettably, several had died.

But by 1874 he was sorry to see that the school building was only half full (31 boys and 32 girls).[1] See Appendix E for details of the dispute between the Master and Schoolmaster/mistress in 1875.

Plan by Chambers of New School for 100 Children at Workhouse (c.1868)

On first floor – Dormitory for 50 boys & 50 girls in 4 rows of beds with dwarf partitions down the centre; plus Master's bedroom & Mistress' bedroom.

4 outer earth closets provide for the girls and an urinal for the boys also earth closets for the master & mistress in the boys' & girls' yards. Doors to be provided in the yard back walls to allow soil to be removed, without being taken through the school building.

On the ground floor boys' school room and day room, Master's day room, Mistress' day room, girls' schoolroom & day room.

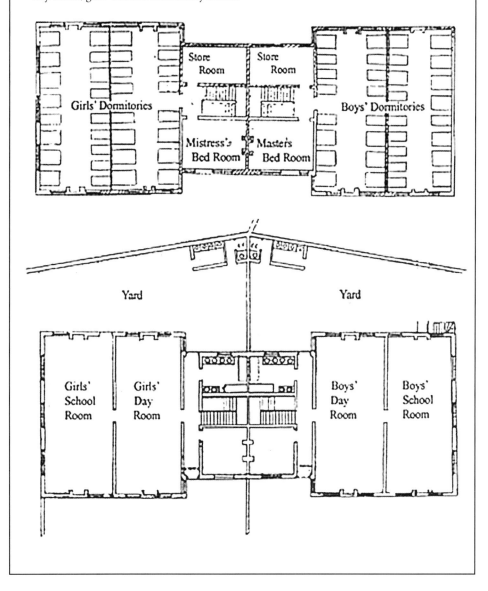

There was surplus accommodation for other children, so the Board of Guardians of Uxbridge Union, where the number of children was posing a problem, came to an agreement with the Henley Union to send some boys here at a charge of 6s 6d per head per week. In August 1878, Uxbridge (Middx) Union requested Henley to make a contract to receive up to ten girls, in addition, into the Workhouse School.[2]

Thereafter, in 1880, the Brentford (Middx) Union clerk wrote that: "Mr Henley, the Poor Law Inspector, suggested that an application should be made to ascertain if you can take some in the schools of your Union?"[1] The agreement was sealed on 11 May 1880 with the Guardians of Brentford Union for the reception into and maintenance and education in the school at the workhouse, of this Union of boys not exceeding 8 in number and of girls 16 in number, chargeable to Brentford Union.[1] The records contain reference to a Local Government Board secret agreement with Brentford Union in this connection.[1]

Boys will be boys and trouble ensued! In July 1880 the Master reported that on 25th June three of the boys in the school belonging to Uxbridge Union ran away while out for a walk with the other boys and the Schoolmaster, that they were detained by the police authorities at Maidenhead (perhaps trying to find their way home to Uxbridge?), from whence the Master fetched them back on the following day. That on the 3rd July two other boys aged 15 and 14 ran away, having escaped over the garden fence. That they were admitted to the Wallingford Workhouse and that he fetched them back on the following Monday.[1]

Children from Cookham Union were also accepted.[3]

eg. In December 1885 Ada Slade from Cookham Union "defective eyesight prevents her going to school or receiving domestic instruction. Please remove girl according to terms of Agreement."

In 1886 Maidenhead Union took the opportunity of sending four of their children to be schooled in Henley Workhouse. Unfortunately, they were found to be nitty, with their clothing in tatters and one child even had scarlet fever. So that was one way of transferring the problems!

Industrial training continued as part of the curriculum. Indeed, in 1881 the LGB had decreed that milking of cows be taught in workhouse schools. One can but wonder at the reaction of the Guardians when, in June 1884, they were confronted with a report on the condition of a cow at Henley workhouse by the vet, Mr Edward Mellett. He was firmly told that an operation on the cow was not to be performed![3]

In 1882 a School Attendance Officer had been appointed for Henley. He was ex Sergeant Major Littlewood of the Oxfordshire Hussars.[3]

In August 1885 there was an advertisement placed in the Local Government Chronicle that accommodation was available in the schools at the workhouse for children belonging to other unions. The school was proving too large for Henley Union's purpose fourteen years after opening.

| Children from other Unions | 20 | cf 12 last year May 12, 1884 |
| | 22 | cf 11 last year August 9, 1884 |

Reading Union was invited in 1887 to send 10 of their boys and 6 girls "on the same terms as heretofore."

In August 1889 "the Guardians, being of the opinion that the future welfare of the children resident in the Workhouse would be best promoted by their being educated at the public schools, in the town, resolved to send them to such schools so as soon as the necessary arrangements could be made, dispensing with the services of the Schoolmaster, with testimonial".[3]

This resulted also in no more work for the shoemaker in industrial training in shoemaking and he was discharged. (However, the whole of the inmates' boots were to be entirely made and repaired on the premises by a shoemaker on an ad hoc basis.)[3]

A tailor, William Courtney, was appointed in May 1890 to the office of Caretaker at the boys' school and Industrial Trainer in Tailoring. All the men's and boys' clothing was to be made and repaired by the tailor. He was to live in the redundant Schoolmaster's accommodation, on a pay scale of £20 pa plus money in lieu of beer.[3]

On 8 May 1891   Lucy Postans was appointed girls trainer at £20 pa, but on
    5 June 1891   She was invited to leave after complaint by the Master of the way she performed her duties.

After 1890 the post of Schoolmaster was combined with that of the extant mistress, Miss Walsh, at a salary of £30 pa. She stayed for 5 years until ill health caused her resignation. Three more schoolmistresses followed in quick succession, much to the concern of the Inspector. For instance, in June 1893 he reported that the school is not so good as it was last year but there have been three changes of teachers and the present one, Miss E Courtney, has only been here a fortnight. Some of the 37 children (no infants) are very weak in arithmetic.[3]

After the resignation of Elizabeth Courtney in December that year, the Inspector reported that there are no schoolmasters, the boys being placed under the schoolmistress. "There are also no Industrial Trainers but I find that there is a Boys' Caretaker and Shoemaker at £20 pa. The Board of Guardians will consider a recommendation of the School Committee to send the children of school age (16 boys, 21 girls) to the Henley National Schools." The LGB concurred with this course of action so long as the girls were not left without paid superintendence.[1] (Moral behaviour being paramount).

The Board of Guardians then sought to obtain the services of a competent woman to act as Industrial Trainer and caretaker of the girls when not in school, in lieu of a schoolmistress. Harriet Furze from Rochford Union in Essex, aged 34, was appointed Industrial Trainer in sewing and knitting for an estimated ten girls under instruction at a salary of £20 pa plus £3 10s beer money.

In January 1896 it was reported that the arrangement by which the children attended the National Schools "continues to work well and the Committee consider it is of great advantage to the children to mix with other children living under very different conditions and that it may be fairly evident that this education will largely influence for good their future life."[2]

After five appointments of Industrial Trainer in three years, in 1897 the Girls' Trainer, Miss Minns, absented herself when her mother was suddenly taken ill. She was allowed to leave. The LGB then decided that there were insufficient children (five) under training to justify this post[1] (see page 99 for subsequent developments).

By January 1901 the LGB Inspector was asking why he had not been furnished with information as to the removal of children from the workhouse (also the number of imbeciles and the amount of outdoor relief).[1] Henley guardian the Revd Coxe commented that it was four months since the children had received any instruction. He moved that a teacher be provided until they could go back to school. Because of illness half the school buildings had to be isolated and used as a hospital for affected children. There were only four cases but they were being treated in the house. The children might go back to school next week.[3]

In response to Mr Watts (fellow Guardian) asking if it was the spiritual or secular side of education it was proposed should be given, because they had a chaplain who very rarely and very occasionally administered, Mr Coxe said that it was nothing to do with the spiritual side. Mr Watts continued that it was only on sanitary grounds that the children were being kept in the house.[3]

By November that year plans were under way for conversion of the schools into infirmaries for 50 beds, costing £1,000, so this large school built for 100 children had a life of less than 30 years as a school but existed for another 80 odd years in hospital use.

9. Outdoor Relief

THE OLD Poor Law encouraged outdoor relief to be used regularly by the parish Vestry to alleviate poverty and suffering in the neighbourhood. This took the form of cash dole: 'casual', 'extraordinary', 'discretionary' and included able-bodied labourers and their families in time of need, (notwithstanding in 1800 that no pauper keeping a dog could have relief!)[i]

So those in need applied to the Overseer of the Poor in each Parish. This system was financed through the collection of rates from those who occupied land and property in the Parish, supplemented by local charity funds.

But the New Poor Law in 1834 stated that all relief whatever to able-bodied persons or to their families "except as to medical attendance" shall be declared unlawful otherwise than going into well-regulated workhouses. Also the less eligibility rule insisted that the situation of the pauper inside the workhouse must be less desirable than that of independent labourers outside in the community.[2]

The 1834 Act, while centralising the administration of relief, at the same time formalised a new approach to the concept of idleness. The official view decreed a more primitive attitude in that a degree of poverty was acceptable but that able-bodied pauperism denoted a sign of bad character.

So the New Poor Law was intended to deter those able-bodied poor who were physically capable of supporting themselves and their family from reliance on public assistance – despite the low level of wages obtaining locally. But the intention was always to reunite family groups (which were separated within the workhouse) and send them out of the House to earn money to keep themselves – while putting pressure on farmers to pay wages high enough for a family to live on.

Although outdoor relief was to be abolished for the able-bodied, nevertheless it could be continued for the aged and infirm and for accident or illness at the discretion of the Relieving and/or Medical Officer. So, in order to discourage the indolent, the new workhouses were to provide living standards which would be below those enjoyed by "independent labourers" outside the workhouse. This was known as the workhouse test, since it was assumed that anyone desperate enough to live in the workhouse must be in genuine need of relief. Therefore, the PLC ruled that no relief should be given **in money** to an able-bodied male pauper in employment except in cases of sickness or accident.

Nevertheless, in December 1835 Henley Poor Law Union was continuing to grant Relieving Officers' requests for various monetary outdoor relief to 17 families in

---

i   "Life in the Victorian Countryside" Pamela Horn, 1976.

the area (see following list). This still amounted to a surprising total of £35 18s 10½ compared to the sum of £52 6s 8½d previously paid in December 1834.

Some casual cases of relief allowed 1835.[i] [ii]

July		
99	Wm Simmonds + wife and 7 children 4-19 Wages 9s pw, family ill with scarlet fever.	allowed in kind 4s 6d.
December 1st, 8th, 15th, 22nd, 29th		
71	Wm Read, age 57 + wife and 2 children, wife very ill.	allowed 8s 11d for shoes.
94	Wm Dormer, age 42 + wife 35 and 7 children: 1-15 wages of man and wife 24s pw, Man and wife ill.	loan of 3s and 4 gallons of bread.
99	Wm Simmonds, age 37 + wife 39 and 7 children, 19,14,12,8,6,7,1. Family ill. Relieved by order of Surgeon, allowed extra and relief continued.	Paid funeral expenses of child aged 12.
114	Susannah Lovejoy + bastard son.	Belongs to Woodley / removed (Berks).
71	Wm Reade + wife. Pauper recovered from illness.	Relief discontinued.
6	Frances Rhodes Widow. Ill.	Extra 3lb mutton.
43	Eliz Hawkins age 33. Son ill.	Relieving Officer gave ½ gall bread / confirmed.
116	Samuel Sellwood, age 32; wife 32; 2 children: 9,7. Man in prison for poaching.	Relief given: 2s + 1 gall bread. approved.
32	Richard Burrows. Ill.	Relief given: 2s + ½ gall bread. to continue.
118	James Clark, age 38, wife 32 + 4 children: 8,6,4 + infant. Man ill for few days.	Relief given 3s + 2 galls bread / approved.
88	Charlotte Coxhead + bastard child. Woman confined, 5 weeks.	Maintenance order to be served on putative father: James Lloyd, butcher in/near Windsor.
5	Amy Broadway, age 54. Can find no work at the time of year.	1s pw.
	Wm Brookes, age 39 + wife 27 and 5 children: 9,6,4,2,1.	relief refused.

---

i   See detailed listing in "Henley-on-Thames Poor Law Union and Workhouse Records 1835-51" Oxfordshire Black Sheep Publications.

ii   ½ gallon = 8 lbs.

Some examples in December 1835 were:

82	Wm Clements, widower.	Relief discontinued, it being supposed has had made over some property to his son.
120	James Swain age 45, wife 42 + 10 children: 18,16,14,12,9,7,6,5,3,1. Wages 9s pw goods to value of 10s. Wants clothes to enable daughter, 14, to keep place.	Guardians recommend 10s.
122	James Maskell + wife + 5 children: 18, 15,15,13,10. Man has broken leg; surgeon says bad case.	6s + 2 galls bread + 1½ pints porter a day after medical orders.
99	Wm Simmonds, wife + 7 children.	Relieving Officer paid burial fees of child / allowed.
88	Charlotte Coxhead + child. Reputed father would appear at Quarter Sessions, but Guardians think evidence is not conclusive.	Case suppressed.

This was despite the new Board of Guardians in July 1835 scrutinising the list of casual cases of relief. The list was tightened up still further in March 1836 after the PLC reiterated to the Board of Guardians that Rule 19 could not be infringed and that the Relieving Officer should give the pauper the amount in kind.[1]

For example, explicit directions were issued by PLC to the Guardians in 1835 in respect of admitting a labourer's children into the workhouse.

> ... Where it is deemed inexpedient to enforce the test by offering the workhouse to able-bodied labourer as well as his family, it must still be borne in mind that relief to the child is relief to the parent, and such mode of administering it as is proposed ought to be carefully watched so as to prevent its application except in cases where some kind of relief is absolutely necessary and it should, as far as possible, be so given as to prevent habits of dependence.
>
> A condition in Article 21 requires that the relief, if given to able-bodied male paupers in employment, should be in kind and not in money as heretofore. It was intended as a preliminary step to the total prohibition of all such relief in aid of wages, for which so much mischief has induced to workhouses themselves and to the community,[i] but it is the duty of the Commissioners to see that efficient workhouse accommodation is provided in every instance so as to enable Guardians to offer the alternative of the workhouse before they issue an order prohibiting all relief to the individuals indicated in Article 21, Section 1.
>
> This Commission sees no objection to the proposal of taking one or two children of labourers having large families into their workhouse school for a season, provided that such aid is actually necessary and provided that such

---

i   Speenhamland system.

children are not considered as permanent inmates of the workhouse, which would be obviously objectionable. The children might be then instructed in the day-time and returned to their parents at night. This would be an eligible mode of affording relief in the case of a large family.... [1]

Henley Poor Law Union Minute Book 1835-6 [2] records the detailed consideration by the Board of Guardians of casual cases of relief allowed parish by parish.

This shows the Guardians coming to terms with new regulations. One month after their first meeting they sat down and went through the pauper list of the parish of Pyrton and the relief afforded. Of the 56 cases under consideration, 16 were discontinued and 5 pauper families were placed in the Workhouse.

A fortnight later it was the turn of Peppard: 26 cases were considered, of which half were allowed a continuation of cash and bread; only 2 were discontinued and 8 placed into the Workhouse.

It was a busy day, Bix had 30 cases for consideration; Swyncombe 26; Nuffield 25 and Nettlebed 29, etc.

These minutes give fascinating details of the individual applicants by age, infirmity or problem and family size and the decision to refuse or to make an allowance, given in cash generally between 1s and 2s 6d per week plus ½ gallon or 1 gallon of bread. These were starvation rations.

Thomas Smith and wife, 42, had 8 children under their roof plus 3 elder children away. The man was willing to go to any manufactory town so the Clerk was instructed to seek advice from the Assistant Commissioners in London as to helping them on their way.

The Overseer of Bix, Mr Cheer (sic) reported on the sums of money lent as loans. As regards Swyncombe, the Clerk was to give notice to employers to attach wages for the outstanding sums at 1s pw.

Albert Simmons, able-bodied, and his wife had 8 children aged from 1 to 11. The man's wages being considered insufficient to support his large family, the Guardians of Caversham Parish requested special consideration to see what could be done for the family before Michaelmas. Allowed meanwhile 2 gallons of bread per week.

Sadly, the mother of the Gearing family was dead and the father transported so the child had been put with Mary Lovejoy at 1s pw and ½ gallon bread.

On the other hand, outdoor relief was automatically refused to bastards, who were labelled as such and sometimes allowed into the Workhouse. Consider the case of Widow Simmons with 3 children "(one bastard) – no relief for a bastard". Allowed for self and 2 children 2s pw and 1 gallon bread (just one more mouth to spread it around).

Martha Austin of Swyncombe had her relief discontinued in order to bring the woman before the Board for refusing work at the commencement of the harvest.

Ann Richardson of Nuffield was in dire straits with three legitimate children aged 14, 12, 10, her husband having been transported, and two illegitimate children aged 5 and an infant. She was ordered into the Workhouse, but one week later was being allowed for the legitimate child of 10 years 1s 6dpw and ½ gallon bread, so presumably was pressing on regardless.

Samuel Whittick and William Woodbridge of Henley were lent one grubbing mattock and beetle in order to grub at Phillis Court; a blacksmith.

Robert Hoard, his wife and children were allowed to come into the House and 5s given him to get his goods from the wharf. They were willing to go into the manufacturing districts in the north so Hoard was allowed the loan of a pair of trousers, jacket, smock frock and stockings but six months later he was still making applications.

William Fisher of Britwell Salome had 5 children aged 13, 12, 11, 9, 8. The Home Migration Office in Manchester had notified the Clerk that the family may be conveyed to Tamworth. The Overseers of the parish were directed to provide the family with necessary clothing and pay the expense of their journey. So this family was thus removed from future parish expenditure.

In February 1836 the PLC advised that in the case of Charles Banbury (33) and wife (32) with 7 children (0-10), to whom outrelief was being paid at 9s per week for rent plus 1s6d, a "safer course is to offer to provide relief to such an able-bodied man in the workhouse".

Henley Union minute books go on to list the following disbursements in April 1836 showing some flexibility in the arrangements still pertaining:

Ian Clark, with a wife and 4 children; he was in prison since February so she was allowed 4 gall bread ...

William Simmonds, a labourer earning 9s pw with a wife and 6 children; wife confused and daughter ill he was given 5s in relief.

Henry Fisher had a wife and 5 children; his application for a midwife's services was allowed.

Mary Wicks was a lunatic housed at Messrs. Warburtons costing £13 8s 6d.

Also at this time James Maskell, who had a wife and 2 children and had suffered a broken leg, had extra meat ordered for him by the Medical Officer at a cost of 1s 9d paid for 5 weeks.

Sam Sellwood also had a wife and 2 children; he had just returned from prison so his wife's allowance was discontinued.

Poor William Haseman's wife had died so he was allowed a coffin and shroud costing 14s 9d for a pauper funeral.

By the Summer quarter of 1837 the Application and Report Book gives detailed listing of the amount of relief then allocated in each Parish. Such treatment in kind compensated for dietary deficiencies.

For instance, Charles Ford, able-bodied umbrella maker at Thomas's lodging house, was given 2s on 21 April and 4s 1½d on 27 April because his Irish wife was ill and destitute and they had three children. Decision was made that temporary assistance be given as the case required.

Richard Wells, a labourer in Well Place, Ipsden with 6 children, was earning 10s per week; allowed supplement of 4s 9d because wife was confined and ill.

Ann Percy, a widow aged 67 of Nettlebed, had been receiving 2s and ½ gallon of bread. This was reduced to 6d as her son was deemed able to assist.

Daniel Buckett aged 60 and his wife Elizabeth, 42, had seven children, aged 14, 12, 10, 7, 5, 3, 1. Daniel was unable to work and received medical relief. Child, 14, earned 3s. Relief ordered by Guardians of 4s, 4 gallon bread and 5lb mutton, value

6s 6d. Likewise, William Lucas of Henley aged 42 with wife Elizabeth and 6 children were allowed 4s and 4 gallon bread because an accident caused him to be out of work due to a broken collar bone.

Poor Elizabeth Sarney, a widowed field worker of Nettlebed with 3 children aged 8, 10 and 11, had been receiving 2s and ½ gallon bread. The Guardians considered that one child was able to work and reduced the allowance to 1s.

Consider the position of Jane Lucas, single, aged 19, Henley labourer, who had been confined with a bastard child, for which a midwife had been paid 7s 6d. Seven weeks later the child was dead and she was allowed 11s 9d for the funeral and coffin etc.

Occasionally, the Guardians were inclined to help out in order to keep someone in work, e.g. Elizabeth Webb, aged 18, who was a servant at the Kings Arms in Henley, having been found a situation out of the workhouse. She was allowed 10s in clothes "to keep her service".

An unusual case of mobility was that of Ann Lewin, aged 27 of Shiplake. Her husband was abroad in the army and over a period of 2 months she and her child were helped on their way to join him in India via Chatham.

There are about 190 entries listed, revealing various crises of injury, illness, prison and degrees of poverty both short-term and long-term; able-bodied with too many mouths to feed or having suffered an accident; old age; husband gone away; ill; feeble or even lunatic. A continuing saga of hard lives led in the rural agricultural economy hereabouts.

Some interesting examples of the work of Relieving Officers in the community are indicated by the following further extracts from entries in Henley Union Minute Books in 1840-1. This illustrates the nature of deprivation and need e.g. crises caused by illness, injury and prison; the expenses incurred by births and deaths; and the problems faced by having large families on small wages.

Apr 14 1840	Cav	Thomas Snow has had an accident in the hand and is unable to do any work.
		George Roberts has erysipelas and is unable to work. (Kidney disease)
	Henley	William Stone – ½ pint of porter daily and mutton.
	Peppard	Jane Hostler requires mutton.
Apr 21	Eye and Dunsden	Louisa Mossiman requires mutton.
		Charlotte May requires mutton.
		Joseph Read unable to work.
		James Beard unable to work.
	Caversham	Eliza Mascall in a weak state; requires mutton.
Apr 28	E&D	The Clerk to go and take the examination of pauper Rose Wild.

Apr	Watlington	Godfrey E not fit to be removed; requires a nurse, sore eyes.
		Ward Wm, fit to be removed.
		Maynard J, oranges, port wine and 2lb mutton fever.
		Maynard J, arrowroot and sherry wine.
		Herbert J, unfit to work; requires a nurse / spitting blood.
		Wheeler Jas, unfit to work sore eyes.
		Coleman J, unfit to work indigestion.
		Robinson S, unfit to be removed / fever.
		Woods Wm, unfit to work, sore eyes.
May 19		Sarah Thorpe and illegitimate child – Clerk to report.
		Charlotte May and Louisa Mossiman ongoing. James King's wife – mutton and brandy.
Jun 1	E&D	Order of affiliation on illegitimate child of Sarah Thorpe.
		Putative father: Henry Eynott of Caversham to pay 1s 6d pw.
Jun 9	E&D	Mutton for Louisa Mossiman, Charlotte May.
		James King's wife (also porter).
Aug 4	E&D	William Hearne – some mutton (Clerk to look into case).
Sep 8		Wm Hearne, Mrs King, Charlotte May still having mutton.
		(Hearne eventually to be removed to Padworth on Oct 6).
Nov 3	E&D	Henry Pritchard into workhouse.
Dec 8	Caversham	Stephen Curtis and Charles Banbury into workhouse.
1841		Medical Certificates were produced as follows:
Jan 5	E&D	Sarah Haseman, an ongoing case; her bastard child died Jan 2.
	Greys	Richard Woods, 2lb mutton.
		Mrs Rawlins, some mutton.
		Ann Neville, unable to work.
	Peppard	Sarah Lawrence, unable to work; 2lb mutton.

		Porter and wife, 3lb mutton; ½ pt beer daily.
	Harpsden	Roberts, 2lb mutton.
	Caversham	Mrs Woodward, unable to work; bad leg.
		Henry and Susan Woodward unable to work.
		Mrs Wells is in a weak state and requires mutton as before.
		Mr Chapman unable to work; 2lb mutton as before.
		Wm Foster unable to work; bad leg.
		Susanna Clark, unfit to work.
		Mrs Burrow's child – mutton broth.
		John Maskell 2lb mutton.
		James Lovejoy unable to work.
		John Lovejoy still in a real state, unable to work.

The PLC had decreed in April 1836 that without their sanction, no money could be expended from the poor rates to help paupers emigrating to America. They later denied a request to clothe an able-bodied man and his wife to enable them to take work in Halifax (Nova Scotia) because it was forbidden to give outdoor relief to able-bodied men.[1] Nevertheless, in 1858 a family of seven was granted £11 in order to migrate from Watlington to South Australia, thus relieving the Parish of long-term out-relief. The extended family consisted of William Franklin, 62, wife 65, son 38, daughter-in-law 33 and child, (Anna Maria) 3 months; son-in-law James Smith 20 with wife 21, seven people.[1]

When, in 1836, William Gill of Gallowstree Common, near Sonning Common, became too old to work and was already on parish relief, he gave his house to his sons James and Stanshill, who apparently had no qualms about allowing him to go into the workhouse at Henley. The Guardians asked for a contribution of 3s a week towards the old man's keep but no pressure was put on the sons to take him into their home.[2]

Of note, given the regulations, is the quarterly return for December 1837:

Total indoor number of paupers	214
Total outdoor number of paupers	111
Maintenance	£309
Out relief	£1124
Establishment charges	£946

There followed, in January 1838, complaints made against Thomas Barnes, the Relieving Officer for Watlington. He was unable to make a defence against allegations that he was careless and inefficient and the Guardians therefore decided that he was no longer qualified to hold the situation; they accepted his resignation. However, the PLC deemed him "drunken, irregular in paying paupers and fraudulent" and they issued an order for his dismissal.[1]

In some places benefit given as outdoor relief was disguised as "medical relief" and so outdoor relief "on receipt of a Medical Officer of Health's certificate" was still paid in 1840 to the following paupers:

William Bunce's wife, Henley	1lb mutton
Widow Bunce	1lb mutton
Henry Pritchard, Eye and Dunsden	some mutton
Louisa Mossiman	some mutton

The less-eligibility rule was reinforced by the Outside Relief Prohibition Order 1844. However, this order included exceptions whereby Guardians might easily relieve able-bodied poor on grounds of sudden and urgent necessity, accident or sickness.[i]

The allowance system thereby continued to operate in many areas, including Henley. This dole was effectively used to keep wholly and partially unemployed labourers alive and available for the next season's work. Henley Corporation minutes record that bread and fuel were given away in considerable quantities in winter to alleviate immediate distress at this time.

The 1851 census lists 39 paupers in Henley outside the workhouse, who presumably were still receiving outdoor relief in order to survive. The allocation of bread for the poor was issued from a building behind the former Red Cow public house, where there is still a trace of the bread ovens.

By the 1852 Outdoor Relief Regulation Order, at least half of any assistance was to be given in the form of food, fuel or other necessary articles. These were purchased on contracts by the Guardians, with the lowest tender being accepted, irrespective of quality of the goods provided. Those men in receipt were to be set to work by the Guardians for as long as assistance continued. The work mainly took the form of chopping wood, breaking stones, digging or some other task connected to road-mending.

The 1858 half-yearly accounts for Henley Union show the cost of in-maintenance (workhouse) at £140 11s 5d, which was 45% of the out-relief at £309 2s 6d; also relief of irremovable Poor under the Settlement Law payable to other Unions: £128 8s 6d. The number of outdoor paupers reported in January 1860 was 1512.

In 1869 there was considerable increase in the amount of mendacity, pauperism and destitution in the general area (of Henley).[3]

January 1871 proved to be a hard winter. A soup kitchen was opened for 486 persons: 137 families were provisioned on one Thursday, amounting to £58 10s and including a large number from Trinity District of Henley.[3]

Subscriptions to the soup kitchens were listed in the Henley Advertiser (including a donation of 5s from S Mortlock) but there were considerable arrears because expenditure over five weeks amounted to £150. Soup had been distributed to 444 families comprising 1604 individuals during the five weeks, with a total distribution of 2000 gallons. A balance sheet was published. At year end it was reported that in Henley there were 449 people in receipt of outdoor relief; 254 in Watlington and 118 in Caversham (½ of the whole population).[3]

---

i   Pamela Horn (ibid).

Expenditure on Outrelief in 1870/1 as listed in Kinch's Advertiser

It will be seen that apart from the period January to March (May not reported), seasonal variations in outrelief were not so applicable to such occurrences as accidents or sickness. The table of outrelief, down to the last farthing, allowed by the Guardians via local Relieving Officers, shows fluctuations month by month but overall with some consistency in allowances given to those seeking outrelief throughout the years 1870 and 1871.

	1870	1871
2 weeks in January	£126 5 7¾d	£138 13 8d
February	£136 5 8d	£142 14 10½d
March	£122 9 4¾d	£135 7 2½d
April	£134 1 9½d	£131 16 2d
June	£121.8.8½d	£114 12 1½d
July	£119 2 5¾d	£112 9 5¾d
August	£116 11 2¾d	£118 19 0¾d
September	£114 4 1½d	£114 12 7¾d
	£115 17 4d	££116 18 9d
October	£130 19 1¾d	£114 14 2¼d
	£118 19 8½d	£114 15 3d
November	£121 4 8 ½d	£117 0 4¼d
	£116 3 11 ¼d	£119 6 3½d
December	£119 15 8d	£118 10 3¾d
	£119 6 0½d	£116 19 9d

The continuing cost of out relief can be gauged from the following return made in early 1872:

	week 12	week 13
Henley	£70 5s 6d	£55 1s 10d
Watlington	£33 17s 0½	£34 10s 11¼d
Caversham	£15 15s 3½	£17 2s 7½d

Philanthropy was displayed in early **January 1872** when 53 children belonging to the Industrial School were supplied with a substantial dinner at the Town Hall, kindly lent for the purpose by the Mayor. Through the so-called liberality of those who contributed, there was an abundance of roast beef, pudding, beer and other good things. In the evening there was a Christmas tree from which every child received a present and, before departing, each had an orange and a bun. The remains of the feast were distributed among about 20 poor people.[3]

In May 1873 the LGB wrote that the outdoor pauperism of the (Henley) Union was high as compared with England as a whole.[1]

There occurred another hard winter in **January 1881** when the "blockage of streets by snow in wintry weather scarcely ever has been equalled". (The cost of clearing it was nearly £50). There followed the opening of a soup kitchen with distribution to a very large number of families. Also Smiths Charity supplied 16 poor widows with bread. In addition they donated flannel and calico to 150 poor persons.[3]

By May 1881 it was resolved, on a proposal by the Revd Almack, that no outdoor relief be given in future to any persons who have taken no care in providing themselves by means of benefit clubs etc;[3] self-help was the order of the day.

However, there were voices of concern. In March 1887 Mr A W Hall, MP for Oxford, was arguing against the Poor Law as the right and proper way of administration, especially in respect of those receiving outdoor relief, being "exceedingly harsh and pressing upon many deserving poor".[2]

So it is noteworthy that outrelief was payable even when a pauper moved in with family: Fred Brooker, in 1888, formerly living in Checkendon on sickness outrelief, was then residing with his daughter at Warren Row, Berks. Cookham Union extracted an agreement from Henley Union to continue paying him 2s 6d per week plus a 4 lb loaf of bread.[2]

On 8 January the Henley Advertiser reported: "The opening of the soup kitchen on Thursday last was a great boon to the many families in Henley, and a great number of applications for tickets were received." Subscriptions were urgently sought. The soup kitchen was stated to be intended for those out of employment or in distress and not for persons with small families and in full work. Another example of outrelief occurred in 1889 when the guardians received a deputation from the Borough school asking if the Board would agree to paying school fees for children whose parents were unable through poverty or other causes to pay. The Guardians presumably viewed education as the route into the job market so that they were "anxious, after enquiry by their officer to give them facility for such payment in cases where there is satisfactory evidence of inability to pay on the part of the parents".[3]

In June 1890 the Relieving officer applied for an order of committal against George Pavey, beerhouse-keeper of Reading, for non-payment of arrears of maintenance order for his father [3] (see page 87).

Outrelief took various forms. For example in March 1892 the Board of Guardians obtained repayment of £2 10s 1d, which was money expended by them in relief given to Mrs McDonald in consequence of the Sanitary Authority having prevented her from taking in washing while one of her children was suffering from diphtheria.[2]

In August 1894 a well-meaning resident wrote direct to the Local Government Board about a poor family with 10 children, one of whom was "handicapped", viz.

> H Ramsbottom, Well Place, Wallingford to LGB:
> There is a poor family here consisting of a man and wife and 10 children. The
> man earns about 12s /wk at present. The two eldest girls are in service but one

is obliged to ruin her own prospects by coming home to help her mother. One boy aged 15 receives 7-8s/wk. All the others are too young to do any good, and the 10th child is only about a month old. But one of these younger children, aged between 5-6, is a hopeless idiot, blind and dumb and not able to move itself out of its bed.

I have written to the Henley Union asking them to receive this child into the workhouse infirmary and pointing out that the whole family is dragged down from comparative comfort to penury. The younger children are perforce neglected and the prospects of the elder ones severely damaged. It is impossible to get a neighbour to help her as none are near who possibly could.

What I am anxious to know is whether the Guardians are not legally bound to receive the child, supposing the facts are what I have stated. And supposing they are not bound, what can be done in this really great trial, as the child is quite as much as one woman alone can properly manage and there are four younger who cannot receive proper care.

LGB replied that they were precluded by law from interfering in individual cases but said that it did not appear that the Board of Guardians had actually refused the application and, in any case, there was "a good deal of money" coming into that house.[1]

In December 1894 the Guardians submitted an application to LGB in respect of:

Frank Foster, Shiplake, who had become quite blind a few months ago from atrophy of the optic nerve. Out-relief at 4s 4d pw.

Attempts have been made but without success to obtain his admission into an institution where he could be taught basket-making, the reason of the refusal to admit him being that he is over 40 years of age. Arrangements can be made for the man to learn the trade of a basket-maker under Mr Hitchman, a tradesman in this town who would be willing to teach him for a couple of years. The Guardians would pay 6s pw. This the LGB sanctioned, subject to production of vouchers to District Auditor.[1]

In 1894 the new Local Government Act provided that all Rural District councillors should also serve as Poor Law Guardians for the parishes for which they had been elected. This seems to have prompted a change of policy by Henley Board of Guardians. "Outdoor relief had greatly increased since the new Board came into existence after Christmas, the new policy of the Board now being to give outdoor and not indoor relief". So in 1895 it was reported that there had been "a great increase, amounting to an extra £416 a year, in outdoor relief during this year and there would probably be a decrease in indoor relief" (inmates).[3] For example, for the half-year to Michaelmas 1895 the following comparison was made:

	1894	1895
R/O Mr Glass's District, Watlington	£20 5s 7d	£23 6s 9d
R/O Mr Stone's District, Henley	£20 17s 11d	£25 13s 6d
R/O Mr Bobin's District, Caversham	£13 9s 7d	£ 13 3s 5d

The Revd H Coxe commented that the increase amounted to £8 a week or £416 a year for outdoor relief, despite the fact that the number in the House was greater now at 108 compared to 90 the previous year.[3]

A letter from LGB on outrelief was circulated in 1896. Mr Ovey proposed from the chair that a committee be appointed to consider the increase in outrelief and to frame rules for adoption by the Board for dealing with future applications. This resulted in the Visiting Committee proposing that the Board discontinue giving outrelief in bread, save in exceptional cases, but instead give payment in money at the rate of 4d per 4 lb loaf to all poor persons over 60 years of age. The Guardians disagreed and decided to pass the following motion: [2]

"That the new Rule of the Board that money instead of bread be given to the outdoor poor of 60 years of age and upwards be rescinded and that the old custom of giving money and bread be continued." And so it did.

Furthermore, the Board of Guardians agreed to the issue of a pair of shoes at a subsidised cost between 2s and 4s 4d, shoes being an important element of being able to go out to work. Also allowed was the cost of a set of clothes to enable young paupers to go into service or apprenticeship, and the attendance of a midwife to a pauper's wife at childbirth; at the other end of the scale, funeral expenses to be allowed for burial. For those men experiencing a hernia there was a truss provided so that they could continue to work.

But even after WW1 the families of people who were unemployed continued to face hardship. In the winter of 1921-2 the mayoress organised a soup kitchen for children, funded by local subscriptions. This was based at the Police Station and ran for four months, attracting about 150 children every day.[3] However, unemployment continued to be a problem in Henley until the late 1930s, with consequent applications for public assistance.

Nevertheless, for Christmas 1929 Lord Phillimore insisted on no extra out-relief, which he viewed as a sentimental gift, other than the usual Christmas fare provided to inmates and staff. He was opposed to it on account of the money coming out of the ratepayers' pockets.[3]

Outrelief from continued residence in one's own Parish was the dominant mode of relief throughout the 19th century, despite sporadic efforts to reverse this, and outrelief became even more pronounced in the 20th century. Indeed, by September 1931 there were nearly one million people receiving assistance in England and Wales compared with 600,000 in 1914. Nearly all of this relief was given to residents in their own homes.[3] This had been evident since about 1900.

10. Diet

THERE WAS a distinction in attitude towards the "deserving poor" and those deemed idle or vagrant but, nevertheless, there was always a stigma attached to living in the workhouse. This dissuaded the poor from entering and becoming an extra burden on the rates. Nevertheless, once inside the inmates did receive a reasonable diet, which was probably better than they could afford to have outside. For example, the dietary table for 1791 in the Poor House was listed as follows:

	Breakfast	**Dinner**	**Supper**
Sunday	Oatmeal porridge One slice of bread	7 oz meat, veg, slice bread; 1 pt beer	Slice bread; 1 pt beer 2 oz cheese or 1 oz butter
Monday	"	12 oz suet pudding & 1 pt beer	A pint of broth & slice of bread
Tuesday	"	same as Sunday	same as Sunday
Wednesday	"	14 oz rice pudding & 1 pt beer	same as Monday
Thursday	"	same as Sunday	same as Sunday
Friday	"	same as Monday	same as Monday
Saturday	"	oxcheek soup with pease or French barley	same as Sunday

NB: Males 18 oz bread on meat days 14 oz on pudding days
      Females 16 oz on meat days 14 oz on pudding days
      Children to have sufficient quantity.[i]

This was much less than the diet in the Poorhouse in 1781 when quantities of £50 of butcher's meat or £25 of Bacon were being ordered for the Poor in the House per day, three times in the week.

However, with the introduction of the New Poor Law in 1834 strict control was exercised as to the amount and cost of feeding the inmates, who were to be no better off than if they were in their own homes on a subsistence diet. Any variation to the prescribed diet had to be authorised by the Poor Law Commissioners in London.

There was a recommendation to the Guardians that the inmates should earn every meal; they should do sufficient work before breakfast to pay for that meal and the same before dinner and supper. This was because it was felt desirable "that where

---

i   MS. DD. Henley C IV. 11a.

there are many men employed, system and regularity are most essential and it was considered improper for the pauper to be allowed to idle away part of their time; it was desirable that he should see and feel that he is made to earn his own living and that the workhouse system is a system of work indeed."[2]

In fact, the Poor Law Commission produced six model dietaries, meagre and uninteresting, from which local guardians selected one which approximated to the diet of labourers in the area. The dietaries contained 160-170 ounces of solid food per week for adult inmates, or about one third more than an agricultural labourer in the rural south could in fact afford to obtain. Much of the diet consisted of cheap carbohydrates, such as bread, potatoes and suet pudding, but there was provision for a meat meal once, twice or three times a week and additional protein was provided by cheese at breakfast or supper. (Vegetables were expensive and unless grown on site were not provided).

In February 1836 the Henley Union chose the PLC's Dietary Table No 1. It is notable that the quantities and variety were considerably less than prior to the New Poor Law. Nevertheless, in May of the following year, the Commissioners considered that the new diet appeared to be higher than diets generally adopted elsewhere. In July 1836 the Henley Union reported a great scarcity of potatoes, so the Commissioners agreed to four ounces of bread being allowed each pauper for dinner on meat days.[1]

In December 1848, following a new PLB General Dietary Order and against the advice of their medical officer, the Guardians proposed to reduce the amount of meat allowed on the three meat days each week in order to make a saving of 4d per

January 1886, Henley Union Minute Book
Dietary Tables: Able-bodied

Ounces:		Breakfast		Dinner								Supper	
		Bread	Gruel	Bread	Cheese	Beef	Pork	Vegetable	Soup (pint)	Fish	Meat Pudding	Bread	Cheese
Sun.	Male	6	1½	7	2							6	1½
	Female	5	1½	5	1½							5	1½
Mon.	Male	6	1½	3			4	16				6	1½
	Female	5	1½	3			4	12				5	1½
Tues.	Male	6	1½	6					1½			6	1½
	Female	5	1½	5					1½			5	1½
Wed.	Male	6	1½	3		4		16		12		6	1½
	Female	5	1½	3		4		12		12		5	1½
Thur.	Male	6	1½	7	2							6	1½
	Female	5	1½	5	1½							5	1½
Fri.	Male	6	1½					16			14	6	1½
	Female	5	1½					12			12	5	1½
Sat.	Male	6	1½	6					1½			6	1½
	Female	5	1½	5					1½			5	1½

*On Wednesday in Winter months, Fish served in lieu of meat.
Oxford Archives PLU4/G/1A1/18.

279

the Poor Law Board –

Table A
Children from 2 to 5

	Breakfast		Dinner						Supper		
---	Bread	milk	Cooked Meat	Meat pudding	Potatoes or other Vegetables	Soup	Rice milk	Bread	Bread	Butter	milk and Water
---	oz.	pints	oz:	oz:	oz:	pints	pints	oz.	oz.	oz:	pints
Sunday	4	1/2	.	.	.	.	3/4	3	4	1/2	1/3
Monday	4	1/2	2	.	6	.	.	2	4	1/2	1/3
Tuesday	4	1/2	.	.	.	3/4	.	4	4	1/2	1/3
Wednesday	4	1/2	2	.	6	.	.	2	4	1/2	1/3
Thursday	4	1/2	.	.	.	3/4	.	4	4	1/2	1/3
Friday	4	1/2	.	8	6	.	.	.	4	1/2	1/3
Saturday	4	1/2	.	.	.	3/4	.	4	4	1/2	1/3

Table B
Children from 5 to 9

	Breakfast		Dinner						Supper		
---	Bread	milk	Cooked Meat	Meat	Pudding	Potatoes or other Vegetables	Soup	Rice milk	Bread	Bread	Butter	Milk and Water
---	oz.	pints	oz:	oz:	oz:	pints	pints	oz.	oz.	oz:	pints
Sunday	4	1	.	.	.	.	1	3	5	3/4	1/2
Monday	4	1	3	.	8	.	.	2	5	3/4	1/2
Tuesday	4	1	.	.	.	1	.	4	5	3/4	1/2
Wednesday	4	1	3	.	8	.	.	2	5	3/4	1/2
Thursday	4	1	.	.	.	1	.	4	5	3/4	1/2
Friday	4	1	.	10	8	.	.	.	5	3/4	1/2
Saturday	4	1	.	.	.	1	.	4	5	3/4	1/2

Children under 2 years of age to be dieted at discretion

The Sick to be dieted as directed by the Medical Officer

Oxford Archives PLU4/G/1A1/18, 1886.

head. This would have reduced the men's dinners to one ounce of meat, half a pound of vegetables and four ounces of bread on the three meat days. The Commissioners thought this a very considerable reduction and suggested that, on the meat days, a small quantity of bread – say three ounces – should also be given with the reduced dinner or that five ounces of meat with vegetables be given twice instead of three times a week, with suet pudding on a third day.[1]

However, in December 1850 many of the children had bad colds and coughs, so the master recorded in his journal that he had ordered that all the children in the house be given hot boiled rice for dinner instead of bread and cheese. In 1864 the Medical Officer endorsed Mr Mortlock's suggestion of a change to the children's diet by substituting apple pudding in lieu of their usual meat dinner on Mondays for the next 3 months (Sept – Nov).[1]

According to the dietary tables dated August 1869, the children's diet was somewhat more varied than for adults, with suet pudding on Thursdays and rice pudding on Sundays and 3 oz bread. For supper, in addition to the 5 oz bread and cheese, the children were given butter on their bread once a week and half a pint of milk and water.

Detailed returns to the Poor Law Board in December 1869 consisted of amended diet tables selected by the Henley Board of Guardians for eg: the able-bodied paupers; the aged, infirm and imbeciles; and growing children: 2 to 5, 5 to 9, and 9 to 16; children under 2 years of age to be dieted at discretion.

So breakfast consisted of bread and gruel every day: 6 oz bread for the men, 5 oz for women and children; and 1½ pints of gruel for everyone (a gallon of gruel was made with 12 oz round Scotch oatmeal). Dinner, taken at lunchtime, varied between cooked meat or meat pudding, made with 7 oz flour to 1½ oz suet and 4 oz raw meat, on three days; bread and cheese or bread and soup on the other days (no differences between able-bodied and aged or infirm). Soup was to be made with raw meat on Tuesdays and Saturdays: "The meat is allowed to remain in the soup, which on Tuesdays is made with the liquor in which the meat was boiled on the previous day.[1] Such detailed cooking directions came down from PLB even into the kitchen.[i]

Supper was always the same, however, with 5-6 oz bread and 1½ oz cheese for all aged over 9; younger children had ½ oz butter on their bread instead of cheese plus ⅓ to ½ pint of milk and water. In September 1887 the inmates were reported as complaining that their allotted shares of cheese were served in a crumbled state. In response, the Board of Guardians ordered the contractor to supply a sound and suitable cheese for cutting into small portions.[3] In addition, the aged and infirm were given one pint of sweet tea per person. This last meal of the day was taken at about 5 pm, leaving a gap until around 8 am next morning.

And so this dreary diet continued year in and year out, as laid down and approved by PLB, except that in December 1871 it was ordered that male paupers aged over 15 would be given 8 oz bread for supper and 6 oz bread and 1 pint of gruel for breakfast – still monotonous but enhanced portions. However, in June 1875, a letter from LGB on the auditor's report re daily provisions account stated "On Thursday 24th December and every subsequent Thursday to 25th March '75 the Master had given

---

i   NB. p.67 that eggs and poultry are used in the House.

soup at dinner instead of the prescribed dietary of bread and cheese for adults and suet pudding for children. The only authority for such a change was the Medical Officer's written recommendation in his report book: I recommend that during the winter months the whole of the inmates in the House be supplied with pea soup on Thursday in lieu of bread and cheese and suet pudding."

MO Jeston replied that he had been told by the Master that many of the old men and women in the House were unable to eat their bread and cheese and he recommended that they have on Thursdays suet pudding with fruit or treacle and on Sundays rice milk with 5 oz bread instead of bread and cheese. The Guardians resolved that the diet table for Class 2 and 6 be altered on Sundays, that rice milk be substituted for the bread and cheese dinners, that on Thursdays suet pudding or soup be substituted for the bread and cheese dinners.[2]

Drinking water was still suspect in June 1879 when an advertisement appeared for supply of beer for use of the inmates (sound family ale).[3]

But an alteration to the diet was ordered in 1880 whereby on Wednesday each week the same weight in rice when cooked was to be used instead of potatoes for dinner.

The sick were "dieted as directed by the medical officer" who was required to sign the application to PLB as being sufficient for the inmate's needs. So an amended dietary table for aged and infirm and imbecile inmates was agreed in 1875, on the undertaking that this would be more satisfactory to the inmates and as economical.[3]

In November 1884 the LGB asked the MO for his response on the effect of fish dinners on the health of the inmates. Not surprisingly, Dr Baines replied that he considered it was most satisfactory and would strongly recommend fish dinners twice a week for the infirmary patients.[1] Mr Ovey's gift in 1889 of rabbits for the sick and infirm presumably related to Mrs Beeton's recipe for invalids of stewed rabbits in milk.

As regards the diet of vagrants' children, this was prescribed by the Casual Paupers Regulations Order 1882 whereby children under 7 years of age, when detained for one night only received for supper and breakfast 4 oz bread and 1 oz cheese, or 3 oz bread and half a pint of soup, the gruel broth or soup to be made of the same ingredients and in the same proportions as used in the workhouse.

However, following a question in September 1895 about supplying milk to the young children of vagrants, these regulations were amended a year later, viz:

0 – 7 months	milk	½ pint max
	sugar	½ oz
7 months – 2 years	milk	½ pint
	sugar	
	bread	2 oz
2 – 7 years	milk	½ pint
	cheese	½ oz

The allowance could be given to a suckling mother instead of the infant, at the discretion of the Matron.

This matter was highlighted following a report in the Henley Standard newspaper on 26 September 1895 under the heading "Refractory Pauper", viz:

Ellen Baker, tramp, was charged with disorderly conduct at the workhouse on the morning of 26th. Harriet Thomas, female porter, said the language used to her was most obscene and disgusting. The husband of the last witness corroborated and said the defendant said she had been on the road for 30 years. Mr Martin, Master of the Workhouse, also gave corroborative evidence. Defendant said the disturbance arose because she asked for some milk to make gruel for a child of 6 months. Harriet Thomas, recalled, said the child was fed on water gruel. The defendant did not ask for milk. It was not in witness's powers to give milk; that was only done by the doctor's orders. Sentenced to 7 days hard labour.

However later, in a report to LGB, it was stated that as a rule, a child of 6 months would still be taking the breast. "It is a defect in the Order that no provision is made for children under 2. I have enquired into this case. It appears that the child in question was not Baker's child, but that of a woman named Mansfield. It is stated that Baker complained of the child crying and then made a disturbance. The mother, Mansfield, had some milk for her child and did not ask for more. It was and is the practice at this workhouse to supply milk to all young children of tramps in the Vagrant Ward. This will be still more carefully done in future." As a matter of fact, Mansfield's child was admitted into the workhouse and the day following its admission was seen by the MO but shortly afterwards died.[1]

The Report went on, "I do not see that the officers are in the least to blame. On the contrary, they were and are doing by arrangement a thing which is wholly unprovided for in the Regulations ie supplying milk to the young children of vagrants. I think a note should be made that the Order is defective in making no provision for the diet of young children of casuals.[1]

Nevertheless on 1 October, C H Cook, Guardian, called the attention of LGB to the report of a case relating to the Henley Workhouse from which it would appear that babies 6 months old were brought up on water and gruel.

"If this is the common practice in workhouses, it accounts for the extremely stunted condition of the children in them. In our Workhouse Union I was unable to find any children of sufficient stature to meet the not very exacting requirements of the naval authorities."

LGB note: "I can quite believe the statements contained in these papers. The question of infant feeding in workhouses is one much neglected by the Medical Officers and only in very few cases, comparatively speaking, are Articles 207 etc properly observed. This case is apparently a tramp's baby requiring food in the Tramps Ward. It appears to me that the Porteress ought to be censured for not calling the Master's attention to the fact that the infant required more suitable food than that directed to be given to tramps."[1]

Later, in February 1901 the Henley Guardians protested to LGB against compulsory adoption of new dietary tables which would cost Henley Union an extra £200 pa to apply to all inmates, without classification of their respectability. For example, they submitted an estimate of the cost of maintaining within the House a family of 5 with the new diet at 19s per week. Mr Neighbour, Guardian, felt that the Workhouse was a better house to live in than the majority of working men had, and very few working men were able to afford a similar diet to that now proposed. He said that it was only right that the aged deserving poor should spend their last days as happily as they could be, and for that class the diet should be improved. He moved "that the Guardians join in a protest ... and that the matter be referred to the Visiting Committee to report what could be done in the way of improving the present dietary tables" (in certain cases).[3]

This motion was not supported, despite the fact that with a total of 698 Unions, 116 had protested against these tables. The Chairman said the Guardians were in the hands of LGB and the new Order would come into force on March 25.

Incidentally, it was reported in January 1920 that an attempt was being made to revert to the old dietary table in existence before the War.[3] Was a form of rationing still in existence?

Furthermore, in April 1931, at a time of national hardship, it was reported that the Ministry of Health had imposed an improved diet on the new Public Assistance Institutions.[3]

11. Health

IN 1790 the workhouse at Henley already contained an isolation unit known as "the pest house" which stood in the middle of the garden – a solitary hut reserved for inmates suffering from infectious diseases such as smallpox. In addition, in 1835 it was resolved to fit up a barn on the site to accommodate "idiots".

The Pest House.

"Furthermore, in June 1792 it was agreed that Mr Richard Pope be allowed £20 to be paid at Easter next to attend and find necessary medicines and do all other business as Surgeon and Apothecary for the Poor of the Town and Parish of Henley whether residing in the workhouse, in the town or Parish or elsewhere; and all such other poor persons not belonging to the said town or parish who shall become chargeable thereto, in any illness or accident whatsoever which may happen or come to any such poor person till next Easter, on receiving an order from either of the Parish Officers. And in the case that said Mr Pope shall neglect to attend any such sick poor persons having first had notice from either of the said Parish Officers, the said officer may employ another apothecary to attend and administer proper medicines to such poor sick person and deduct the charge thereof out of the said £20; upon frequent neglect, to remove the said Mr Pope… NB Cases of midwifery and inoculation to be paid for separately from the above agreement." He was replaced by James Brooks in 1800.[i]

---

i   Oxfordshire Record Office BOR3/C/V/PW/12b.

1834 was seen to be a milestone in the provision of Poor Law medical relief to sick poor via Parish Relieving Officers, but from 1834 – 1847 it was not contemplated that poor persons who were sick would be received into the workhouse, rather to continue the practice of granting them outdoor relief pro tem.

List of Medical Officers 1847

Name of each District	Names of Parishes in each District	Area of each in Acres	Population of each Parish according to the census of 1841	Names and addresses of Officers with the date of their respective appointments and time for which appointed	Their respective salaries
Henley District	Henley and Workhouse Bix Remenham Pishill Pyrton(small part of) Fawley	1737 2826 1591 495 495 2681 9320	3617 422 485 147 100 280 5051	James Henry Brooks, Henley March 2nd 1847 from the 25th March then next for one year	£ 106
Hambleden District	Hambleden Medmenham	6615 2298 8913	1241 384 1625	Thomas Ward Jeston 6th July 1847 till the 25th March next	£ 34
Greys District	Rotherfield Greys Rotherfield Peppard Shiplake Harpsden	2609 2159 2693 1993 9454	1536 439 564 205 2743	Edward Young, Hart Street Henley March 2nd 1847 from the 25th March then next for one year	£ 60
Caversham District	Caversham Eye and Dunsden	4625 3108 7733	1641 868 2509	John Woodrofe Workman Reading March 2nd 1847 from the 25th March for one year	£ 45
Nettlebed District	Nettlebed Nuffield Ipsden Checkendon	986 1645 2484 2967 8084	690 215 610 398 1913	Thomas Ward Jeston Henley March 2nd 1847 from the 25th March then next for one year	£ 50
Watlington District	Watlington Swyncombe Britwell Salome Britwell Prior {Pyrton except the Liberty of Assendon} Cuxham Brightwell	3384 3705 727 481 3963 501 1520 14281	1850 399 233 62 612 222 310 3678	John Edward Boyton, Watlington March 2nd 1847 from 25th March then next for one year	£ 90

Medical Officers

Under the New Poor Law, from the outset in 1835 three Medical Officers were appointed for the Districts of Henley, Caversham and Watlington and in the first nine months 806 patients were treated by the Union doctors. Of these, 775 were ordinary cases, 9 were accidents and 22 midwifery (all such designated as "bastards"). The Guardians reported that the system of medical relief was most efficient.

PLC instructions to the Board of Guardians in May 1835 specified that "the Medical Officer shall in every case, when required by the Guardians or the Relieving Officer or by the pauper on whom he is attending, give a certificate under his hand of the sickness of such pauper ..." [1] Thereafter, the minute books contain lists of nourishment (usually mutton) to be provided as outdoor relief to those certified as "unable to work". (See pages 114-6). For example, the Medical Officer allocated to a poor man in Eye and Dunsden, who was in a weak state and unable to work over a number of weeks early in 1842, some mutton plus half a pint of gin – used to treat dropsy. By March, the relief was reduced to mutton (no gin) which continued into May, when he was allocated mutton broth only.[2]

In April 1838, Medical Officers' salaries came under review and the following instance was cited. "The gentleman serving the Greys District has ruined a valuable Horn this year in the Eye and Dunsden Parish, where roads are very bad. His predecessor, Mr May of Reading, twice broke his gig. Mr May found the labour so great that although the Parish of Eye and Dunsden is but two miles distant from his residence, he refused to accept it with Caversham Parish and, as no medical gentleman in Reading or elsewhere answered the advertisement, the Board felt justified in accepting the offer of Mr Young at an increase of £4."[1]

Also in 1838 the Guardians maintained that pauperism had decreased under their management, but that the species of pauperism by which the salaries of Medical Officers must be regulated had not decreased, nor could it do so while the "able-bodied and other necessitous classes of the poor receive only such wages as will supply the common necessities of life, their small savings, if any, being barely sufficient to prevent application for relief in times of distress."[2] This is undoubtedly an expression of understanding on the part of the Guardians of the conditions prevailing in the real world outside.

The list of medical officers of the Henley Union in 1847 with the parishes they covered and their salaries is in the Public Records Office and is reproduced on page 130. Regrettably, the copyright of the beautifully hand written original is chargeable at £104 by the National Archives.

The appointments were renewed annually by the Board of Guardians and confirmed by the PLC. In overall charge of health, the doctors mainly gave long service, as will be seen. By 1847 the list had been extended to six doctors to include areas around Hambleden, Rotherfield Greys and Nettlebed, with the contracts as shown.[1]

As will be seen, meagre salaries were paid: anything from £34 pa to £106 pa, the latter to include responsibility for workhouse inmates; in addition 10s 6d was paid for each midwifery case attended for Watlington and Henley, 15s elsewhere involving more travel. According to an advertisement placed in the Reading Mercury on 3 March 1849, the contract between the Guardians and the Medical Officer "is to include all medicines and medical and surgical appliances in all cases of sickness, surgery and midwifery within the district of the Medical Officer, to attend to which he shall receive a written order from the Relieving Officer or other competent authority."

Poor Law Orders stated the duties of Medical Officers to attend the workhouse at periods fixed by the Guardians and when sent for by Master or Matron. The period fixed for Henley was 9am – 1pm, so as well as visiting the sick in the community, the Medical Officer was called upon within the workhouse.

Already in October 1835 the Medical Officer considered the ventilation in the bedrooms insufficient to ensure good health and required fresh arrangements. Action was promptly taken by the Guardians. Later, in 1842, two ceilings were raised for the same reason.[2]

In 1840 there was an outbreak of contagious fever which temporarily closed the building to all further admissions. The Medical Officer, Edward Young, reported that "the rooms where the patients were placed, particularly the boys, were very ill-adapted for sick persons of any description, especially fever. They are situated on the ground floor paved with bricks, small windows facing a higher building within five yards of them. The beds are too near together and the boys sleep two, sometimes three to a bed."[2] It took a year before agreement was reached that a separate infirmary should be erected.

In May 1841 Edwin Chadwick wrote to say that the PLC had had under its consideration the plan and specification prepared by Mr Billing, the Reading architect, for the proposed infirmary to be erected at the Henley Union Workhouse and that they desired to make detailed comments thereon for consideration by the Board of Guardians, including the fact "that there were neither water-closets nor bathrooms provided therein, both of which are requisite to an infirmary". Nevertheless, the PLC did not withhold their formal sanction and approved the erection of a new infirmary[i] at the northern boundary.[1] (see map) A building containing four wards was completed by the end of 1841 at a cost of £417.

So thereafter sick paupers were admitted to the workhouse infirmary for such nursing care as might be provided.

Early in 1847 there was typhus in the district and also in the workhouse, and no fewer than forty cases of measles; already two houses in New Street had been taken over for boys and girls with the disease. One of the Relieving Officers, employed to distribute relief to those who were entitled to support outside the workhouse, had himself died of typhus.[1]

Women's Infirmary. © Assendon e-museum, 2009.

---

i   That building no longer standing.

The needs of sick outdoor paupers were as much for adequate nourishment as for medicine but doctors who prescribed meat and wine as "medical extras" were regarded by Guardians as usurping their authority over relief. For instance in 1858 the medical extras ordered by the Watlington MO under investigation were not according to the amount and nature of the extras allowed. MOs had no power to order extra nourishment for the sick under their care but only to recommend and certify that it was required. The ordering of such extras rested with the board of Guardians and the Relieving Officers.[2]

In fact, in 1866 the Inspector stated that he considered the medical extras given by Relieving Officers on the certificate of the Medical Officer "heavy in this Union". He requested them to exercise care in giving medical certificates for meat, milk, wine, porter etc for the pauper patients.[1]

On the other hand, doctors' contractual responsibilities were under scrutiny, sometimes with dire consequences: In 1858 Dr Young was censured by the LGB for not paying attention to the order to attend Samuel Blackall, for sending medicines onwards without visiting the case and for failing to visit the pauper.[1] Again he was taken to task in May 1862 by the Board of Guardians. Having heard the complaint of the pauper, Edward Atwell of Peppard, they were of the opinion that the Medical Officer was guilty of neglect of duty in not complying with the order of the Relieving Officer to visit him. Nevertheless he stayed as the Medical Officer for Caversham until 1879.

Eyesight of inmates was taken into account by paying an annual subscription of 5 guineas to the Royal South London Ophthalmic Hospital since ophthalmia was a concern; likewise a subscription to Bath Memorial Water Hospital in 1862.[2] (also see reference to Margate sea-bathing page 96).

In 1865, the PLB issued a circular letter recommending that in future cod liver oil, quinine and other expensive medicines shall not be provided at the expense of the Guardians. Despite this, in June 1867 Dr D'Oyley Brooks was taken to task by PLB for supplying John Pratt, age 60, at Greys Hill with cod liver oil (half a pint per week).[1] As Pratt was suffering from disease of the lungs, the Board of Guardians agreed to continue supplying the above.

Occasionally there were outbreaks of infectious diseases within the workhouse, especially among the children. For instance, in 1870 the Doctor reported 16 cases of scarlet fever among the boys, who were placed in two rooms adjoining the women's infirmary. Also at that time a woman, Sarah Brickland, had three children with ulcers and ringworm following measles.

The MP, Edward Hermon copied his letter to the Board of Guardians to LGB in July 1872 asking whether there was sufficient medical aid for the poor. He pointed out that a poor woman named Bishop living in Peppard had been taken seriously ill on the Saturday. Despite Dr Brooks' promise to visit that evening, he still had not done so on Sunday so Mr Hermon sent a man on horseback to the doctor. Nevertheless the Guardians insisted that they had sufficient cover for outdoor poor.[2]

However, Dr Munro who covered the Nettlebed area was in trouble in February 1873 when Martha Savage of Ipsden sank from exhaustion and died, despite having been prescribed meat, which she did not get. Likewise a complaint was made that Dr Munro had neglected to attend a pauper, John Gibbons, at Berrens Hill in the parish of Ipsden and the Guardians had called in Mr Horne of Wallingford to visit the case.

The Board ordered that Dr Munro be requested to attend the next meeting when it was resolved that Dr Munro had been guilty of neglect in the case of John Gibbons in not visiting him between 22 and 27 August.

On the 22 October LGB requested Dr Munro to furnish the Board immediately with an explanation. In November 1873 the LGB described a letter from him as being "a very improper one". By 1875, following an LGB official inquiry into three serious complaints in Nettlebed of neglect by Dr Munro, he was forced to resign (see Appendix F).[1]

The following table shows the range of disabilities recorded in the census of inmates over the years. These were all under the care of the appointed Workhouse Doctor.

Disability	Year 1851	1861	1871	1881	1891	1901
Blind	3	4	1			
Bronchitis						1
Cripple		1				
Deaf						3
Deaf and dumb		2	1	2		1
Deformed						1
Epileptic					1	3
Feeble minded						1
Idiot			3		3	
Imbecile			11	10		1
Lunatic						1
Paralysed						3
Phthisis (tuberculosis)						1
Weak minded		14				2
Grand Total	3	21	16	12	4	18

In January 1873, following the Public Health Act 1872, District Medical Officers were appointed by the new Oxford Sanitary Authority as Local Officers of Health; initially Relieving Officers were to act as Inspectors of Nuisances in accordance with their existing duties of visiting paupers at home who were seeking relief.

Childbirth was a continuing threat to women's health and that of their babies, not to mention the impact on families where older children may be orphaned thereby and end up in the workhouse. For example:

An Entry in District Medical Officer's Relief Book on Feb 26, 1884 reads:

> Puerperal Fever occurred at Smiths, Crowsley, after attendance by a midwife. The sanitary arrangements of the house were neglected. The baby died from erysipelas on 18 Feb and the mother died on Feb 21.
>
> From this house the disease was conveyed by a nurse to the lying-in woman named Tuckwell about 300 yards off. She is now very bad and under treatment and her infant died of blood poisoning on Feb 22.

To attend to these cases with the necessary precautions it was incumbent on me to telegraph for and employ the services of a double qualified medical man, Dr M L Hearne, who will continue to attend these to their termination.

I respectfully ask you to take into consideration the great extra expense entailed and make me some compensation.

This outbreak is not subsequent to my attendance.

G Owen Willis. (£15 proposed) [2]

In October 1886 LGB set out new arrangements to enforce the 1854 Vaccination Acts to secure the vaccination of all children against smallpox. Three appointments were made in the District to take on the role of Vaccination Officer at one shilling for each case of successful vaccination registered. In fact, the existing Relieving Officers had this added to their duties until re-organisation in 1899.

Even as now, Medical Officers provided long service in their locality. Dr James Brooks retired in 1883, having served for about 40 years in Henley. Dr E C Baines held the appointment of Medical Officer of Nettlebed district from 1875 to 1886 and the post of Henley District for 12 years.

Hambleden was served for 37 years by the Jestons, R P Jeston following in his father, Thomas's footsteps. Such service was surpassed by Dr Dixon in Watlington, who resigned due to ill health in 1892 after 43 years, having spent his whole working life since 1849 aged 28 in that large area of Watlington, population 3678. This resulted in the award of a superannuation of £50 pa. Unfortunately, towards the end of his long career, there was a complaint by the Guardians in 1891 that he "did not exercise sufficient care on 29 April (a) in not having carefully examined David Loveday to ascertain the extent of his injuries from scalding, having received an order from the Relieving Officer to do so; (b) in giving directions for him to be sent 10 miles on a cold day in an open cart to Henley Workhouse in his wet clothes and without dressing his scalds." [1]

It was reported in May 1893 that there was an outbreak of five cases of scarlet fever at the workhouse and one of diphtheria. This caused their removal to the new Smith Isolation Hospital in Fair Mile, Henley which had opened in 1891, costing Mr W H Smith £11-12,000. In fact, during the preceding year 12 children had been admitted suffering from scarlet fever.

From 1891 the isolation facilities offered by Smith Hospital were used whenever outbreaks of serious disease occurred. In August 1896 the Medical Officer reported that the two girls Higgs were free from typhoid fever; they should be removed from Smith Hospital to the Workhouse so as to thoroughly build them up.[3] An account sent to LGB for maintenance and nursing, also included "vagrants from the Vagrant House suffering from smallpox." [3] By April 1901 Smith Hospital admitted five cases of scarlet fever from Henley Workhouse, from among the 64 cases dealt with.[1]

Originally, Dr Baines of Henley had been appointed to cover Nettlebed as well as Henley. This arrangement lasted until 1886, when a complaint was made after the LGB Inspector discovered that Dr Baines of Henley-on-Thames had subcontracted for £49 pa his duties in Ipsden and Checkendon to "a medical man resident in Wallingford". Article 199 was invoked: "Every Medical Officer shall be bound to visit and attend personally as far as may be practicable the poor persons entrusted in his care and shall be responsible for attendance on them". A new MO for Nettlebed was promptly appointed at a salary increased from £80 to £100 pa.[1]

The medical cover in Nettlebed was in complete contrast to Rotherfield Greys, where the local Guardian, the Revd North Pindar, proposed the re-appointment of George Smith, Medical Officer for Greys, as an "admirable man and prompt manner in which his duties were discharged and was always hearing of the kindness and readiness with which he answered to the calls made upon him".[3]

In contrast, in August 1890 Dr Baines was reported in the Master's Book for the delay in obtaining medicines for the sick, sometimes of four days, even for a man seriously ill. Dr Baines was asked to attend the next meeting of the Board of Guardians and explain.[2] Dr Baines was again in trouble in January 1891 after his Medical Relief Book showed too few visits especially to the late Samuel Hailey. He was ordered "to visit at least once per month all permanent cases where medical extras were recommended".[1]

August 1892 saw emergency arrangements being made by the Henley Union "in consequence of the prevalence of cholera on the Continent and the danger of its importation into this country".[3] Therefore, the Local Government Inspector had advised Henley Union to make arrangements for the preparation of one of the wards of the hospital for the reception of patients forthwith into the (Smith) isolation hospital before its official opening at the end of September. The Sanitary Authority was already active in disseminating precautions to be taken against cholera. The Medical Officer was asked by the Guardians to report on action thought desirable for the authority to take since 30 cases of cholera were reported in September by the Metropolitan Isolation Board. Authorities of the various infirmaries, hospitals and workhouses had been communicated with, chiefly for the purpose of ascertaining what number of cholera patients their respective institutions could, in case of need, accommodate. However, by September 16th England was declared free from the epidemic.[3]

Several fresh cases of scarlet fever at Nettlebed were reported to the Inspector of Nuisances [3] and later in September 1892, a letter was published promoting the need for all drinking water to be boiled. "The authorities in little towns shrink too much from annoying their neighbours, and a multitude of villages still remain in a disgraceful condition. The subject is one which the central authorities are bound to attend to and one which has been brought before the central authority at the Board of Guardians Henley as regards Nettlebed. The recommendation of the Medical Officer for the County that a report should be made as to the means of supplying water there by a duly qualified engineer was quietly ignored."[3]

According to the annual report of Dr Dyson Wood, County Medical Officer of Health, for the year 1894, there were no deaths in the area from smallpox, scarlatina, diphtheria or typhoid fever, from measles or from whooping cough. In fact, there was no death at the workhouse from infectious diseases and during 11 years in succession, only two deaths occurred in the workhouse from zymotic diseases.

This report also states that in 1894 20 deaths occurred in the workhouse against 12 for the previous year and 18 in 1892. In 1895 the 18 deaths recorded in the workhouse were due to diarrhoea (1); phthisis (TB) (1); heart (6); bronchitis (3); – other (7). Twelve deaths occurred in paupers over 65, 3 aged 25 – 65 and 3 under 15.[3] In 1896

Dr Smith, Medical Officer for Greys, could not be reappointed as he did not reside in the Parish. Mr Neighbour said it would be a great loss to the Union as he was most attentive to the poor people. Dr Macpherson was appointed instead at £90 pa.[3]

The LGB Inspector came upon an outbreak of measles among the children in April 1898. He was concerned that this had not been reported earlier but he found 12 patients treated in the workhouse, isolated with a special nurse in charge, after the first 3 were sent to Smith Hospital. Two wards in the Men's Infirmary had been converted into Infectious Wards. No serious complications were reported directly due to measles.

He noted that the Medical Officer, Dr Rigge, had repeated Dr Baines' call for a place in the grounds where cases could be moved immediately when an infectious case was discovered so as to stamp it out quickly. Furthermore, attention was drawn to the approaching season of the year "when an army of tramps begin their peregrinations from and to the large towns. One never knows how soon a case may be discovered among them." Therefore, the MO asked LGB to strongly urge the Guardians to carry out this plan without delay.[1] Of course, such an expensive development by the Guardians did not happen.

1901 was a bad year for the doctors. Dr Baines was in the bankruptcy court in June.[i] Much worse was the death of Dr Rigge, a partner of Messrs Jeston, Baines & Rigge in July at the age of 41. This was followed by the death of Dr R P Jeston in October, aged 75, whose father had recently died aged 97.[3] Following the death of Dr Rigge, Dr Peake was appointed to the post of Medical Officer Workhouse and Henley district; also Dr Stevenson as MO Nettlebed at £100 pa.

Nursing

On inception of workhouses in 1834 no special nursing care appears to have been given to sick inmates in the "average" workhouse, apart from the services of a matron who was the Master's wife. Pauper inmates could be used as untrained nurses but in Henley Union, following the opening of the Infirmary in 1841, there was a succession of so-called nurses appointed who failed to perform their duties in a manner satisfactory to the Medical Officer. Nursing was not considered to be a respectable occupation for any educated woman so the illiterate filled this gap.

These nurses were a continuing problem within the Workhouse. The nurses duly appointed from outside at £20 pa plus board and £3 10 0d money in lieu of beer (from 1886), seemed, as well as low paid, to be untrained and/or "incompetent".[2]

For example, in August 1850 the Master reported that Mrs Kemp, the Infirmary Nurse, was found so drunk in her room in the evening about 8.30 that she could not stand, and it required the assistance of several of the pauper women to get her to bed. In doing so, she fell down and cut her head so badly the MO was obliged to be sent for to dress the wound.[ii]

In 1885 the attention of the Board of Guardians was called to the general inefficiency of the then nurse, "She is in no way qualified for her duties. She is deaf, vacant, inactive, unintelligent and leaves much of the nursing to the paupers." The

---

i   By 1903 Dr Baines was acting as Certifying Factory Surgeon.

ii PLU4/W/A1/1.

Board resolved that her services be discontinued after one month. She then requested a gratuity but this was not granted! [1]

Another case in point was Maria Musselwhite, first appointed in June 1886. In November 1886 she agreed to keep sober and attend to her duties in future. The Guardians agreed to keep her in office so long as her conduct was satisfactory. However in September 1887 she obtained an appointment elsewhere and left without notice.

Annie Knightly was appointed forthwith but was found unfit to work (drunk) and dismissed immediately. Then Mrs Godfrey stayed for 2 months before dismissal and Ursula Daniels resigned 4 months later. Thereafter, the Board of Guardians in May 1888 had little choice but to re-appoint Maria Musselwhite; four years later she was dismissed after "failing to carry out instructions given to her by the Workhouse Medical Officer".[3]

Meanwhile, is it any wonder that in June 1891 the Nurse was reprimanded by the Chairman of the Board after inmate Kate Cole gave birth to her fourth illegitimate child. The Master reported that she had been in the Infirmary since March, that she had not been out of the workhouse since May 1890 nor was she known to be pregnant. On appearing before the Board, the Nurse was censured for not having seen that the woman was properly bathed; and consequently not having discovered her condition previous to her confinement.[1]

During the 12 year period 1885-1897 there was a succession of nine nurses appointed, of which six were dismissed and three resigned (including Annie Cox after 5 years service 1892-7, having obtained a £5 pa increase after 2 years).

An order of the LGB in February 1892 gave power to appoint Nurses to attend upon the sick poor relieved by the Guardians out of the workhouse. This is interesting in these days of Care in the Community!

In 1897 the Medical Officer complained of the incompetency of Nurse Eliza Curtis after two months of service "who is totally incompetent and has not the least notion or knowledge of nursing. She cannot apply the simplest dressing to a wound or make a linseed poultice." He went on to say that the easy manner in which persons obtain testimonials is open to serious abuse.[1] She finally went in October, to be replaced for 6 weeks by Hannah Howard. Sarah Webster then came from Oxford Lunatic Asylum in 1897 for 3 years at £25-30 pa with a furnished apartment plus rations and washing plus £3 10 0d pa.

Reasons for dismissal were recorded in workhouse minutes books but not necessarily reflected in the reference obtained by the outgoing nurse. In one instance in October 1897 PLB demanded an explanation from the Henley Board of Guardians for misleading future employers by not spelling out the fact of dismissal. Perhaps they should merely have stated that "they would be glad to see her back, having shown herself capable of anything!".[i] But the Guardians blamed the easy manner in which persons obtained testimonials from officers. This was open to serious abuse when new employers accepted the service of candidates who were afterwards found to be unfitted to fill such important posts. In this instance the Guardians had given Nurse Curtis one month's notice to terminate her appointment.[1]

---

i   BBC Woman's Hour, Nov 2003.

Within the workhouse by 1901 there was a scarcity of able-bodied women in the House so no-one to assist the Nurse to keep the infirmary clean. The Chairman gave a casting vote to approve the appointment of two wardswomen and helpers in the infirmary at £16 pa plus rations.[3]

At the same time, the Chairman recommended that hot and cold water be laid on throughout the infirmary (so hopefully that would have improved the hand washing required).

After 1909, with the transformation of the school building into infirmary accommodation, a series of Assistant Nurses were appointed. Fourteen of these came and went between 1909 and 1915.

After becoming a Public Assistance Institution in 1930, when a Public Health Committee took over care of the sick, Henley Workhouse infirmary continued in use, particularly for the aged and sick of the surrounding community. But the stigma of the old association with the workhouse was not eradicated, even after assimilation into the National Health Service in 1948 when all hospitals owned by local councils were automatically transferred to the Minister of Health.

In the 1980s the old infirmary buildings were finally vacated in favour of a reduced size, single storey ward, for short-stay community hospital care erected in front of the school building. So Townlands continues to provide community health care for the people of South Oxfordshire into the 21st century, with the prospect of redeveloped facilities in 2016.

Women's Infirmary. © Assendon e-museum, 2009.

12. Lunacy

WITHIN the workhouse, lunacy was identified and eventually acted upon, labelled as anything from lunatic, imbecile, idiot and also women suffering from post-natal depression. Indeed, childbirth out of wedlock could be considered as a form of mental insanity and the offending woman committed to an asylum.

The 1834 New Poor Law prohibited detention in any workhouse of any dangerous lunatic, insane person or idiot for more than 14 days. For this purpose it was resolved in August 1834 to fit up the barn to accommodate idiots. From 1871 onwards the census returns recorded if an inmate was considered "lunatic", which meant someone who had lost their reason but had periods of lucidity; "imbecile" was someone who in later life had fallen into a state of chronic dementia; or an "idiot" who suffered from congenital mental deficiency.

By the Lunacy Act of 1845, Parliament passed a law compulsorily requiring every County to build and run an asylum for pauper lunatics and single lunatics who were at home. Therefore, Littlemore Oxford County Asylum was opened in August 1846 to provide accommodation for Oxfordshire's lunatic paupers. In such large asylums of over 1,000 patients there were few cures and few patients were discharged; many remained incarcerated for life.

Littlemore Oxford County Asylum.

List of Idiots Chargeable to Common Fund, 1858						
					Cost per week	Term
Ann Sharpe		Fawley	Bucks County Asylum, Stone, 1853	Dangerous	10s 6d	Years
Rebecca Teylor	54	Bix	Littlemore Asylum, 1846	Dangerous	9s	Life
William	51		Workhouse		3s 4¼d	Life
Susannah	49		Workhouse		3s 4¼d	Life
Catherine Webb	31		Workhouse		3s 4¼d	Life
Ann Lawrence	59	Brightwell	Littlemore, 1851		9s	Years
John Dennis	73	Britwell Salome	Workhouse		3s 4¼d	Years
Ann Pain	26	Caversham	Reading Gallowstree Common, with her mother		3s ¼d	5 years
John Bunce	60	Caversham	Reading, Widmore End with John Ambrose	Melancholic	3s ¼d	1 year
George Lewis	38	Caversham	Littlemore, 1857 (died 1858)	Lunatic	9s	1 year
Elizabeth Brooks	26	Cuxham	Workhouse	Weak intellect	3s 4¼d	5 years
Thomas Harris	31	Henley	Littlemore, 1847	Idiot	9s	Life
William Wise	51	Henley	Littlemore 1850	Lunatic	9s	8 years
Rebecca Sharpe	55		Littlemore, 1850	Lunatic	9s	7 years
Ann Bunce	53	Henley	Littlemore	Lunatic	9s	10 years
Ann Allaway	62	Henley	Littlemore, 1855	Lunatic	9s	9 years
Mary Wicks	17	Henley	Littlemore, 1857 (discharged 1858)	Lunatic	9s	1 year
Hester Clarke	51	Henley	Workhouse	Weak intellect	3s 4¼d	dead
George Toomer	61	Henley	Workhouse	Weak intellect	3s 4¼d	years
George Langford	45	Pyrton	Littlemore, 1857	Lunatic	9s	1 year
James Warner	53	Pyrton	Workhouse	Weak intellect	3s 4¼d	1½ years
James Sarney	27	Rotherfield Greys	Littlemore, 1847	Lunatic	9s	11 years
Ellen Leader	32	Rotherfield Greys	Littlemore, 1857	Lunatic	9s	1 year
Frances Wood			settlement order Grove Hall Asylum, Bow, 1856	Lunatic	14s	1 year
Ann Black	23	Rotherfield Greys	Workhouse	Weak intellect	3s 4¼d	years
Fanny Patrick	22	Rotherfield Greys	Workhouse, removed to asylum	Weak intellect	3s 4¼d	4 years
John Chase	80	Shiplake	Littlemore, 1846	Lunatic	9s	21 years
George Wright	86	Shiplake	Workhouse	Weak intellect	3s 4¼d	years
Mary Norcott	30	Swyncombe	Littlemore, 1849	Idiot	9s	Life
John Gillett	46	Swyncombe	Littlemore, 1854	Lunatic	9s	years
Martha Light	64	Swyncombe	Workhouse	Weak intellect	3s 4¼d	years
Thomas Neighbour	63	Watington	Littlemore, 1853	Lunatic	9s	4 years
Grace Austin	26	Watlington	Littlemore 1854	Lunatic	9s	6 years
Ann King	65	Watlington	Workhouse	Weak intellect	3s 4¼d	years
Eliza Betteridge	62	Watlington	Workhouse	Weak intellect	3s 4¼d	years
Elizabeth Nobes	52	Common Fund	Littlemore, 1846	Lunatic	9s	12 years
Ann Hitchcock	52	Common Fund	Littlemore, 1850	Lunatic	9s	10 years
Mary Ann Francis	38	Common Fund	Littlemore 1854	Lunatic	9s	3 years
Elizabeth Wood	54	Common Fund	Littlemore 1855	Lunatic	9s	3 years
George Chefsall	46	Common Fund	Hoxton HR Asylum, 1852	Lunatic	14s	6 years

Under this Act, Board of Lunacy Commissioners were created in 1845 and they were required to make unannounced visits to the 250 asylums and workhouses and were empowered to release any improperly confined patients. So-called harmless patients remained in the workhouse, whereas the "furious" and "dangerous" were to be admitted to the asylum. This was to ensure that conditions in the workhouse were adequate and that such lunatic cases received the attention they needed.

Following the General Consolidated Order 1847 stating that lunatics be put into a separate category requiring suitable accommodation and treatment for them, the annual report on pauper lunatics noted 23 in Henley Union; three in Oxford Asylum at 11 shillings a week, two "in lodgings" and one dangerous. However, in February 1849 the number of lunatics was reported in Henley Workhouse as six males and eight females, with 29 chargeable (presumably at asylums). In December 1850 the Master wrote to five asylums seeking admission of a lunatic pauper, Hannah Young, "who was not fit enough to be transferred out" – but all asylums were said to be full then.[2]

The cost of maintaining pauper lunatics in asylums was a considerable drain on the Union's resources. For example, the published accounts for the half year ending Michaelmas 1858 showed a charge of £58 16s 8d for "maintenance of lunatics in asylums" (see detailed listing).

By 1862 the workhouse accounts were showing expenditure of £158 to the Dayman Lunatic Asylum (the NHS Oxfordshire Authority Archivist thinks that this was a small private institution) but there were still 17 imbeciles and idiotic inmates in the House in May 1865.

9 January 1864 Littlemore Lunatic Asylum
"The Committee of Visitors have published their annual report for 1863. We much regret to find that the progressive increase of the terrible disease, mental aberration, has compelled the managers to submit for consideration the most feasible means for procuring additional room… The number of patients, both male and female, has been in excess of the maximum which the house was intended to accommodate. Thus the expense of maintenance of the supernumerary patients in out-of-County establishments.

"Littlemore Asylum was first opened for Oxfordshire only in August 1846; in December 1846 for the city of Oxford; the County of Berks and the Borough of Abingdon were added in March 1847. In December 1847 the Borough of Reading became united with the County of Oxford and at the commencement of 1850 the present union of counties and boroughs was in full operation, excepting Newbury.

"Calculated to accommodate 440, the actual number of beds is 500.

Propose: 1. extend existing asylum and land;
          2. erect in Berks additional asylum
          3. erect new asylum for Berks, Reading and Abingdon." [2]

Year	Males	Females	Total
1846	45	47	92
1863	239	307	546

The Commissioners in Lunacy made one of their regular ad hoc visits to Henley Union in June 1865 and examined the weak-minded inmates: and again in October 1866 when Dr Navine reported, "There are today 6 males and 12 females classed as of unsound mind. They were all mobile, quiet and orderly. They were all in fair bodily health and personally in a satisfactory state. James Merson and Elizabeth White, specially noticed at the last visit, have been sent to Littlemore Asylum. Nurse Elizabeth Cox has been in the House since the last visit and has conducted herself well. Inspected the dormitories. They, as well as the dayrooms in which I saw the lunatics and idiots, were very clean."[1]

In February 1868 the Inspector noted that there were 15 lunatics and imbeciles in the House, with one old man under mechanical restraint. In August 1867 the following account was paid:

For Lunatic Asylum, Littlemore   £206 9s 6d
County rate, Dayman Oxon   £418 15s 5d

The Commissioners in Lunacy report for August 1869 noted 16 inmates of unsound or weak mind: 4 male and 12 female in Henley workhouse. All were harmless and many were usefully employed in the workhouse. Their beds were mainly of straw, with some of flock. Four seemed to have been on a special diet, which included tea (which would have been a special treat for other inmates) and daily meat.[2]

In January 1869 there was a dispute with Reading Union over who should pay the costs of maintenance of Ann Slaughter in Littlemore Asylum. After, unfortunately for Henley Union, she was judged to be settled in Caversham, Henley was required to pay for her, her husband George, having absconded. Her future maintenance would cost 9/6d per week.[3]

In August 1873 Mr Henley, LGB Inspector, reported that in going through the wards he had found a woman named Weller, a pauper of unsound mind, restrained in bed by straps. He noted she had attempted to escape from the Workhouse. The Master and Matron and nurse should be cautioned not to use such restraint without immediately calling the attention of the Medical Officer.[1] Likewise, he reported in March 1874 that, "there is an imbecile inmate named Frances Weller who has on several occasions been placed under restraint in the workhouse and in respect of whom the MO is prepared to certify that she ought to be removed to the asylum. Application was made a fortnight ago to a magistrate for an order but without success." She was sent to Littlemore on 15 May.

Later in 1884 the Shiplake Station Master, Thomas Henry Davies, aged 60, with 24 years' service, was sent to Moulsford Asylum, chargeable to Henley Union but his son was required to pay Henley Union 3s per week towards his maintenance.[1]

By January 1885 the Commissioners had decided that an important proportion of pauper lunatics in County asylums might be adequately and more economically (sic) provided for in workhouses. LGB referred to three cases relating to Henley Union, including one 89-year-old admitted to Littlemore 10 years previously. The Board of Guardians responded that there was no accommodation at Henley Union for pauper lunatics.[1]

In February 1886 the Medical Officer wrote to the Guardians asking for suitable wards to be provided for idiots and persons with mental disease who "according to the new regulations under the Idiots Act we cannot send to asylums". The Board of Guardians appear to have reacted otherwise by announcing in May 1886 that "thanks to the ladies who so kindly collected money for this purpose, the boy Thomas Buckett was, on the 29th ult., elected an inmate of Earlwood Asylum for Idiots for five years. At the end of that time, if no more able, or unable to earn his living by a trade he will be taught, he will be eligible for re-election for the remainder of his life. The amount subscribed was £10".[2]

On 27 July 1886 in an LGB report for the Commissioners in Lunacy about a visit to the Workhouse on 16th by Dr Southey, one of the Visiting Commissioners, the Board requested the Guardians to consider the following suggestion of the Commissioners:

> I found upon the Classes listing 4 males and 7 females, all, with one exception (a male epileptic idiot lad) very suitable cases to be left at this workhouse. This boy, however, is at times very troublesome and always noisy and cannot, for want of proper attendance to take charge of him, be taken out for exercise so

much as he requires. Confined in the small airing court that is provided in the hospital here, he is very annoying to the other cases there, and would be far better off himself and better managed in an asylum.

The day rooms and dormitories were clean and tidy and the beds in good order; night dresses are allowed to all the women. Bathing is on both sites, the use properly and regularly carried out, in good baths well supplied with water.

Building was going on which will afford better accommodation to the Infirmary wards and provide a second exit by a staircase in case of fire to both sexes sleeping in this part of the house. And drains are to be connected with the new town sewer. It is intended, I understand, to remove and/or alter the present middens in the imbecile area court with water closets.

No complaints were made to me. The imbeciles were clean in person and tidily dressed and are, I have no doubt, well cared for. Most of them are usefully employed.

The Clerk sent an extract from the report referring to the duty allowed to the Medical Officer to the Workhouse and requested him to give the requisite certificate for the boy's admission into the Littlemore Asylum.[1]

In August 1888 11-year-old Maud Davies was admitted into the workhouse from Caversham. She was reported to be suffering from epileptic fits and Medical Officer Baines had her under observation: he declared her to be an idiot. The Guardians agreed that she would be transferred to Eastern Counties Asylum for Idiots as the workhouse was not a suitable place for such a case.[3]

In May 1891, Mr A Grove attended in reference to the claim made by the Board for the demand of the amount due under a bond given by him to Elizabeth Grove, his mother, a lunatic chargeable to the Union.

Bills for Lunatics were a continuing and rising expenditure for Henley Union.

For example, in September 1891 payments were made to:

Colney Hatch (Herts)	£2 12 0d
Littlemore (Oxon)	£245 4 0d
Bucks	£12 0 0d

To which was added in February 1892 Berrywood Northampton when Harry Sopp was sent there as "an idiot" at a cost of 14 shillings a week.[1]

By July 1896 the cost of maintenance for K Leach in Littlemore amounted to £18 19s 2d for one year – almost the salary of the Industrial Trainer.

Boards of Guardians were ever mindful of cost to the rates and eager to offload payments to other Unions. Thus, in June 1891 Henley Union was involved in a claim relating to Daniel Gibbons, late of Harpsden, who had become chargeable in Croydon Union, who wished Henley to pay the bill.[3] Gibbons had previously spent two years in Littlemore Asylum.

Contributions were demanded from relatives (where possible). For instance, in August 1891 William Wakefield, a coal merchant, was summoned to pay £10 8s 0d, being 26 weekly instalments towards the maintenance of his wife at Littlemore Asylum. Defendant had paid 5s per week since 1882. This was now raised to 7s 6d per week.[3] Likewise, Mr Chant of Watlington was asked in November 1891 for 21s 7d expenses incurred in removing his son to the asylum plus 4s per week towards maintenance.

Incidentally, the death was reported in the local newspaper in October 1892 of Emma Warner, blind, of Harpsden, aged 57 at Littlemore Asylum.

Around this time the Chairman of the Board of Guardians drew attention to the large increase in the number of lunatics being paid for externally, especially for Caversham which sent 5 lunatics this half-year against only one in the last (was there a high incidence of incest in Caversham?). There were now 58, an increase of one-third, costing £3,947 per annum of which Oxfordshire County Council grant was only £1,658, leaving £2,289 to be found, requiring a rate of 5d in the £.[3]

The Commissioners in Lunacy visited again in October 1892 and reported:

> Of the four imbeciles seen previously, one of each has since died, the two remaining, both women, are still here and are the only persons classed as being of "unsound mind". They continue to be fit for workhouse care and are both usefully employed in the laundry. The one, Mary Ann Caterer, is subject to occasional attacks of epilepsy. Her fits are said by the Matron to occur chiefly, if not entirely, at night. Should they occur by day and increase in frequency, it may be unsafe to employ her in the laundry, and work elsewhere would be desirable for her (following death of Mary Ann Lovejoy the previous year, see p.88).
>
> Lizzy Sargeant is another young woman also thoroughly unfit to be in the House except under statutory powers of detention, and her remaining in the House otherwise is a clear breach of the Lunacy Act 1890. She is so weak as to be of unsound mind, to the extent of being unable to take ordinary care of herself. She should be placed on the list of imbeciles, in conformity with the Act. I conversed with her and she told me that she was about to be married immediately – her replies to my questions were not (making) any sense. She is, however, happy and content to stay in the workhouse and it seems to be the best place for her. All these three persons are on the House diet. I trust that the occasional outdoor exercise of women classed here of unsound mind, beyond the workhouse grounds may be under proper control and a constant object, as such persons should not be made, on account of their mental fraction, close prisoners.[1]

The Idiots Act of 1886 also required the creation of special education facilities in homes for "feeble-minded", especially girls, who may be felt to be in need of protection against a risk of producing illegitimate babies. In 1893 there occurred correspondence from the Clerk to Henley Guardians, asking LGB to consent to payment by the Board of Guardians of 2/6d per week towards cost of maintenance of Emily Elizabeth Tubb aged 16 to go to The Training Home, West Brompton per Mrs Arding of Braziers Park, Checkendon, who would share maintenance while defraying entire cost of maintaining the girl's sister in another institution. "The two girls are both imbeciles and have been living with their widowed mother at Checkendon, and she is no longer able to maintain them owing to the difficulty of finding sufficient work."

The Guardians considered that there was great risk in allowing imbecile girls to remain at home unprotected in a lonely country place and the mother was unwilling to let the girls be received into the Workhouse; in fact, had they been admitted, there would have been difficulty in teaching them useful work ...

Reply from LGB stated: no objection and asked for printed report, if any, showing the character of the home and its management. In reply, the Clerk reported that the girls were trained for domestic service and also taught plain laundrywork, needlework and stocking knitting. There were also classes five days a week for the special teaching of bible knowledge, reading, writing and arithmetic. He attached the 10th annual report of the South Kensington Association for the Care of Friendless Girls Training Home at West Brompton.

LGB responded "This seems to be a school and, if so, it should be certificated if Guardians wish to send children to it to be trained. However, Emily Tubb is over 16 and is therefore beyond school age."

"I fail to see what the Guardians can do except to subscribe. The case, however, seems to be one which we should assist if we can. The Guardians say the girl is an imbecile. Probably she is of the feeble-minded class." LGB sanctioned a subscription at £6 10 0d per annum so long as the girl was maintained in the institution.[1]

Six weeks later there was a letter from Checkendon Rectory: "I beg you to try and get an official answer from LGB in relation to Emily Tubb. I have already made myself liable for more than I had intended to pay on her behalf and I cannot afford to keep her at the Training Home at my own expense. I fear that unless help can be got, she will have to come back and go into the Union. This would be a very great pity.

"I saw 2-3 days ago a lady who goes to the Home where she is to help give instruction. She says she is undoubtedly improving and developing very satisfactorily and thinks that if the training is continued for a while, she is quite likely to get a livelihood. Great care is being given her." [1]

In a similar vein, the Clerk wrote to LGB in August 1893 asking for consent to send to the Revd Dr William Stainers Home for the Deaf and Dumb Children at 70-80 Pentonville Rd, London N, Gertrude Emily Fuller, aged 8½ yrs, who is deaf and dumb and the child of Henry Fuller, a biscuit factory labourer residing at 10 Kings Rd, Lower Caversham in this Union. The annual payment to be made by the Guardians was £19 4 0d, towards which the father of the child undertook to pay the Guardians 2s per week.[1]

A contentious case arose in regard to the death of a Henley Workhouse inmate who had died in prison. In March 1893, the Henley Advertiser reported "On Friday last an inquest was held at Reading Prison on the body of Edwin Smith, aged 56, who was sentenced to imprisonment by the Henley Magistrates for wilful damage at the Henley Workhouse. Death arose from exhaustion following upon cellulitis. It was stated that the poor fellow's mind was deranged and that he was to have been moved to an asylum, and the jury expressed an opinion that the Workhouse authorities should have taken steps to remove him to an asylum rather than to prison."

This caused consternation among the responsible officers, the Henley Board of Guardians. The Chairman, Mr Brakspear, said the man was most carefully examined by the MO and by a magistrate, and he told several of the inmates that he should pretend to be mad so that he might be taken to the asylum. The Master said that Smith was in the workhouse from October until the day he was given into custody. He was wardsman but he had one or two cases he did not like and discharged himself (from the workhouse) on Monday morning, returning in the evening. He went to work in the gardens for two days. The Master was called to the man and found him on his back. He professed that he could not stand. He was sent to the hospital but they could not make anything of him and he was sent back to the ward. He pulled the old men out of their beds, tore up the bedclothes and broke eight panes of glass. He was afterwards seen by two doctors and they would not certify that the man was insane.

Revd Coxe asked the Master if he knew the man had been in an asylum. The Master replied that he didn't until he saw Smith on his back. He said he would sham mad as he was much better cared for in the asylum than in the workhouse. Mr Wiggins asked if throwing the man out of bed was not the act of an insane person? The Master thought if he had been insane, he would have knocked the man about but he did not do that.

Mr Barnett, Guardian, thought the Coroner should have adjourned the inquiry and let the Guardians be represented. Mr Brakspear agreed. The jury appeared to think the man was neglected; if the inquest had been adjourned they could have produced evidence to show it was not so. The Master said Smith was as calm and as quiet as any other inmate as long as he had work he liked.

It was agreed that a reply be sent to the Reading Coroner stating that the deceased had been examined by two medical men, who pronounced him to be sane.

The reply from the Coroner, Mr W Weeden, stated, "I must leave with you the question of publicity suggested in your letter. I may perhaps be allowed to say that you do not mention when the examination you refer to in your letter took place but if just before the deceased left the workhouse then it seems to me simply a case of difference of opinion between medical men."

Mr Brakspear proposed sending the correspondence to the Press for publication, with mention made of the fact that the medical examination was made just before the man's removal to jail.[3]

In February 1895 the Clerk (Mr Lloyds) reported on the case of John Oakley who had recently been visiting Littlemore Asylum, which was now billing Henley Union. The Clerk first went to Moulsford Asylum to inquire where the man came from and his settlement. He ascertained that the man was admitted there in December 1894 and was discharged on the 29th. Oakley next attempted suicide at Nuneham and was sent to Abingdon Union, whose Clerk was instructed to make a County case of it. Oakley was thereupon sent to Littlemore Asylum, where Lloyds went the next day. He was told that the man needed 48 hours of good feeding on account of being much depressed and then he was to be discharged.

Mr Lloyds interviewed the man, who said he was born at Henley Workhouse and he was 28 years of age. When 10 years old he went to Grimsby as a fishing boy and then joined a training ship.[i] The Clerk added that unfortunately he could not find the man's birth notice on the register ... However, the man said correctly the names of the various officials in the House during his boyhood. Oakley was to be discharged on

---

i   See p.99.

January 20th and intended to make his way to London in order to seek employment as a ship's cook.[3] So Henley's obligation to John Oakley was at an end.

Later, in July 1897 there was a sad case in the community. A Report was made by MO McPherson of Greys on the condition of Fred Morton, eight years old, "a healthy and unusually strong boy suffering from very highly arched palate. Owing to this (chiefly) is unable to speak – mentally his condition averages on idiocy. If living under more favourable conditions, would probably improve considerably. Is very troublesome and always up to something, and mother declares she cannot look after him ... A suitable case for Earlswood Asylum."

Subsequently they reported: "The boy attended at our Society's office to be medically examined – The boy is an idiot and should go to an institution for idiots, e.g.

Western Counties Idiot Asylum, Star Cross, Exeter
Eastern Counties Idiot Asylum, Colchester
Royal Counties Idiot Asylum, Lancaster
Children's blocks at Middx West or Northampton County Lunatic Asylums."

But by the end, having made application to each of the institutions named, the Guardians had not succeeded in obtaining admission of Frederick Morton into any of the institutions owing to the demands of their own candidates.[1]

This problem prompted the Guardians to ask the County councils of Berks, Bucks and Oxon to take steps to provide an institution for idiots and imbeciles, either in addition to one of the County Lunatic Asylums or some other way. The Guardians urged LGB to induce the County Councils to proceed because "the presence of imbecile children was frequently a trouble to the neighbourhood and they were allowed to roam without any attempt to control them or to train them in any trade, thus becoming paupers for life." [3]

But by 1901 it was recommended that all curable imbecile children be sent to the Star Cross Asylum, Exeter. Adult curable epileptics to be sent to St Giles Asylum, which would build an extra wing at £1500 – Unions in the County to be charged pro rata towards the outlay.[3]

In 1901 "feeble-minded" was substituted for "idiot"; this led to an increase in numbers listed.

Report on a visit to Littlemore Asylum, March 1907: One man had been there for 52 years and a woman had been an inmate there for 46; two others for 38. There were 53 cases from the Henley Union.[3]

The introduction of the Mental Deficiency Act in 1913 hardened the powers of the Commissioners of the Board of Control. On a visit to Henley in July 1914, Mrs Pinsent reported that there were now no certified cases in the workhouse, the woman seen in 1911 having been transferred to Reading. She drew attention to two epileptics who should be sent to an epileptic colony. One had been living there all the 50 years of her life (Mary Ann Caterer?) and the other, aged 20, was thought to be "useful and strong". Two male "imbeciles" were not certified (one having been discharged from Starcross as unimprovable), for reasons of administration.

Most important was the case of Sophia White, a feeble-minded 17-year-old girl who was pregnant with her second illegitimate child. Her first baby was born in

Abingdon Workhouse. She had only left the house a fortnight, having been taken out by her mother, when she became pregnant again.[3]

Mrs Pinsent hoped that action would be taken at once under the new Act. She also noted three generations of the Blackall family in the workhouse, comprising at one time or another at least 12 individuals, some of them "feeble-minded". The Salvation Army had tried to help but could make nothing of the woman whose four children were now in the Poor Law School and she should be certified to prevent her discharging herself from the workhouse. Another woman was described as "feeble-minded and morally defective."

This report provides an interesting insight into the past when someone who suffered from an epilepsy (no drugs available to control the condition) or was simply a little slow, was locked up in the workhouse to live out their days.

In 1920 the Master reported the death of 57-year-old Mary Ann Caterer, born in the Institution and who never left it.[3] Some women remained in an asylum for life and some were only discovered in the 1950s as being confined for having given birth to an illegitimate child.

After World War I the board were facing greatly increased charges: by 1920 Bucks County Asylum were charging 26s 10d per week; Littlemore in Oxford 23s, increased to 27s 1½d by July, (compared with 9s 11d before the War), National Association for the Feeble-minded 19s 6d per week and the National Society for Epileptics had advanced by 2s per week. The Board had received an "unsatisfactory" reply to their request that their asylum patients be brought closer to home instead of being scattered so far about. Mr Neighbour urged the Board to continue to agitate for a redress of the hardships entailed by relatives in going long distances and by Visiting Committees in performing their duties.[3]

Therefore the annual subscription of 10s to the Buckinghamshire Voluntary Association for the Care of the Mentally Defective was agreed to.[3]

A Royal Commission report in 1926 led to the Lunacy Reform Act in 1929. However, with the inauguration of Public Assistance Committees in 1931, the soon-to-be superseded Board of Guardians expressed concern about the future welfare of local people in various mental homes. This is an indication of the degree of care that was shown to those in their care, even though off the premises.

"For the past 25 years the late Board adopted the duty imposed on them by the Ministry of Health and annually sent a deputation of five to the several mental homes where people whom they all knew were always glad to see them. It was on the grounds of humanity that they felt that these poor people should be periodically visited and not be sent to an asylum and no-one knew anything about their wellbeing except for the very rare visits made from relatives. No-one knew more of these people than they did who were responsible for sending them to the asylum and it did not seem right that those who knew them should be prohibited from seeing them once a year. The PAC not acceding to their recent request, application to be made to the County Authorities for permission to send a deputation. Revd. Irwin said that by visiting them they had been able to help some of the patients." [3]

It was not until the second half of the 20th century that Victorian asylums were finally closed and small units opened for care of those with mental illness and/or learning difficulties under Care in the Community developments in 1987.

13. The Gatekeeper

ACCESS TO the workhouse had to be strictly controlled so as to admit only those deemed eligible. Tramps in particular had access limited to overnight stays and they had to offset the cost of their free meal by carrying out a task such as oakum-picking or stone-breaking. The work was allocated and superintended by the Gatekeeper/Superintendent of Labour, whose wife acted as assistant, especially in the Tramps Ward.

On admittance the vagrants were put through the disinfectant bath area by the Gatekeeper (or his wife for the females), after being questioned about having any money or food on them. A false statement for gaining relief at Henley Union could result in 21 days hard labour in Oxford Gaol if a search next morning revealed cash in the belongings – and the money could be forfeited. So John Sullivan was treated lightly by the magistrates in Jan 1869, only being committed for 7 days hard labour for having applied for lodging at the Union House, having one shilling in his possession.[2]

Porter's Lodge, 78 West Hill former gates were here.

Furthermore, there were often reports of tramps appearing before the magistrates accused of tearing up workhouse clothing in which they had slept. The Superintendent of Labour/Gatekeeper then had to testify in court as to the charges being brought.

The Superintendent's duty was an important element in keeping down costs and the appointment was crucial to the management of the workhouse. As Superintendent of Labour, his duties included overseeing production of home-grown vegetables in the workhouse grounds (see page 73).

A minute of the Board of Guardians dated 26 November 1841 records: "Ordered that the Master be allowed to supply the person who cleans the Tramps a little beer and tobacco as extra allowance, the Board having taken into consideration the difficulty of the washing done in the House at this season of the year and regarding the allowance of beer to the persons engaged in doing it essential to the maintenance of their good health".[2]

Upon the death of Henry Wheeler, Porter and Superintendent of Labour, and between 1869 and 1886 the role was carried out by James Spickernell and his wife Martha, who had four children. In 1871 they obtained £2 10s pa in remuneration for extra services on the erection of the new schools. In September 1879 James Spickernell asked for a further increase in salary following the introduction of baths to the Casual Wards. He said that the number of tramps who passed through during the previous 12 months was 2368 and that the number would increase. The Board of Guardians granted him an extra £8 pa and his wife £3 pa (fewer female tramps).

However, after 16 years service and the appointment of a new Master in December 1885 the atmosphere changed and in February 1886 the new Master reproved the Gate Porter for sending fire-wood off the premises. Mr Spickernell replied, "Look here, I am not going to put up with any more of your humbug!" The Master's report was laid before the Guardians, who interviewed Mr Spickernell, who "expressed his willingness to submit to the requirements of the Board in the future".[2]

Nevertheless, his relationship with the Master had broken down and six months later the Master expressed regrets to the Board that he was unable to work with the Gate Porter. "He renders me little assistance and does not comply with the instructions given him by the Board. He is also most uncivil in his manner." The Master's viewpoint prevailed and the Board of Guardians resolved that the services of Mr and Mrs Spickernell be discontinued at the expiration of one month (though a testimonial was granted them).

This led to a procession of 10 incumbents in the next 13 years. The rate of pay on offer was £25 pa + £10 pa for the wife to attend to the Female Tramp Ward and act as assistant gatekeeper, to include board and washing, to reside in the lodge (West Hill) and each to have an allowance of £3 10s 0d in lieu of beer; a sum of £5 pa also to be paid to the porter for cutting the hair and shaving inmates, his wife to be given 3d per head for bathing female tramps.

A problem arose in September 1893 when the incumbent, George Moss, absented himself from his duties during his wife's week's leave of absence and, being depressed, he resigned. On her return, the Board agreed to reinstate him but reduced his salary by £5 pa.[1]

By April 1895 Archibald Totman was Porter and superintendent of Labour at the Workhouse, with his wife Hannah, Porteress and attendant at the Female Tramp Ward. He went to court on April 6th to prove the case against Edward Lewis, who was charged with tearing up his clothes whilst an inmate of the Henley Workhouse. The prisoner was sentenced to 7 days hard labour in Oxford Gaol.[1]

The Totmans resigned in March 1896. Rev Coxe drew attention to his case. The Guardians were losing the services of a good man. He fancied the Visiting Committee were more against him than they really were. From conversation with him he fancied that he would stay on if he were asked to do so. Mr Groves thought it best that the notice should be accepted. Whilst the gate porter had been a good man in the garden, there had been, since he had been porter, more cases brought before the Henley Bench than had been for 10 years previously.

By September 1896 his successors A Diamond and Thomas Garland Shipley had ceased to hold office, and a new appointment was made of Porter/Supt of Labour and Assistant Relief Officer for Tramps William Edgecombe, aged 26, and his wife who came from Kingsbridge Union Workhouse in Devon. They were well thought of and, indeed, the Guardians awarded them a gratuity of £1 for protecting the water pipes during five weeks of winter weather by shutting off the stop cocks and emptying cisterns every evening and filling them next morning. However, LGB insisted that such a gratuity, while not unreasonable, required their prior sanction.[2]

The next appointment was John A Martin with his wife and 2-year-old child (for whom he was required to pay cost of maintenance in the House at 3s per week plus 1s pw for lodging and washing = £10 pa from a wage of £30 + £25 pa each, unsurprisingly, this meant that he promptly resigned after only a few months in post.[2] Charity was not extended to staff! Appointees came and went: like Albert Frith from Islington Workhouse, aged 27 – appointed in February 1899 at £30 pa with no beer allowance; resigned six months later. (Were the lights of London too far away from him?)

There followed in 1901 Edward Norman Knight as Labour Master, whose harsh stance was viewed unfavourably by Henley Magistrates (see next chapter).

What a contrast to the report in 1916 of the death in office of Mrs Emily Knight, Gate Porteress. The Guardians felt she was "the most cheerful official ever" and promptly engaged her sister-in-law, Miss E Knight.

14. Vagrants

A SUCCESSION of Medieval statutes strove to deal with the suppression of vagrancy and were evidence of an on-going concern by the authorities as regards public order. However, one clause in the 1535-6 Statute required that those who entered into possession of lands of religious houses should provide hospitality and service for all the poor as of old.

But vagrants were regarded as "foreigners" to the locality and, as such, a problem for the local vestry to deal with over the ages. Vagrants were the most despised group – usually referred to as "casuals", incorporating seasonal tramps, itinerant labourers and homeless persons on the move and were an on-going concern to the authorities as regards public order. Special accommodation where vagrants could sleep one night was set apart from that for regular inmates of the Workhouse to maintain morality within the workhouse and to isolate the potential for disease-carrying.

Vagrants were received at the Porter's Lodge on West Hill. A disinfecting stove was provided in their adjacent Receiving Wards, which were to be warmed and provided with water closets, baths and lavatories, with a means of drying their wet clothes.

In early 1847, after an explosion in numbers received into the House caused renewed concern for public order, the PLB approved a new tramps ward for Henley. Incidentally this did not incorporate separate cells as per other Unions but consisted of open wards (male and female) with stanchions containing hammocks.

Tramps used to gather outside the workhouse gates beside the Red Cow public house in West Hill waiting to be admitted to the Casual Wards after 6.00 pm. After inspection and disinfection, they were locked up in the building, near the Porter's Lodge at the main entrance where they were allowed to stay overnight.

Hammock slung on stanchions.

In return for a meal and a night's rest, they had to perform a task before leaving. Some casual inmates refused to undertake the tasks allotted to them eg oakum-picking: nevertheless in May 1850 there was 18 cwt of oakum ready for sale. Indeed, experienced vagrants might find the conditions in prison (where such indiscipline led them) to be more satisfactory and, with few exceptions, those men, when once in gaol, completed their daily tasks and gave no trouble.[2]

The comings and goings of vagrants were a constant source of attention. In 1849-50; the master kept a tally of the numbers of vagrants admitted, how much money they had on them and the cost of provisions for them.[2]

Date		Vagrants Admitted	Cost to Union	Cost of Provisions
19/5/49		70	6/-	
2/ 5/49		105	1/4½d	
2/6/49		95	1/5d	7/6d
9/6/49		125	1/10½d	8/4d
16/5/49		104	5½d	7/6d
23/9/49 (sic)		45	1/10¾d	2/8¼d
7/7/49		21	1d	
14/7/49		23	9½d	
21/7/49		11	3½d	
28/7/49		46	24/9¼d	
4/8/49		34	7d	
22/9/49	Quarter total	330	£1 10s 6d	£1 1s 0d
22/12/49		471	6/5½d	£1 13s 10d
	Last year	1321	£12 13 2½d	
31/9/50	Total vagrants	161	2/6d	9/10½d
29/12/50	Total vagrants	388	1/1½d	£1 1s 9d
15/3/51	Total vagrants	397	1/2½d	£1 9 3d
31/5/51	Total vagrants	143	10/9½d	
	Last year	981	£12 19s 5½d	

The Master suspected that tramps were depositing money in the town before claiming to be destitute and entering the workhouse. On one occasion, therefore, he had a man with a 12-year-old boy followed to a house in West Hill, where they were found to have left money for safe keeping. They were promptly taken before the magistrates, who discharged them with an admonition.

In August 1849, George Roberts, a vagrant in the tramp house, tore up all his clothing. He was thereupon supplied with old rags[i] and discharged without any breakfast. He was said to be "very disappointed at not being sent to prison".[2]

Offences were not confined to men. Three days later two women, Mary Ann Davis and Ann Whiting, able-bodied vagrants, were sent into custody for breaking windows at the tramp house. They were sentenced to serve one month with hard labour in Oxford gaol. That did not deter two Irish women, Ann Welch and Mary Morgan, who, two weeks later, on 12 April, broke 11 panes of glass in order to be sent to Oxford gaol. This time the Master did not put the County to the expense but locked them up for four hours and then discharged them. All these examples of problems with vagrants are in the Master's report and journal.[ii]

---

i   By tearing up their clothes, vagrants could hope to be given a better replacement suit.
ii OA PLU4/W/A1/1.

West Hill, 1904. Painting by Lucy Cooper.
Reproduced with permission of Town Clerk, Henley Town Council.

Such indiscipline sometimes spilled over into the pauper inmates. In November 1849 there was insubordination leading to the breaking of windows in the day-room. The five ringleaders were taken before the magistrates and sentenced to two months in gaol with hard labour. Nor were problems confined to the inmates. In December 1849, the Master had to report John Woodley, who was in charge of the Tramp House, for neglect of duty. Twenty-one tramps had been admitted at 8 pm that day and it was reported that all had been searched and nothing found but 1½d on them. The Master did a spot check, together with the Schoolmaster, and found all the tramps in bed with their dirty clothes on and, upon searching them, he found pipes, tobacco, matches and provisions plus 3s 8½d in cash.

In January 1850, two tramps, John Baker and Albert King, were locked up for refusing to work. They then broke windows in the lock-up cells in order to be sent to gaol. The Master did not send them to the magistrates but, after six hours of confinement, he sent them out of town, escorted by a constable.

This was echoed by two able-bodied tramps, Henry Evans and Thomas Gard, who, in December 1850, were locked up for four hours for refusing to work. "They wished to be sent to prison." The regime there must have been seen as a softer option. Perhaps this incident led to a more general outbreak of disorderly conduct because, three days later, the Master had to deal with 18 tramps, of whom three were indeed sent to prison and 15 were punished by the Master and discharged.[2]

It was a troublesome month because on 19 December Thomas White, William Smith, Mary White and Catherine Driscoll, four able-bodied tramps, broke 21 panes of glass in the Tramp House. The Town Magistrates committed the men to two months in prison, with hard labour; the women also, but for one month.

At the same time, Alice Kemp, a pauper, was sent to Oxford Gaol for one month under the Vagrancy Act for wilfully making herself chargeable to the Parish when she had means of supporting herself; presumably money was found on her when searched.

On 3 February 1851, William Bell of Watlington was sent into custody under the Vagrancy Act for neglecting to maintain himself when he had the means of so doing. "This man was discharged from the Army in May last in consequence of sickness, with a pension of 6d per day, which he denied he had received at the time he was admitted into the Workhouse. This afterwards proved to be untrue and he was committed to Oxford for 1 month with hard labour." [2]

There was more trouble in March when two tramps were corrected by the Master for refractory conduct at the Tramp House. It was probably suspected that these two were looking to go to Oxford Gaol as an easy option. Instead, when they were taken before the Town Magistrates they were merely reprimanded and sent out of town, escorted by the constable.

The Master's Journals do not survive beyond 1851 and the newspaper reports in the Reading Mercury are sparse until the Henley Advertiser began printing in 1860. Thereafter the reports of tramps appearing before Henley Magistrates reveal a continuing and increasing problem.

For instance, the attention of the Chief Constable was called to a riot occurring at the gate of the workhouse on the evening of 4th September 1860, which continued more or less from 7 o'clock until 11 o'clock at night. [2]

However, in June 1861 the Board of Guardians sat down to consider the best method of administering relief to tramps after the Magistrates had stated they wished no harsh treatment shown to tramps. The Board exhorted the Master to be especially careful in the exercise of his discretion, eg a woman found in a state of exhaustion in the town was subsequently admitted to the Tramps Ward, having been refused previously. Other cases the Master had rejected as being tramps who were able-bodied. [2]

On Aug 10 1861, the Henley Advertiser reported John Mitchell and William Reed, two men of colour, charged with refusing to labour at the Union House having received food and lodging. Committed to gaol for 21 days each.

By October 1861, the Poor Law Inspector of the Union was requested to investigate an account of the number of tramps committed to Oxford Gaol for offences in Henley Union Workhouse being greater than the number committed for similar offences in any other workhouse in this country. The inspector was to investigate the system adopted for their relief at this union workhouse and afford the Board his future guidance. [2]

Unremitting problems with tramps continued. On January 2nd 1864 John Turner, William Taylor, Joseph Sears, William Nicholas and William Read, all tramps, were sentenced to 21 days imprisonment each and hard labour for having on the same morning refused to perform a certain task of work at the workhouse in return for food and lodgings which had been afforded them. And Aileen Turner, also a tramp, for having on the above day wilfully damaged the windows of the Porter's Lodge at the workhouse to the value of 1s 6d, was committed for 14 days. [3]

The opening of new Vagrant Wards in 1867 coincided with the concern voiced by Oxford Magistrates over the question of dealing with the great amount of vagrancy reported to prevail within the County of Oxford. An emergency meeting was called with Boards of Guardians to discuss the matter. This caused the Henley Board of Guardians to focus their attention on how other Unions managed to reduce the number of tramps and thereby the cost to the Poor rate. Therefore in January 1868 a comprehensive report by a Committee of Henley Guardians was laid before the Board of Guardians following correspondence with other Unions in this and adjoining Counties. The Report found that at Stroud, Guildford and Cookham the Guardians had appointed the Supt of Police as Assistant Relieving Officer at a salary and that in consequence the numbers of tramps had decreased more than ten-fold.

It was resolved, on the recommendation of the Committee, that the Clerk communicate with Oxford Police Committee and ascertain upon what terms the Henley Board of Guardians may secure in future the assistance of the police as Assistant Relieving Officer for casual poor for the Union of Henley. The response came in February 1868 from the meeting of the County Police Committee who had resolved that as a provisional arrangement the services of a policeman as Assistant Relieving Officer be made, upon the Guardians undertaking to pay the County £25 a year, as a share of the appointment made in Woodstock Union for the area. The additional duty would involve the expense to the County of £300 a year for five additional men, whereas the Henley Board now paid £59 pa for rent and superintendence of tramps; this it was said by Henley Guardians "really tends to the maintenance of the evil". The Henley Board of Guardians propounded the desirableness of uniformity of action throughout the County.[3]

By December 1868 John Burn felt compelled to write to PLB on the matter of tramps, (as a private individual rather than as a Guardian). This letter is shown at Appendix G and comments on searches for money; work, food and length of stay; wayfarers as compared to professional tramps; punishment and imprisonment; recording of tramps. Interestingly with reference to the above, he writes, "... if a policeman were employed, and that he did his duty ..."

For example, John Sullivan, a tramp, was found to have one shilling in his possession when applying for lodging at the Union House in January 1869. He was committed to Oxford Gaol for 7 days hard labour.

Concern continued and in 1869 J J Henley, the PLB Inspector, reported that the vagrants were to pound a peck of flints, which the Master considered a deterrent to the habitual vagrant, though numbers had not much decreased. However, Mr Henley commended the Vagrant Wards in which "each man has a pretty coconut matting hammock on iron stanchions".

From reports in the Henley Advertiser in 1871, it is possible to plot the weekly movement of tramps into and out of Henley Union Workhouse during that year (see next page). From this it can be inferred that most mobility occurred in Spring time until June, when the numbers fell off during harvesting; on the road again in October and November. The hard winter months of December to February were presumably too cold and fruitless to be venturing forth.

For comparison, the number of tramps admitted March to September 1881 was 1657 (an average of 55 per week, I estimate) and was an increase of 137.

Tramps admitted weekly 1871

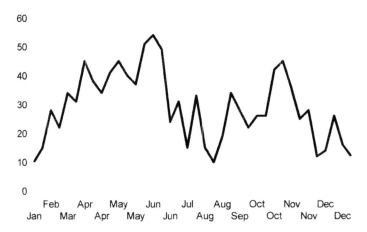

Although vagrants preferred to stay away from workhouses on census nights, it is interesting to see from page 79 the occupations of those passing through 1871-1901, for example carpenter, baker, riveter and of course general labourers.[3]

Problems continued. In June 1871 Emily Lees, a tramp, was charged by Mr Mortlock, the Master, with breaking two panes of glass at the Tramp Ward, doing damage amounting to 4s. The prisoner pleaded guilty and was sentenced to 21 days hard labour.

This contrasts with two other cases in the same court when no damage was caused: Rebecca Birch, tramp, was charged with being drunk and riotous in Duke Street; she was locked up and fined 5s plus costs. Likewise, Sarah March. Perhaps they were so drunk that they never got up the hill to the workhouse!

In November 1871 William Brown and James Smith, tramps, were charged with refusing to perform a certain task of work – breaking a peck of stones – in return for food and lodging at the workhouse; both were sentenced to 21 days hard labour.[3]

The Board of Guardians were considering a yard for storage of materials. In January 1872 the Henley Advertiser reported Mr Watts as saying that circumstances had occurred at the Union which he thought might relieve the Board from the necessity of procuring a site. The Local Government Board had recently issued fresh instructions about the employment of vagrants: they would have to break stone. He thought that probably some arrangements might be made with the Board of Guardians whereby the Local Board might buy their stones ready broken. The report went on to say that Mr Outhwaite, Guardian, thought it would be desirable that the Board should be granted the power to send inmates to break stones if at any time there should be a deficiency of labour. He said it would be a mutual benefit to both Boards.

In December 1872 the Assistant Inspector reported that vagrants were not regularly bathed (if at all) and they were without sleeping garments. He advised that there should be a bath attached to the ward.[2]

Cottages further up West Hill, since renamed West Street, continued to cause problems in 1878. William McDermott was charged with keeping an unlicensed lodging house, which was regarded as a refuge by thieves, tramps and suspicious characters. It was said that there were about a dozen tramps in the kitchen and in the house every night, each paying 4d per night. A licence had been refused as the rooms were too small, so the proprietor was fined £5 plus costs.[3]

In March 1879 further alterations and additions to the Tramp Wards were agreed and a tender let to Charles Clements at £268, to include hot and cold water and fittings. The following illustration shows the layout, from which can be gauged the process of admitting tramps through the 7 ft high gates beside the porter's lodge;

**Proposed Alterations & Additions to Tramps Wards at Henley Union
(incorporating stone-breaking yard)**

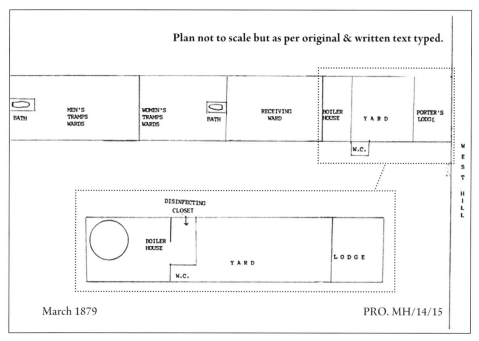

Plan not to scale but as per original & written text typed.

March 1879   PRO. MH/14/15

through the yard (where stone-breaking would be carried out the next morning), with its boiler house where a disinfecting closet would decontaminate their clothing; into the Receiving Ward for a search for any money and removal of clothing; then admittance into either the men's or women's ward, where a bath would be taken before a meal and sleep in a hammock.

In November 1879 tasks of work were set out for male casual paupers: breaking of 2 cwt of stones, or such other quantity not less than 1½ cwt and not more than 3 cwt depending on the nature of the stone.

The stone-breaking yard continued in use. For example, in October 1882 the Board of Guardians ordered that 6 yards of flints be purchased for providing work for tramps, and in December they ordered that the pounded flint be advertised for sale.[3]

Vagrancy being a constant source of concern to the Victorians, a Casual Poor Act was enacted in 1882 tightening up the rules. Minor alterations were made to Henley Tramp Wards, costing £49. This Act at last resulted in a dramatic fall in numbers; in 1883, numbers admitted to Henley Union Tramp Wards were 1,135, down from

2,592 in 1882 – a reduction of 43%. Prior to the Act in 1881 the half-yearly figure was 1,657, an increase of 157 over the previous half year. In January 1884, the Reading Chronicle commented on the significance of these figures and the necessity for the Act, the belief being held that indiscriminate hospitality encouraged vagrancy. Indeed, John Burn, Guardian in 1868, had suggested that when vagrants tore up their clothing they should be left in the Casual Ward without any clothing for 2-3 days. PLB declared this to be "not legal".[1]

Nevertheless, despite the reduction in numbers emanating from the new Act, there were still tramps passing through Henley and trying to use the Casual Ward for relief. For instance;

> James Swan, tramp was charged in September 1886 with applying for relief at Henley Workhouse, having at the time money in his possession. Archibald Totman, Labour Master of the Workhouse said that the previous evening about 7 o'clock the prisoner applied for admission to the Casual Ward. In answer to the usual questions, he said he had no money about him. Witness searched his clothes and found a penny in his pocket, 10½d in his bundle and 2d in a little tin box, making 1/1½d. He reported the case to the Master. Mr Martin said the money was all in coppers. Swan was committed for 7 days hard labour and the money to be forfeited.[3]

Alarmingly, James Bell aged 33, George Hall aged 36 and George Lantoness aged 62 were three tramps admitted into the workhouse infirmary from the Casual Ward in March 1889 suffering from itch. The Medical Officer said two of them had a very severe form of itch and it was most desirable that more isolated accommodation for such cases be provided.[2] (Such contagious disease could otherwise spread among the inmates).

A case arose in January 1891 when Peter Friend, the Workhouse porter appeared as a witness to Henry Watkins, tramp, who was charged with having destroyed his clothing at the workhouse. The prisoner said he would rather go to prison than tramp the country [3] (it being winter).

On 4th November 1892 it was reported that Arthur Sconce "a queer looking man with long sandy beard and hair" was charged with refusing to do his allotted task of work at the workhouse. The prisoner made a statement in answer to the charge but not a word could be understood. George Moss, Porter of the Workhouse, stated that the prisoner was admitted to the Casual Ward on November 1st. Witness gave him a choice of either stone or oakum but he refused point blank to do either. He was quite capable of doing the work. He had his lodging and food the same as the other men. Sentenced to 7 days hard labour.[3]

On June 2nd 1893 Borough Police Court – Abusive Tramp:

> George Wilson, described as a labourer from Richmond, was charged with being drunk and disorderly in West Street on Sunday evening. Prisoner presented a very miserable appearance. He had no shoes or stockings and his coat was in tatters. Mr Martin, Master of the Workhouse, stated that at 10 minutes

past 9 on Sunday night he answered the bell. Prisoner at once abused him. Witness refused to take him in as he was drunk, when prisoner used disgusting language. During the whole of his 13 years experience, he never heard such abusive language. Witness had 8 other men in the Tramp Ward. At the Police Station prisoner abused witness in the most vile manner. His conduct was so bad that Mr Keale heard it and sent word down that the man was to be locked up. PC Green deposed to taking prisoner into custody against the Workhouse gates. He abused the Master very much all the way down to the Police Station. The Master told him he could not go into the workhouse in such a state. His language in the Station too was disgraceful. Prisoner said he had never been in the town before. He was sorry if he used bad language. He was sentenced to 3 weeks hard labour.[3]

By 1895 a Conference was called in Oxford to discuss "The growing evil of vagrancy".[3] Nevertheless the steady stream of vagrants continued to go through Henley Union, only the recalcitrants leaving a record as they passed through Henley Magistrates Court:

On 27 April 1901 John Sewell, tramp, was brought up in custody charged with refusing to perform his allotted task and refusing to work whilst an inmate of the Casual Ward at the Workhouse on April 24. Edward Norman Knight, Porter at the Workhouse, said that the defendant was admitted to the Casual Ward on Tuesday night and had his supper. After having his breakfast on Wednesday morning, defendant refused to do his work, saying he would not break stones on dry bread. Defendant said he had never been in a Casual Ward before and was not shown how to do the work. Evidence having been given by the Master of the Union, prisoner was sent to gaol for 7 days hard labour.[3]

Some Labour Masters at the Workhouse were harsher than others. For instance, in November and December 1901 three tramps were put before the Borough Bench, having refused to work after being refused hot water to drink. In these cases, the magistrates felt it was inhuman of Edward Knight, Porter/Supt of Labour, to refuse a man something warm during the cold weather before commencing work.[3]

Again in January 1904 there was a spate of cases before Magistrates of tramps refusing to work because of cold sleeping quarters and work shed. This led to an altercation:

"Treatment of Tramps: Magistrates and Guardians at variance. Observations by the Henley Borough Bench.

Mayor Alderman Clements JP remarked on the Henley Bench some weeks ago dealing with eight cases of tramps who refused to do their labour task at the workhouse. At time there was extremely bitter and cold weather. Alderman Simpkins JP and himself thought there was some reason in what the men who were charged alleged. They said they were very cold during the night and that the workroom was also very cold, and made that the excuse for not performing their task.

The Henley Board of Guardians replied: Tramps are, in the vast majority of cases, vicious and idle, and the Guardians do not consider it advisable to make life inviting, nor do they consider it necessary to provide them with artificial warmth while at their work or to artificially warm their bedrooms to a greater extent than is done by the present hot water pipes. They have three blankets and a flannel nightgown, which is more than can be afforded by the majority of ratepayers in the Union (if it be true that the occupier of a house pays his rates in rent, if in no other way).

The diet given to tramps is regulated by LGB. The refusal to work, which has been recently manifested two or three times recently at Henley, appears to be part of a concerted action set afoot by tramps all over the country."

However, JPs Ald Clements, Simpkins, Monk and Chamberlain had all visited the tramp wards.[2] The Bench thought the circumstances warranted some little consideration being shown to these men, in the shape of something more than a cup of water and bread. The contention was that a warm room, a good heavy nightshirt and three moderately heavy blankets, a man should have nothing whatever to complain about. The Mayor thought the tramps had a better acquaintance with the Magistrates than with the Guardians.

The matter was allowed to drop by the Magistrates.[3]

Assault by a tramp: George Foster, tramp, charged with assaulting Edward Norman Knight, the porter at 8 am. Prisoner threw a bucket of water at him and then threatened him with a large iron bar. Prisoner said he was cold all night and lost his temper.

But there was no excuse allowed that Summer in June 1904 when William Burrows, a labourer of no fixed abode, was charged in custody with having refused to perform his allocated task work, stone pounding, whilst he was an inmate of the workhouse labour ward. Edward Knight, Labour Master at the workhouse, said the prisoner was admitted to casual ward, and next morning he put him to work. At noon he had done very little and as he had not finished the work at four, Knight spoke to him about it. The prisoner said he could not finish it in one day and that he therefore would do no more, with the result that he was sentenced to 14 days hard labour.[3]

The old problems continued: in March 1905 Charles Palmer of no fixed abode, a tramp, was charged with having made a false statement for the purpose of gaining relief at Henley Union. Edward Norman Knight, Labour Master, said that when he admitted the prisoner to the workhouse he asked him the usual question whether he had any money or food upon him. Palmer had replied in the negative but, on being searched the next morning at work time, the witness found 1s 4d in his bundle. Palmer was sentenced to 21 days hard labour.[3]

According to a report in the Henley Advertiser, there was a large increase in the number of tramps admitted to Henley Union in the half year to Lady Day 1907, causing concern to the Guardians, viz;

Year	1904	1905	1906	1907
Half year to lady day	747	1057	1090	1201
Half year to Michaelmas	655	854	819	
Total	1402	1911	1909	

But, in 1908 there were humane sentiments being expressed, this time by one of the Guardians and by some of the magistrates:

In June 1908 the Revd Hart-Davis, guardian, proposed that tramps in the Henley Union receive tea instead of water. He said there were two conceivable ways of dealing with tramps. One was at present in vogue at the Union: treating them scarcely as human beings, giving them very scant food, and work which was unremunerative to the Board and very distasteful to the men. There were some tramps, he agreed, with regard to whom they could hardly use repressive measures, but there were others who would, he thought, respond to kinder treatment.[3]

Even so, there followed continuing cases being brought before the Police Court, as with John Walker, labourer, and Matthew Montague, seaman, in August 1908, who refused to pound stone because they disliked and refused to do such work. Likewise in October Edward Snell and Frederick Whale. By then it was thought that some of the magistrates were getting tired of the Workhouse Master bringing such cases before them and that some cases were brought up unnecessarily.[3]

October 1908: Four more tramps were sent to gaol on Monday for having refused to do their tasks at the workhouse. They said that when they did work they expected proper payment for it. Three of the men were sent to gaol for 14 days hard labour and one man, who threatened to do bodily harm to workhouse officials, was ordered to serve 21 days hard labour.[3]

It is noteworthy that in November 1908 about 30 members of the Hunger Marchers came to Henley on Saturday evening and addressed a meeting in Market Place. The speakers spoke from their van and were emphatic in their condemnation of society. At about 10.50pm they proceeded to the workhouse where they demanded admittance into the Casual Ward.[3]

By 1909 there appears to have been a change of policy in regard to tramps having money on them. When John Alexander, a labourer of no fixed abode, was charged with committing wilful damage to a door at the Union to the extent of 1s., the Labour Master of the house said the prisoner was admitted to the Casual Ward and had said "no" when asked if he had any money. A search discovered 3d, which was confiscated. The prisoner did not like this and caused the damage. He said he wanted the money to buy some food in the morning. He was told that if he had admitted possessing it, it would have been returned to him on leaving the workhouse. As it was, he was sent to prison for 14 days.[3]

In an attempt to prevent begging, a notice was erected in the town in 1911 by the Berks, Bucks and Oxon Joint Vagrancy Committee warning the public not to offer food and drink to beggars, who could obtain a meal at the workhouse. Any occurrence of begging was to be reported to the Police Station (see next page).

Vagrants from far and wide still used Henley Union casual ward. In 1913 a young man named Victor Archambaud, said to be Canadian, was charged with performing only a quarter of the task set him by the Labour Master, Mr E Knight, and refusing to complete it. Sentenced to 14 days imprisonment.

During the course of World War I casuals continued to pass through Henley: 100 during a fortnight in January 1916, but more usually 65 – 75. In April 1916 the Army Council requested notification of all cases of men apparently of military age and receiving relief to be reported to the Recruiting Officer. In the following few weeks this resulted in a downward trend in what would usually have been increasing numbers; for example in June 1916 73 compared with 139 in the equivalent week of 1915.

By Spring 1920 the number of vagrants relieved suddenly doubled to that of the previous year, eg from 32 to 60 in April and from 36 to 60 in May. This led to an emergency meeting of the Bucks/Berks/Oxon Joint Vagrancy Committee, at which Mr Cave of Henley, on behalf of the Masters Association, raised the question of the number of soldiers of the labour type on the road. They held an army discharge and that entitled them to preferential treatment. There would perhaps soon have to be made some regulations as to the keeping of these men and to make them do a class of work; oakum-picking had been banned and stone-breaking discouraged.

The Master reported that there appeared to be more men, many of them coming in thinking they could get their discharge next morning, which was bringing the place down to a common lodging house, which was never intended. One casual had come in with 1s 8½d on him. He stayed two nights and performed the task allocated of picking 1 lb oakum; when he left Mr Cave deducted 1s from his money towards his maintenance cost. He appeared to be very dissatisfied and went to the police. In the Master's opinion he was a habitual casual and not a seeker of work.[3] In the case of discharged soldiers, the Master did not enforce a task. After discussion, the Guardians decided to charge a shilling in future.

By now there was work in progress to refurbish the Casual Wards at a cost of £240. In July 1920 the number of vagrants had jumped from 34 to 88. But by January 1930 the number of casuals relieved during that month had leapt to 1638; March 1105; April 1129. The massive increase in 1930 resulted from single men being denied Parish relief and, with few jobs available during the Great Depression, having to tramp from one workhouse to the next for sustenance as they sought scarce work.

By that time the Joint Vagrancy Committee had ordered that all vagrants were to be detained on three consecutive Sundays so as to get some reliable information as to accommodation available. It had been ordered that a day room be set apart for the vagrants so detained but in Henley that would involve considerable constructional alterations so the Public Assistance Committee would be asked what to do when on a recent evening there were 68 casuals and accommodation for only 20? – so that "the onus would rest on that body".[3]

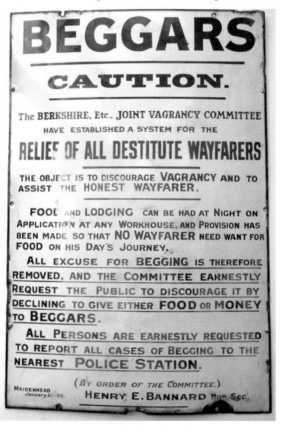

1911 poster now displayed in the entrance to the Hart GP Surgery.

In July 1931 the Master reported 605 casuals relieved in the month (compared with 748 previously but Henley casual wards were closed on July 1st (harvest time?). No further applications had been made except for one, but when he was told he would be detained for two nights and would have some of his money kept, he did not insist on staying.[3]

There is a graphic description of what it was actually like to be a user of a tramp ward, known as "The Spike", written by George Orwell in his down-and-out days in 1931.[i] There was still an abiding memory in Henley into the early 1960s of a queue of tramps outside the workhouse gates awaiting admission at that time.

---

i   *Down and Out in Paris and London*. George Orwell, 1933.

15. Entertainment

HENLEY has always been known for its philanthropy. For instance, in 1839 the PLC, having refused to sanction any extra allowances to the poor in the Union, the inmates of the Henley Poor House were reported by the Reading Mercury as having been **as usual** regaled with an excellent Christmas dinner of beer and pudding, the funds for which were raised by public subscription. Christmas apart, there was little relief from the humdrum nature of life in an institution.

However, following a general softening of attitudes to poor relief in the latter part of the 19th century, there are some references to an occasional treat for inmates, ranging from musicians coming in to play and to greater amusements in the form of outings, when the outside world began to invite inmates out for recreation.

For instance, some of the old women went to a tea party at Mrs Whitelaw's in July 1883. In the following year at Crowsley Park, Col and Mrs Baskerville, preferred to give the children a treat: "the Master reported that all the children went to Crowsley Park today, Aug 5. Mrs Baskerville gave them an excellent tea and they spent a most enjoyable afternoon. Thanks from the Board were conveyed to Mrs Baskerville for her kindness".[3] Mrs Whitelaw was also thanked for having twelve old women to tea on 23rd September.

Christmas became a special time within the workhouse. For instance, in January 1884, the Reading Chronicle reported the Henley Union inmates regaled with an annual Christmas treat thanks to Lady Stapleton (of Greys Court), Mrs Baskerville (of Crowsley Park) and Miss Ackroyd. Cheers were given to Master and Matron, Mr and Mrs Mortlock "who have done so much to promote happiness and enjoyment of both old and young".

"In January 1885, on Thursday the 3rd, all the people were assembled in the large dining room shortly after four o'clock and had a most excellent tea provided them through the kindness of Lady Stapleton, who was accompanied by her daughter, Miss Stapleton. After all had done justice to the meal, Lady Stapleton said how pleased she was to see them so enjoying themselves and also spoke a few friendly words to the children.

"In the evening an entertainment was got up by Alderman Chamberlain and a few friends for the benefit of the inmates ... The programme of entertainment consisted of a piano and violin accompaniment to songs and also the Congregational Junior Band of Hope.

"At the conclusion of the entertainment the gifts presented by Lady Stapleton were given out. These consisted of tobacco for the men, tea for the women and sweets and toys for the children. In addition, all the inmates had an orange each. The Master, Mr Martin, thanked all those who had tried to give them some pleasure on that day and called for three hearty cheers, which were given lustily by the boys, bringing the entertainment to a conclusion".[3]

"In September 1885 the Vice-chairman of the board of Guardians paid for a steam launch to take all the children in the schools for a pleasure trip on the River Thames" what a thrill for them that must have been.

At Christmas 1885 the festivities began as usual with the service in the chapel of Henley Union. The "usual Christmas fare of roast beef and plum pudding was served to the inmates, who afterwards were supplied with oranges and tobacco and amused themselves with singing songs".[3]

Christmas started early in 1886 when members of Henley Temperance gave a concert at Henley Union Workhouse on Thursday, December 17th, as reported in the Henley Advertiser. "All the inmates, with the exception of those in the infirmary, were present in the dining hall, where a platform was erected at the south end for the performers. The officers of the establishment were also present. After the concert was over, each of the inmates was given a bun, a cup of coffee and an orange, provided by the kindness of a few tradesmen of the Town, the articles being handed round by members of the choir, affording no small pleasure to the recipients.

"The Master, Mr Martin, thanked the performers on behalf of the inmates, to whom he said it had been a treat and had helped to break the monotony of a workhouse life. He hoped to see the choir there again as he was sure the inmates would look forward with pleasure to another similar concert. Cheers were then given for Mr Simpkins, who acknowledged the vote of thanks. All present joined in singing the national anthem, bringing a very pleasant evening to a close."

Entertainment continued into January when, "by the generosity of Mr and Mrs G Brakspear, the inmates were provided with a bountiful tea", in addition to which tobacco and sweets were distributed amongst the inmates. "Hearty cheers were given by the inmates to all who had contributed."

Queen Victoria's Golden Jubilee was celebrated in fine style on June 21, 1887. The inmates of the workhouse had a good dinner consisting of roast beef and plum pudding served in the dining hall, which was gay with flags and mottoes. The officers of the establishment all joined together, after which, headed by the 2nd Oxon RV band, a procession was formed and all went to the meadow at the back of the workhouse where a number of games were indulged in, including obstacle and three-legged races, and fetching out oranges from a pan of water with the teeth. A plentiful supply of tobacco and snuff was handed round to the adults, and sweets and nuts to the children. Tea was also taken in the meadow. The amusements were kept up til a quarter to nine, when the inmates again sang the national anthem and, after giving ringing cheers for the Queen, returned to the House.[3]

Lady Stapleton again provided a treat at Greys Court in July 1887 for the children in the workhouse. The Master also reported that Mrs G Brakspear (wife of the Chairman of the Board) had sent some cherries for the inmates.[3]

In January 1891 it was reported that Lady Stapleton was again giving an annual treat to workhouse inmates, with a spread of bread, butter, jam, cakes and buns, with music by the band of Henley Volunteers. The Henley Advertiser reported that the inmates retired at 10 o'clock "highly gratified".

Tobacco in those days was a great treat so the Master's suggestion of an allowance of 1 oz of tobacco weekly to male inmates aged more than 60 must have caused great delight. After due consideration and recommendation by the Board of Guardians, the LGB agreed to this largesse costing £10 pa.[1]

An exciting treat came in September 1892 when Sir Frank and Lady Crisp chose to commemorate their Silver Wedding by conveying the inmates on board two steamers to Goring-on-Thames. "All but a few timid ones who could not be induced to go on the water started off at 8 o'clock in the morning, returning at 8.45 pm. Refreshments were supplied to all 91 participants but wretched weather rather spoiled an otherwise memorable day".[3]

Recently, in 2003, the Henley Standard published a photograph of a similar outing in about 1930 for families in Henley Workhouse, all crammed aboard, some with babies in arms (see page 170).

June 1893 was the occasion of a royal wedding. More treats were in store as the Board of Guardians declared that the inmates were to be treated as if it were Christmas Day (with a menu accordingly). Mr Ovey, a Guardian, invited them to Badgemore House for entertainment.

Annual Christmas festivities in 1894 were reported in the Henley Advertiser. "On Christmas morning the usual service was held in the chapel of the Henley Union at which all the inmates were present, when an appropriate sermon was preached by the Revd W Chapman. The room had been most tastefully decorated by the Matron, Mrs Martin ... The usual Christmas fare of roast beef and plum pudding was served to the inmates, who afterwards were supplied with oranges and (more) tobacco, and amused themselves with singing songs and similar recreation until half past nine, when they retired to rest with light hearts."

At this time Miss Henrietta Chamberlain, "a young lady residing in Henley", was accorded appreciation by the Board of Guardians for "voluntarily playing the harmonium at the services at the Workhouse of this Union for the past five years". She was offered a reward of 5 guineas with the request that she purchase with it any article she likes.[3] (NB: Contrast this with the annual wage of £15 paid to the laundress!)

That must have been her swan song because in 1901 Mr Chamberlain (by then a Guardian) moved that the best thanks of the Board be given to Mr Monk for so kindly playing the harmonium at the Sunday services at the Workhouse during the past 5 years.[3]

The Henley Advertiser listed the following gifts provided by local benefactors at Christmas 1895:

Col and Mrs Noble	tobacco for old men and tea for women; crackers for the children
Mr and Mrs Ovey	toy for each child
W H Smith Esq	12 lb tobacco
	gifts of oranges
Mr Savage	invitation to the theatre
Mr Buckham	sweets and oranges for the children
Lady Stapleton	treat for inmates
Mr A Monk	musical entertainment

Another cause for celebration occurred with Queen Victoria's Diamond Jubilee in May 1897. The Board of Guardians were authorised by LGB to provide a tea with cakes, bread and jam; in addition, for the men 1 oz tobacco in Jubilee paper (sic) and a pipe; snuff for the women (sic); and sweets and oranges for the children. Furthermore, the inmates were allowed to see the sports held in the Town.[2] So a memorable occasion it was for the inmates.

All this time there had been the opportunity given for friends to visit inmates. Rules for this seem to have been relaxed by 1899 because the Visiting Committee of the Union had cause to investigate the custom which had been obtained in allowing visitors to see their friends outside visiting hours. They declared that there were no grounds for complaint and recommended that friends of the inmates be admitted only on Sundays between the hours of 11 and 12 o'clock and 1 and 2 o'clock.[3]

While local ladies' munificence had been accepted by the Board of Guardians for all these years past, even by the turn of the century there was no actual involvement of ladies with the Board. Therefore, in 1900 the Revd J W Nutt proposed that a committee of ladies be appointed to visit the inmates. He said that it simply meant they should be appointed to call in and read to the inmates. "Everyone must see what a dull life they had." If the ladies saw anything (untoward), they would report to the Visiting Committee.[3]

Entertainment at Christmas that year included a concert arranged by Mr Branman and friends. During the interval, tea and coffee, mince pies, cakes and fruit (and tobacco for the men) were handed round by the Master and other officers.

In summer 1901 Mr Holbrow was owed £1 for plants by the Guardians. He insisted that this should go towards giving the children a treat. The Master, Mr Simmonds, was anxious that this should form a nucleus towards an outing on the river, and Mr Simmonds asked if he might collect subscriptions towards it. The Board thought Mr Simmonds could not collect as Master of the Workhouse but only in a private capacity. The Clerk was directed to convey the best thanks of the Board to Mr Holbrow for his generous offer.[3]

Ad hoc entertainment continued during 1901 at Easter; in August when Lady Crisp entertained the inmates to tea at Friar Park; and in December when Mrs Brakspear gave presents for the inmates.[3]

"In early March 1904 entertainment at the workhouse was provided by the kindness of the Master and Matron, Mr and Mrs Simmonds. It was stated that the inmates of the workhouse had the tedium of their existence relieved by a capital entertainment on Friday evening. This took place in the Dining Room, where a pleasant time was passed in the enjoyment of an excellent programme provided by Mr Brown of Nottingham, Mrs Brown and other entertainers. Also the inmates were regaled with tobacco, sweets and biscuits during the evening. A month previously there was Friday evening entertainment by the Henley Lodge of Druids, who gave out gifts of tobacco for men and tea for women." [3]

By 1906 the local newspaper was reporting, "Christmas Day at the Workhouse was indeed a bright spot in the lives of the inmates. They had breakfast at 8 o'clock in the dining hall, which was ornately decked with evergreens, whilst the general effect was enhanced by the clever work of the matron (Mrs Hodgkinson), who had made from tissue paper sweet peas, poppies and very elegant clusters of clematis etc".[3]

Lady visitors were in evidence by November 1907: Mrs and Miss Baskerville had visited the infirmary and given tea and sugar to the inmates. Two large parcels of periodicals had been received from Mrs Brakspear. Mr Leonard Noble wrote intimating that he would give his annual treat to the inmates at the workhouse on December 20th.[3]

The following summer all 45 inmates of the Henley Workhouse, men, women and children, enjoyed the hospitality of Col and Mrs Baskerville at Crowsley Park on a Thursday afternoon.[3]

Lady Crisp was still entertaining a large number of workhouse inmates at Friar Park in summer 1910, where they attended in the charge of Mr Cave, the Master. After a substantial meal, tobacco was given to the men, tea to the women and sweets to the children. Lady Crisp even thought to send presents to those inmates unable to leave the workhouse.

In February 1911 the inmates were entertained by members of the Henley Lodge of the RAOB (Royal Antediluvian Order of Buffaloes) who gave a "very successful" concert at Henley Workhouse. It was reported that the programme was a long one which, "judging by the applause and calls for encores, was much appreciated. A sketch given by boys from the National School caused much laughter." During the interval, small gifts of tobacco and pipes were given to the men, with tea and snuff going to the women.[3]

On Saturday, 21st January 1916, there was a particular treat when the inmates were invited to attend the Picture Palace by Mr Hamilton Gordon (whose application for renewal of a music and dancing licence may have been incidental!).

By 1920 the Druids were reported as entertaining the inmates and giving them 6d each. And the Rector thanked the Guardians and those who had contributed to the fund for a Christmas treat to the inmates at the children's homes. The residents had been very generous and the children spent a very happy time.[3]

During 1925 in the Henley Standard subscriptions were invited to provide a wireless at the workhouse. Presumably this would have been in the control of the Master.

So the boat outing in 1929/30, as pictured, forms a fitting farewell to those inmates still being cared for under the Poor Law before being overtaken by revised arrangements under the control of a new Institution. The Mayor, S J Holton, is shown welcoming them aboard.

Boat outing for the inmates, photograph by courtesy of Mrs Cynthia Brown.

16. Conclusion

IT HAS to be said that Henley was fortunate to have had in place at an early date a facility for relieving the poor, the sick, the mentally infirm and the disabled and elderly paupers. This meant that in Henley the foundations had already been laid when the New Poor Law was introduced in 1834. Although conditions were now prescribed by a central commission in London, a measure of local autonomy remained possible and the continuing preference locally for outdoor relief was evident. The introduction of schoolrooms was a welcome benefit to the community, as were the hospital beds and access to a medical officer.

Since 1834, attitudes to the poor changed significantly over the years, in particular with the onset of the Great Agricultural Depression of the 1880s and increasing unemployment. Boards of Guardians were then encouraged by the LGB to provide work other than stone-breaking or oakum-picking. Towards the end of the 19th century social investigators increased people's understanding of the complexities of poverty and pauperism.

Indeed, workhouses in the second half of the 19th century provided more and more specialised care to the different classes of inmates. Whilst true that the workhouse was still seen as a grim and forbidding place even at the end of the century, much more thought was being given to the needs of paupers. Nevertheless, the workhouse was still dreaded by the working classes as it symbolised failure, heartbreak and degradation. The humiliation of entering the House was still deeply felt, as had always been intended.

1902 saw further advances in public health and a softening of attitudes to poor relief, along with a greater accountability of the Boards of Guardians.

By 1905 dissatisfaction with the Poor Law nationally and disagreement over its objectives and principles of the 1834 Act as applied to undeserving poor and the need to create improved facilities for the deserving poor led to the setting up of a Royal Commission. That failed to agree on the extent to which the 1834 principles were still relevant and the appropriate demarcation between philanthropy and poor relief, as well as the growing number of welfare agencies.

But it was the introduction of an old age pension in 1908 and of state sickness and unemployment insurance in 1911 which radically altered the situation. In 1913 workhouses became "Poor Law Institutions" but this was little more than a cosmetic change to the workhouse. It was not until 1930 that the administrative structure of the New Poor Law was finally dismantled, when the existing boards of Guardians were dissolved and their responsibilities transferred to County Councils. They also set up Public Health Committees to take over care of the sick. Workhouse infirmaries would become municipal hospitals, maintained by the rates, and a co-ordinated system of health care established.

In 1930 the workhouses were closed by Act of Parliament – officially, that is. But in practice it was impossible to close them. They housed many people who had nowhere else to live. Such people could not be turned out into the streets. Apart from that, many of them had been in the workhouse for so long, and subject to the discipline and routine that they were completely institutionalised and could not have adjusted to the outside world. Also, the 1930s were a decade of economic depression, with massive unemployment. Workhouse inmates suddenly thrown onto the local labour market would have made matters worse.

So the workhouses were officially designated "Public Assistance Institutions" and would be referred to locally in Henley as "The Grubber". But in practice they carried on much the same as before except that uniforms were scrapped; comforts such as easy chairs and better food were introduced, and inmates were allowed to go out. The inhumane practice of splitting families was stopped but it was still an institutional life. The staff was the same and discipline was maintained, though life for the inmates was certainly made easier.

Thus, the abolition of the Poor Law Unions on April 1st 1930 sought to remove the stigma of pauperism from those who sought assistance. A co-ordinated system of health care was established and the old workhouse in Henley became Townlands Hospital, with 87 beds; it incorporated the infirmary within the former workhouse.

20th century West Street from a painting by John Piper. Reproduced by kind permission of the Piper family.

The whole of the functions once done by the Guardians were transferred to a Public Assistance Committee to support the needy and to the Public Health Committee of Henley Borough Council, which took over care of the sick. Thus, the workhouse hospital became a municipal hospital maintained by the local rates. Any resident of the area needing medical treatment would be admitted to the hospital and asked to make a financial contribution, if affordable.

The national system of poor relief which began in 1601 finally ended with the 1948 National Assistance Act whereby "existing poor laws shall cease to have effect". So the establishment of the Welfare State between 1946 and 1948 effectively removed the last vestiges of the poor law and the ethos that lay behind it.

Even so, in 1980 an elderly couple living in Friday Street still viewed the modernised Townlands Hospital on the workhouse site with horror: "I never thought he'd end up there!" declared the wife to me when her husband was discharged home. The reputation of Henley Workhouse lingered on.

Appendix A

Government Enquiry into
Henley Charities Distribution 1820

From S Holton ledger[i].

(65) gifts of William Massam, Abraham Pocock, Joan King, William Barnaby, John and William Gravett.

1 July 1651 It appears that the Mayor of Henley and other persons purchased about that time of Richard Boult certain premises (upon which the workhouse now stands) "for the use and benefit of the Poor of Henley" and annexed to the deed is a receipt by Richard Boult, the vendor for £170.

From the receipt and from different entries in the Corporation ledger, it further appears that the purchase money was paid in the following manner:

By £100 Mr Jeaves
£70 William Massam

In 1790 the Bridgemen were called upon to pay in towards building a new workhouse £80, for which they paid interest to the Overseers.

Also part of the charitable gift of William Massam £30
William Barnaby £10
A Pocock £10
Joan King £30

So that there seems to have been expended in the purchase of the site and towards the building of the workhouse the sum of £250 said to have been given to the use of the Poor.

Up to the year 1790 the rent of the land purchased of Boult and the interest of the several sums that were then called in for the purpose of building the workhouse were paid to the Overseers and were probably applied by them in aid of the poor rates. We can discover no traces of any other mode of application.

---

i   Held in HA&HG archives, Henley Town Hall.

From the year 1790 to the present time (1830) the premises have been used as a workhouse. No rent has been paid, nor has any interest been allowed upon the £250 laid out upon them; so that though in fact the Poor have been set to work by means of this money, the Parish at large has received the whole benefit accruing from it.

The present value of the property would certainly very far exceed the interest on £250 but that was only a small part of what was laid out in building the workhouse; the whole of the expenditure incurred by the Parish is stated to have amounted to upwards of £1500.

Taking all the circumstances into consideration, it may be a question of whether the application of the legacies has or has not been consistent with the intention of their respective donors and whether the policy not to pay interest for some at least of those legacies to be applied for charity so as to preserve a distinction between that provision for the Poor which is made by law and that which is afforded by charitable individuals...

There appeared to be the utmost readiness in the Corporation of Henley to rectify any irregularity which may have taken place with regard to these charities and it will be proposed at the next meeting of the Corporation to take proper measures for reshaping all these charities and giving the poor inhabitants of the Parish the benefit at least of the interest on £250 laid out.

In 1821 a Meeting of the General Vestry of St Mary's, the parochial vestry, passed the following resolution:

"That in consequence of the great amount of Poor Rates of the Parish of Henley at this time, when, from the low price of all the necessaries of life the means of subsistence are within the reach of most men and the funds from whence the rates are paid are daily diminishing, it has become absolutely necessary to adopt some plan to remedy, if possible, this growing evil. And it appears to this Vestry that no plan can be effectual which has not for its basis the bettering the condition of the poor and exciting in them as far as may be, a spirit of industry and a desire to exert themselves for the benefit of the families."

The Select Vestry of Henley was formed and immediately set to work. Four Committees were formed. It was found amongst other things that the Overseers had been casual in the collection of rates and in the first six months ratepayers in default were brought before the Magistrates and all arrears were collected.

Appendix B

Henley Workhouse Employees

Clerk

1837	Mr Chapman		
Oct 1840	Nicholas Mercer	£100	Resigned March 1889, old age
Mar 1889	Arthur R Lloyds	£100	Salary increased June 1919 to £200

Assistant Clerk

Nov 1918	Thomas L Easby	£105	Age 26

Treasurer

Mar 1838	John Simonds		Resigned September 1874, ill health
Oct 1874	John Simonds Jnr		No salary

Master

1837	William Jackson	£70	
Jul 1848	Samuel Mortlock	£100	Office vacant on death of Mrs Mortlock
Oct 1866	Samuel Mortlock	£65	Re-applied. Died December 1884
Feb 1885	Henry Edwin Dominy	£65	Vacated by Matron's resignation December 1885
Dec 1885	John Martin	£65	Vacated Office March 1900 on resignation of Matron. Board objected to Master's acting as Dep Reg
Apr 1900	George B Simmons	£65	Resigned June 1906, voluntarily

Matron

Jul 1848	Ann Mortlock		Salary inc in Master's. Died September 1866
Oct 1866	Eliza Pearman (who became)	£35	
Dec 1884	Eliza Mortlock		Office vacant on death of Mr Mortlock
Jan 1885	Eliza Mortlock	£35	Re-applied. Resigned December 1885, voluntarily
Dec 1885	Sarah Martin	£35	Wife of Master. Salary increased to £50 April 1890. Resigned March 1900, ill-health
Apr 1900	Mary E Simmons	£35	Salary increase to £45, January 1903. Resigned June 1906, Voluntarily. Also Superintendent of Radnor Children's Home. 2 year until 28 February 1906 at a salary of £10 per annum. (sic)

| July 1906 | Kate Hodgkinson | £40 | Resigned March 1910, Master's resignation. Board assent to Mrs Hodgkinson acting at Superintendent of Children's Home for a period of 1 year with a salary of £10. Another year March 1908. |

Matron

| Mar 1910 | Nellie F Cave | £45 | Salary increased to £50 April 1913. Plus £5 per annum for acting as Superintendent Nurse. Also Superintendent of Children's Home at £15 per annum. |

Assistant Matron

| Aug 1861 | Elizabeth Mortlock | £1 | Resigned September 1861, voluntarily. |

Superintendent

| Mar 1910 | Nellie F Cave | £10 | Matron of Workhouse Salary increased to £15 March 1911. |

Chaplain

Nov 1863	Rev C A Longland	£50	Resigned June 1870.
Aug 1870	Rev William Chapman	£50	Resigned September 1906.
Oct 1906	Rev Charles Sadler	£50	Resigned October 1910, leaving Henley.
Nov 1910	Rev John G Williams	£50	Resigned November 1918.
Jul 1919	Rev W M A Penyston	£50	

Boilerman

| Sep 1858 | Matthew C Swift | £18 | |

Medical Officer

Mar 1857	Thomas W Jeston	£50	Salary increased May 1872 to £60. Resigned March 1883, voluntarily.
Mar 1883	Egerton Charles Augustus Baines	£60	Resigned November 1895.
Nov 1895	John Arthur Rigge	£60	Died July 1901.
Aug 1901	Arthur E Peake	£60	Salary increased June 1910 to £80. Resigned January 1911, voluntarily.
Jan 1911	Thomas B Dakin	£80	As to question of fees for operations, voluntary resignation.
Apr 1920	George Smith	£80	

Porter

Mar 1862	Harry H Waine	£20	Resigned May 1866, voluntarily.
Jun 1866	Henry Wheeler	£20	Salary increase to £25 August 1867. Died July 1869.
Sep 1869	James Spickernell	£25	Salary increased to £30 March 1878. Dismissed by Guardians June 1886.
Aug 1886	John A Martin	£38	Resigned November 1889, voluntarily.
Dec 1889	Peter Friend	£38	Resigned July 1890, appointed at Hereford.

July 1890	George Moss	£38	Plus £5 as barber. Resigned December 1894, cause not stated. George Moss absented himself from his duties July 1893. Guardians then declared the office vacant but on an expression of regret, Moss was reinstated, although at a reduced salary of £33 and £5 as barber.
Dec 1894	John Dear		Resigned before appointment was reported. Inefficiency.
Feb 1895	Archibald Totman	£25	Plus £5 as barber. Resigned February 1896, cause not stated.
Mar 1896	Thomas Garland Shipley	£4 9s 5d for period. Resigned June 1896, cause not stated.	
June 1896	William Dare Edgcombe	£25	Resigned June 1898, appointed indoor porter.
Aug 1898	John Turner	£30	Resigned November 1898, cause not stated.
Dec 1898	Albert Frith	£30	Resigned August 1899, cause not stated.

Superintendent of Tramps

Mar 1862	Ellen Waine	£5	Resigned May 1866, voluntarily.
June 1866	Harriet Wheeler	£5	Her husband, the porter, died July 1896.
Sep 1869	Martha Spickernell	£5	

Nurse

Mar 1864	Mary S Hubbard	£20	Resigned October 1867, voluntarily.
Jun 1868	Eliza Stevens	£20	Resigned July 1872, voluntarily.
Dec 1872	Annie Sherwood	£20	Increased to £25 March 1878.
1878	Lucy L Bickley	£20	Resigned May 1886, inefficiency.
June 1886	Maria Musselwhite	£20	Dismissed March 1892. Unsatisfactory performance of duties.
May 1892	Annie Cox	£20	Resigned June 1897, voluntarily. As to conduct of nurse in case of Kate Coles.
Aug 1897	Eliza Curtis	£25	Dismissed November 1897, incompetent.
Dec 1897	Sarah Webster	£25	Resigned September 1900, neglect of duty.
Oct 1900	Alice Fleetwood		Dismissed Dec 1900.
May 1901	Emma Pocock	£30	Suspended for insubordination and left August 1901.
Sept 1901	Mary Robb	£30	Resigned October 1910, voluntarily.
Oct 1910	Evelyn M Allan	£30	Resigned February, voluntarily.
Apr 1911	Florence M Pinfield	£30	Resigned May 1912, voluntarily.

Assistant Nurse (additional)

Nov 1910	Julia Coughlan	£20	December 1912 increased to £25. Resigned August 1913, voluntarily.
May 1912	Mary J Crowe	£30	Resigned October 1912, voluntarily. Re-appointed at increased salary.

Assistant Nurse

Dec 1909	Fannie E Heselton	£30	Resigned September 1910, voluntarily.
June 1910	Gertrude E Murray		Resigned August 1910, voluntarily.
Sep 1910	Eleanor E Glynn	£30	Resigned May 1912, voluntarily.
Sep 1910	Emmeline Dear		Resigned December 1910, voluntarily.

Feb 1911	Florence M Brown	£22	Resigned August 1913, voluntarily.
Jun 1912	Adrienne E Lane	£30	Resigned December 1912, voluntarily.
Nov 1912	Julia Murphy	£35	Resigned May 1913, voluntarily.
Dec 1912	Gladys L W Poole	£25	
Aug 1913	Ellen M Macallan	£25	
Nov 1913	Beatrice Worsley	£25	Resigned July 1914, voluntarily.
Mar 1914	Ethel E Cave	£35	
Jun 1914	Emily M Bishop	£25	Resigned 11 February 1915, voluntarily.
Jun 1915	A L Sparks	£25	
Jul 1915	L A Adams	£25	

Schoolmaster

Aug 1861	James S Saunders	£30	Resigned September 1866, voluntarily.
Jan 1867	John H Cotterill	£30	Resigned September 1867, no cause assigned.
Nov 1867	William Griffiths	£30	Resigned December 1868 at the request of the Guardians.
Mar 1869	David Coy	£30	Resigned May 1870, voluntarily.
Jul 1870	David Coy	£30	Re-appointed, Resigned September 1871, voluntarily.
Feb 1872	David Cleary	£30	Resigned January 1873, voluntarily.
Feb 1872	Henry Langley	£30	Resigned November 1875. Convicted of assaulting the Master.
Feb 1876	William White	£30	Resigned June 1887, voluntarily.
Jun 1887	William Cape Waine	£30	

Schoolmistress

May 1864	Elizabeth Way	£30	Resigned November 1866, voluntarily.
Jan 1867	Leah Benjamin	£25	Resigned November 1868, voluntarily.
Feb 1869	Mary A Bradfield	£25	Resigned May 1870, voluntarily.
Jun 1870	Alice Dickson	£25	Resigned December 1872, voluntarily. As to charge against A.Dickson.
Feb 1873	Kezia R Langley	£25	Resigned November 1875, husband's resignation.
June 1876	Annie White	£25	Resigned June 1887, voluntarily.
June 1887	Honoria Walsh	£30	Resigned December 1892, ill health.
June 1893	Elizabeth Courtney	£30	Resigned December 1893, no cause stated.

Industrial Teacher (shoe making)

Jan 1868	William Woodward	12s pw	Resigned December 1869, family being ill.
Dec 1869	Jesse Cornish	12s pw	No report of resignation.
	Matthew Stevens		Death recorded 1882, no record of appointment.
Sept 1881	Lewis Tombs	15s pw	

Industrial Teacher (Laundry Work)

Jan 1868	Sabina Cook	£15	Resigned January 1868, no cause.
Jun 1868	Helen Heather	£15	Resigned May 1870, voluntarily.
Dec 1870	Elizabeth Thomas	£18	Dismissed November 1880, intoxication.
Jan 1881	Elizabeth Miles	£20	Guardians dispensed with services Sept 1883.

Industrial Teacher (Sewing and Knitting)

Jan 1894	Harriet Furze	£20	Resigned May 1894, voluntarily.
Jul 1894	Emmeline F Button	£20	Resigned September 1894, voluntarily.
Nov 1894	Esther Holmes	£20	Resigned June 1895, voluntarily.
Jul 1895	Eliza A Rolfe	£15+£5	Resigned 1895, ill health
Nov 1895	Lily A Minns	£15	Resigned May 1898, cause not stated Successor appointed as caretaker of children, 1898.

Industrial Teacher (Tailoring)

1874	James Josiah Pike		Resigned July 1874 (?…of infirmity).
Jul 1874	Henry Ashby	12s pw	Death reported 1882.
Sep 1881	Thomas Wise	15s pw	

Radnor House Childrens' Home, Medical Officer

Jan 1911	Thomas B Dakin	£15	Also District Medical Officer and Workhouse Medical Officer.

By permission of Oxfordshire Black Sheep Publications.
Henley-on-Thames Poor Law Union and Workhouse Records 1835-51.

Appendix C

17 September 1867 Tender prices accepted

Butter	/lb	10½d	Mr Burgis
Sugar		4½d	Crouch
Tea		2/-	Gibbs
Rice	/cwt	17/-	Carter
Oatmeal		22/-	Burgis
Peas	Bus	9/-	Burgis
Soap	/cwt	36/-	Burgis
Salt		1/10	Carter
Candles	doz	5/5d	Carter
Soda	/cwt	7/9d	Crouch
Meat	/lb	5½d	Bullock

Linen-Draper per Messrs John and William Hopkins of 61 Minster Street, Reading

5/4	Lancashire sheeting by the piece	per yard	pence	8½
36"	Forfar			8½
6/4	Linen Huckaback			8½
36"	Drabbett			1/2½
36"	Muslin check			6½
36"	Welsh flannel			1/1½
36"	Stout Wigan calico			6¾
36"	unbleached calico			6¾
9/8	super calico			4¾
5/4	navy-blue print			5½
36"	grograin			6¾
36"	linsey			1/2½
36"	blue and white satin stripe cotton			11¾
10/4	Army blankets	per lb		1/8½
5/4	Blue Romall handkerchiefs	per doz		7/6

Hosier (per Hopkins)

Men's worsted hose, three-thread (roughs)	per doz pairs	13/9
Men's worsted hose, three-thread (outsize)		14/9
Boys' worsted hose	no 3 (roughs)	8/9
	No 4	9/9
	No 5	10/6
	No 6	11/3
	No 7	12/-

Haberdasher (per Hopkins)

Best Holland tapes at doz pieces of 18 yard each	No 25	2/8
	No 135	3/11
	No 145	4/11
Thread, black and white, brown	No 35 Marshalls per lb	2/11
Best sewing cotton in skeins	18 Brooks per lb	4/4
	24	4/-
Best three-thread wristed in skeins		1/8½
Best mixed pins	per lb per 100	1/-
Best drill-eyed needles		5½

Bonnets (per Hopkins)

Women's strong Dunstable	per doz	10/-
Girls'	per doz	9/-

"Slop seller" (per Hopkins)

Men's felt hats	per doz	6/9
Boys' cloth caps	doz	8/6
6/4 Brown woollen cloth	by the piece per yard	3/4½
3/4 Drab corduroy	per yard	2/2
36" Twill cotton	per yard	5½

Shoemaker (per Mr Pearman)

Men's strong nailed boots	No 4-10 sizes	per pair	8/4
Boys'	No 1-4		6/7
Boys'	10-13		4/6
Women's strong boots	3-7		4/11
Girls' strong boots	1-3		4/6
Girls'	10-13		3/9
Girls'	5-9		2/6
Child's	2-5		1/-

Carrier and Leather-Seller (Mr Pearman)

Crop Butts of 30 lb ea (bark tanned)	per lb	1/6
Hip grain shoulders		1/8
Wax hip		1/9
Wax offal		1/2
English crop bellies		10½d
Welting English shoulders		1/5
Fine flax		1/10
Common hemp		1/2
Closing flax	per doz	11d
Hob nails	per 1000	1/2
Cut Brads	per cwt	18/-

Appendix D

Board of Guardians 1869

Bix	Mr Edmund Wyfold A'Bear
Brightwell	Revd George Day
Britwell Prior	Mr Thomas W Hicks
Britwell Salome	Revd James Thomas Jackson
Caversham	Revd Joshua Bennett; Mr T Green
Checkendon	Mr George Collett
Cuxham	Mr Robert Palmer
Eye and Dunsden	Mr W Pottinger
Fawley	Revd Henry Almack
Hambleden	Mr T Deane; Revd William Henry Ridley
Harpsden	Revd Frederick Bagot
Henley	Messrs T N Watts;[i] Chas Healy; J S Burn; Chas Lucey
Ipsden	Mr James Richens
Medmenham	Mr Philip Hobbs
Nettlebed	Mr W H Gardener Cornwall
Nuffield	Mr Alfred Speck
Pishill	Mr Silas Lovegrove
Pyrton	Messrs A Cooper; J T Wells
Remenham	Mr Charles Plumbe
Rotherfield Greys	Messrs Alfred Piercy; Edward J Plummer
Rotherfield Peppard	Mr Charles Langford
Shiplake	Mr E Saker
Swyncombe	Mr George Griffith Dixon
Watlington	Messrs William Wiggins; Thomas Alexander Allnutt

Board of Guardians 1884[3]

George Edward Brakspear, Hart Street. Brewer
Charles Lucey, Surrey Lodge. Gentleman
William Thos Hews, Hart Street. Auctioneer
William Plumbe, Market Place. Clothier/draper
Charles Headington, Aston, Remenham. Farmer/dairyman
Revd. North Pindar, Rectory, R Greys, Rector
Bailey Tuckey, Peppard House, Rotherfield Peppard, Income from funded property

---

i   Mr Watts having been recently elected to LGB, was reported to be in an action for assault after defamation by Mr Tagg.[3]

Ex Officio (all local land owners)

Col. John Baskerville, Crowsley Park
John F Hodges, Bolney Court
William Dalziel Mackenzie, Fawley Court
Col Wm Thos Makins MP, Rotherfield Court
Sir Francis Stapleton Bart, Greys Court
Rt Hon Lord Camoys, Stonor Park
Rt Hon W H Smith MP, Greenlands
Lt Col Hew Dalrymple Fanshawe, Friars Field
John F S Jeune, Watlington Park
Clerk to Guardians: Nicholas Mercer (who held office 1840-1889)
Meetings held at Workhouse every alternate Tuesday.

Medical Officers:

Henley District	Egerton C A Baines, (surgeon)
Hambleden District	R P Jeston
Greys District	G O Willis
Caversham District	C H Cockran
Nettlebed District	E C A Baines
Watlington District	Henry Dixon

Relieving Officers:

Henley District	William Harding
Watlington	Benjamin Glass
Caversham	William Leach

Governor of Henley Union Workhouse – Samuel Mortlock, Matron, Mrs E Mortlock, Chaplain Revd Wm Chapman MA, Schoolmaster Wm White, Schoolmistress Mrs A White.

Mr Watts had died the previous year having been elected to the Local Board at its formation.[3]

Guardians elected 1899[i] Henley Rural District

Will retire in 1900

Ipsden	H Morris
Kidmore	H B D Vanderstegen
Nettlebed	Revd H A Baumgartner
Nuffield	J Willis
Pishill	J E Groves
Pyrton	E S Hammersley
Stonor	W Persey

---

i Stevens' Directory of Reading & neighbourhood.

Will retire in 1901

Rotherfield Greys	G E Brakspear
Rotherfield Peppard	W Bennett
Shiplake	C Gutteridge
Swyncombe	E J Vernon
Watlington	T A Allnutt and W Wiggins

Will retire in 1902

Badgemore	R Ovey
Bix	Capt Steward
Brightwell and Cuxham	Revd H Coxe
Britwell Prior & Britwell Salome	T Neighbour,
Shiplake Checkendon	R F Duff
Eye and Dunsden	Revd R H Hart-Davis
Harpsden	Revd J W Nutt

Hambleden Rural District

Will retire in 1900

Hambleden	C J Barnett, W F Holt Beever and E West

Will retire in 1901

Medmenham	R W Hudson

Will retire in 1902

Fawley	W D Mackenzie

Urban Parishes

Will retire in 1900

Greys	Ald E Chamberlain and W Hamilton

Will retire in 1901

Henley	A Groves, J Watts and G Jay

Will retire in 1902

Caversham	S Bristow and Revd Sydney H Case

Appendix E

A SERIES of contentious issues also arose in 1875 regarding the incumbent Schoolmaster, Henry Langley and Schoolmistress, Kezia Langley. They had been appointed on 4 March 1873 at salaries of £30 pa and £25 pa respectively.

However, by April 1875 relations with the Master of the House had degenerated following an anonymous letter to Mr Langley viz.

> "… On the meeting of the Guardians the first Board day after Christmas, 'Mortlake' (sic) made two statements, first that the Schoolmaster refused to allow some of the boys from the school that he had selected to go to a treat he had provided … the next was a statement with regard to your wife, a statement so gross, base and unjustifiable that I will not trust my pen to describe an opinion of such cowardly conduct; He said the schoolmistress had an ailment or illness that three medical men could not cure – intemperance was the cause. Later Mr Mortlock withdrew or retracted this. Having felt that other schoolmasters and schoolmistresses have been victimised by Mortlock's unscrupulous conduct, I feel you should be informed of the defamation of character. sgd A Friend of Fair Play."

After an inquiry by the School Committee, they reported: The Committee believes that the complaints to which this report refers have, as in the case of many former complaints, originated in a mutual jealousy and a mutual desire to arouse antipathy on the part of the Master and of the Schoolmaster. It would be well if these feelings could be removed, not only for the sake of the two masters, with whom the continuation thereof threatens to engender other and still more hostile feelings but also for the cause of the School Committee who, in consequence of disagreements and wilful misunderstandings are so often called upon to listen to and or direct inquiries into merely frivolous and unfounded complaints.

This resulted in the Schoolmistress writing direct to the President LGB, as follows:

> "Relating to a charge made against me by the Master of the House whilst I was absent from my duties as Schoolmistress through illness (sic) … I have been engaged in Union Schools for more than 20 years and was formerly Schoolmistress in the Eton Union for 16 years, a Matron for 2½ years and have held my present appointment since January 1873 and have never had the slightest cast upon my character till now …

"I humbly solicit a full enquiry into the matter at the next meeting of the Board of Guardians (an anonymous letter attached)." [1]

A letter sent by LGB to N Mercer, Clerk to the Guardians, and which disregarded the anonymous letter, stated, "I am directed to request that the Board may be furnished with the observations of the Guardians on the representations contained therein."

This coincided with another matter of contention raised by the Schoolmaster over the cleanliness or otherwise of a new schoolboy being sent into the School.

On April 1875 Copy of report of the School Committee: "Having investigated the circumstances referred to by the Schoolmaster as to the dirty condition of certain boys above 7 years sent to the School by Mr Mortlock, the Master, on their admission into the House, I found that his complaint is justified by the facts.

"The Master excused himself by stating that there are no means available for washing boys or girls except such as are provided in connection with the schools, on which the Committee must express their opinion that he has neglected his duty in not saying anything before on a matter so directly concerned to him, as the Master, while they are themselves of opinion that this excuse is not adequate to justify his neglect of duty.

"The Master of the Workhouse, having complained that in our report of the 20th inst as to the charge brought against him by the Schoolmaster of the boy, Francis Taplin, having been sent into the School in a dirty state, we had proceeded on insufficient evidence, we have again gone into the matter and we find that the boys Taplin did not go immediately to the School after the admission into the House but were retained in the hospital till the following day when they were examined by the MO Mr Baines and the Nurse, who both assert that they considered the boys not in a fit state to be removed into the school. Mr Baines also says that after our previous comment he again examined Francis Taplin and found that the state of his skin was such that, though perfectly clean it had the appearance of being dirty, and this materially alters the opinion as to the filthy condition of his body but the evidence of the boy Grainger, who combed his head, remains the same, and prevents us coming to any other conclusion than that his head was not in a clean condition. We still think it was the duty of the Master of the House to have seen that the boys were perfectly cleansed before they were sent to the School." [1]

2 May 1875 Copy of Letter from Mr Mortlock

As the reports from the Visitors Book have not yet been before the Board of Guardians, I think it my duty to state the facts of the case in forwarding them to you.

Elizabeth Taplin, aged 35, a widow and three children: Francis 10 years, Anne 8 years and James 4 years, were admitted into the Workhouse with an Order from the RO on 6 April. I saw them myself upon their admission and noticed that the family looked particularly clean. I sent for the Nurse, who took them to a Probation Ward, where the MO saw and examined them the next day and pronounced them all clean, except the mother, who was unwell and ordered to remain in the hospital. I then sent them for the barber to cut the children's hair; they were then sent to the following Wards: Francis to the Boys' School; Anne to the Girls' School and James to the Infant Nursery.

I heard nothing about the boy being in an unclean state till the 20th April when, after the Board Meeting, a School Committee met to consider a letter sent by the Schoolmaster to a member of the School Committee complaining that I had sent the boy Taplin into the School in a filthy condition. Two boys were brought from the school to corroborate this statement. I complained to the Committee that I had heard nothing of the case and that everything had been done in this case as in all others. The Committee, however, made their report, as I considered, hastily.

The following day I interrogated the MO, the Nurse and the barber, who all assert that the family were quite clean. The boy Francis has a kind of leprosy on the skin, which was pointed out to the MO by the boy's mother at the time of his examination. The Committee still held to their opinion as to the dirty state of the boy's head, which is only borne out by the boy Grainger, who combed Taplin's head and who most likely mistook the scurfy appearance for dirt.

I think I have the right to complain that this boy should not have been kept in the school and said to be in a filthy state for a whole fortnight without any complaint being made to me upon the subject. The Schoolmaster cannot say that I have not paid immediate attention to everything which he has had occasion to bring under my notice. Samuel Mortlock.[1]

Coincidentally on 21 May the Inspector examined the Workhouse School and reported[1]
Henry Langley, Schoolmaster
Kezia Langley, Schoolmistress

Present at examination:

Boys – 26 Average attendance during term: 29
Infants – 28   33

Skills as a teacher: Good/good
Spelling: Fair/fair
Whether school has improved or otherwise since last visit?
Boys – Very fair/Girls – Very fair

Both boys and girls have passed a very fair examination and have acquitted themselves well in reading, writing and arithmetic. There is, however, room for improvement in their spelling from dictation.

It appears that the infants have not been of late as regularly instructed as they ought to have been and they do not know their letters well. I have spoken to their Schoolmistress on the subject and she promises that they shall attend regularly in future.

Elizabeth Timms, Laundrywork	Average 10 children under instruction
George Stephens, Shoe-making	Average 6 children
Henry Ashby, Tailoring	Average 6 children

On 27 May the Chairman of a Committee of Guardians reported, viz: I found two entries in the Visiting Committee's book containing a report of the School Committee upon certain complaints addressed to them by the Schoolmaster. My enquiries into the matters reported disclose a state of things which appear to be very prejudicial to the interests of the school as well as to the general discipline and good order of the Workhouse.

The report of the committee refers to a boy named Taplin, one of a family admitted a short time back after the usual detention in the Probation Ward and inspection by the Medical Officer. A fortnight after the boy's admission to the school the Master of the House was called upon by the Guardians to answer a complaint which had been addressed by the Schoolmaster to the School Committee to the effect that the boy was sent into school in a dirty state, both as to his person and his head. The matter was referred to the School Committee for investigation and report. There, two entries show that they investigated it imperfectly, and the Master of the House complains that the censure passed upon him in the first report, and only partially withdrawn in the second, is wholly undeserved.

Apart from this, it seems important that if the boy was sent into the school in a dirty state, it was clearly the duty of the Schoolmaster to bring the matter at once to the notice of the Master, to whom he is bound by the Orders to render every assistance in his power, in carrying out the discipline and administration of the Workhouse. In spite of doing this, he wrote to the Committee and, in the meantime, attempts were made by the Schoolmaster's directions to remove from the boy's body certain marks which were ignorantly supposed to be dirt but which were discolouration. I saw them myself and I also was appraised of the severe scrubbing which had been employed to get rid of them. This absurd blunder, which might have had serious consequences, would never have been made if the Schoolmaster had done his duty in the first instance.

I asked him why he had not communicated with Mr Mortlock and he said it was on account of the "insolent" treatment he had received from him.

In fact, there is a violent feud between these officers dating from a certain complaint made by Mr Mortlock that he had found the schoolgirls on one occasion by themselves in the road several miles from the Workhouse, the Mistress having taken them out and (it is stated) left them. This led to every unpleasantness and there has been a complete breach between them ever since, with constant complaints and recriminations on both sides. That this state of things is in the highest degree detrimental to the School cannot be doubted, and the following is an illustration of the effects.

I found 4-5 children between the ages of about 3-5 spending their time in the Old Women's Ward. They went to the School up to within the last few weeks and had made some progress. One of them, recently admitted, had attended school regularly outside. I asked why they were not at school now and was told by Mr Mortlock that the Schoolmistress "would not have them". Upon questioning the Mistress, she said they certainly ought to be in school but Mr Mortlock "would not send them". Meantime, these children have ceased altogether to attend school. Their names are James Taplin, Will Woodleigh, Jesse Brakspear and John Simmonds.

The attendance book in the Girls' School is very irregularly kept. I found the attendances of entry for the next day in advance. Also certain children who never attended school on Saturday were marked on that day. Also found a girl, during school hours, washing some stockings belonging to the Mistress. An explanation given of this was that the child had a bad finger and this operation was supposed to be beneficial.

Six months later,

11 November 1875 the Master, having been assaulted on 5th by the Schoolmaster, consulted someone in whom he had confidence as to the course he ought to pursue. He was advised to take out a summons against the Schoolmaster, to be heard before the Town Magistrates; the result was the conviction of the Schoolmaster.

The Schoolmaster and Schoolmistress have this day both sent in their resignation.

The Visiting Committee, aided by a member of the School Committee, have ordered advertisements to be issued for another Schoolmaster/mistress, being a married couple.[1]

William White and Annie White neé Scott were appointed in May 1876.

They stayed in the post for 11 years until after Mr Mortlock's death.

Appendix F

Cases of Neglect by Dr Munro (extracted from correspondence between Poor Law Commissioners and Henley Board of Guardians).[1]

On a Complaint by Mr Dixon, one of the guardians, against Dr Munro, MO Nettlebed.

1. On 16 March 1875, Dr Munro was sent for to see the wife and child of Bayliss of Priest Hill, a pauper living in Nettlebed, at 10 o'clock in the morning. Dr Munro was not at home. The order was again sent at 4.30. He then was at home but he said he never attended after 4.30.

    Bayliss then goes to Dr Munro that evening at 9 o'clock, when medicine and attendance was refused and Bayliss was told he ought to be in Munro's medical club. Bayliss states he has been obliged to pay Dr Munro for medicine before he could obtain it.

2. In this case, Dr Munro had an order given by the Overseer of Nettlebed on 16 Feb to attend a child of William Lovegrove. He visited the case on the 17th and reported scarlet fever and gave a certificate for medical extras – meat for (beef) tea.

    He did not visit the case again until 12 March, an order having been given by the Relief Officer on the 11th. But on 24 February and 3 March he gave recommendations for beef tea and in his report he entered "attendance at patient's house on the 20th day of February – case better".

    In the week ending 27 February he entered "meat for tea" without any date or note of attendance or medicines furnished, and on 6 March "attendance at patient's house, now better". On 11 March: Order of the R/O was taken there "Attendance at the surgery – debility after fever"; on 12 March: "attendance at patient's house"; on 18 March ditto. No entry is made of the termination of the case or of any subsequent attendance.

    Resolved that the Board, having heard several complaints against Dr Munro, Medical Officer, three of which are contained in the foregoing statements, do request the attention of the Local Government Board to the question of the continuance of the MO in the Nettlebed District.

Findings
   Case of Henry Shail
   Case of Bayliss, wife and child
   Case of Lovegrove's child

In each of these three cases the charge of neglect of duty was fully established by the evidence. In the case of Henry Shail, the facts, namely that on February 17 Dr Munro sent a certificate that the pauper was fit to be removed to the Workhouse, he not having seen him since the 12th and inserted a wrong date in his return, which represented him to have visited the case on the day on which the certificate was signed, though he did not really do so till two days later, and were practically undisputed; the only defence set up consisting of excuses and explanations which were wholly unsatisfactory.

In the second case, that of Bayliss' wife and child, the charge of neglect of duty was proved to our satisfaction and, although this case presents features which point to an extremely lax system of administering medical relief in this District of Henley Union, that circumstance does not exculpate Dr Munro, he having accepted it as a pauper case and entered it as such upon his return.

In the third case, that of Lovegrove's child, the conduct of Dr Munro is deserving of very gross censure upon professional grounds; there were also inaccurate entries in the Medical Officer's return and there was a conflict of evidence respecting the fact whether certain visits to the house were paid or not, with respect to which we are of the opinion that Dr Munro took credit, as regular professional visits, for occasions on which he had merely seen the children at the cottage windows in passing.

Having in the above remarks given an outline of the general aspect of the charges, we now proceed to lay before the Board in detail the points in which Dr Munro, in our opinion, failed in his duty with respect to each of them.

In the case of the man Shail, Dr Munro was undoubtedly guilty of neglect in reporting a case of palsy as one of debility, in signing an Order for Removal several days after he had seen the man, without again seeing him; in his misdescription of the man's state at the time of his admission to the Workhouse, in relation to which his statement is a variance to that of the MO who saw and treated him; and in the general carelessness which characterised his proceedings with regard to this man.

As respecting the case of Bayliss, there was some conflict of testimony but, on the whole, we were unfavourably impressed as to the manner in which Dr Munro discharged his duty. It was probable that he considered the Baylisses to be in a position to join his Sick Club and to pay a small fee for medical attendance but this did not justify his grave inattention and, in this as in other cases, it was manifest that his books are carelessly kept, and that he relies too much on his memory; as to where his statements were at variance with those of the people concerned, it was impossible to avoid the conclusion that the balance of probability was in favour of the latter.

From a purely professional standpoint, the worst case of all was that of the child Lovegrove. The evidence of the father and mother proved beyond doubt that the child was seriously ill, that it was only twice personally examined by Dr Munro in the course of a somewhat protracted attack; that where his statements differed from those of the mother, that of the mother was most deserving of credence; that he incurred a serious personal responsibility in dealing so perfunctorily with such an extremely contagious disease as scarlet fever, both in the interests of the child and in those of the inhabitants of the village, and that in allowing the mother to procure medicine (castor oil and a gargle) elsewhere or in withholding it himself, it is impossible to acquit him of serious blame.

Extracts from the Minutes of the proceedings of the Henley Union Board of Guardians, 23 March 1875

Resolved that the Clerk do write to Dr Munro requesting his attendance at the meeting of the Board on Tuesday 6 April at 12 o'clock, together with an explanation of his apparent neglect in not attending Henry Shail at Hailey from 12-19th of the month, whilst on the 17th he issued a certificate without visiting him that he was fit to be removed to the Workhouse, and having inserted in his return that he had visited him on the 17th, he did not do so until the 19th.

Letter: 3 April From Dr Munro: Dear Sir, You have overlooked the fact that it is my Vaccination Day on Tuesday the 6th that you have asked me to attend the Board of Guardians meeting and, as the Vaccination Inspector, who was only here the other day, not only insists on my going at the proper times but to vaccinate some children at the stations the week before the vaccination terms actually commence so as to have some children from which at once to commence arm-to-arm vaccination, all I can do for you is to give an explanation which you can lay before the Board Meeting on that day.

"I was waited on one day (likely, as you state, the 12th but I have nothing beside me to fix the date) to see Henry Shail. I went immediately (without Parish note) to see him, directing the person who came to go for one when I was away. He did so and when I saw Shail I was able to fill up a Parish Order for beef and porter, which was all Shail required, who was labouring from nothing but debility and required no medical attendance. As it was after the day that week that the RO visits his Districts, on the next Wednesday, which is that day that all the Parish notes are at my house, one was filled up for Shail also and on it was marked that he was fit to be removed to the Workhouse. I saw him again on the day you mention but it was not for any purpose but to find if he got his meat and porter. A few hours before last Board Meeting I left with you a note explaining how the mistake about the dates arose. I think this is all you require and it is a matter I can lay with confidence before my profession, at any time assured of their support.

Yours truly, W Stuart Munro MD."

LGB asked for an explanation from Dr Munro

20 April Response: "I have great pleasure in being able to give you explanations at any time and also now if you consider it necessary, to lay it before the Lancet, I will be happy to do so, as I have kept a copy of it all."

Mr Henley LGB: "This is the second complaint against this officer within a very limited time. His reply to this charge is so incoherent that I think an official enquiry must be held. It is probable that a medical defence will be set up. I should therefore be glad if the Board would afford me the assistance of Dr Monck if I am instructed to hold the enquiry."

3 May: Directed to hold an official enquiry; the Board do not consider that your explanation of the complaints referred to is satisfactory.

J J Henley, General Inspector, wrote on: **15 June:** "In conformity with the instructions contained in your letter of May 3, we have held an official enquiry into certain complaints proffered by the Guardians against Dr Munro MD for the Nettlebed District of Henley Union and we have now the honour to submit our report, together with copies of the depositions. The enquiry took place at the Henley Workhouse on 22nd day of May. The charges which form the subject of this inquiry are set forth as follows in the extracts from the minutes of their proceedings which accompanied the letter from the Guardians of 12 April."

Re Dr Munro

The general evidence proved that Dr Munro does not possess the confidence of the community among whom he dwells and it also showed that the Guardians are somewhat lax in their administration of out-relief, to the prejudice of the MO who has a right to look to that to protect his interests in regard to those who ought to afford some little assistance towards their treatment in sickness.

Taking the circumstances here set forth into consideration and having regard to the fact that this is the second time that serious complaints have been made against this Officer within a very short period, we feel that there is no alternative before us but to advise the Board that Dr Munro is unfit any longer to discharge the duties of a District Medical Officer and that he should be called upon to resign.

Witnesses	Expenses	
Dr Baines	1 gn	Surgeon, Henley
John and Elizabeth Bayliss	6/6d	Brickmaker/journeyman, Nettlebed
Geo Dixon	3/6	Farmer, Guardian, Swyncombe
John Eyre	7/6	Corn dealer, Nettlebed
Benjamin Glass	5/0	Relieving Officer, Nettlebed
William and Mary Lovegrove	6/6	Ag lab, Nettlebed
Nicholas Mercer	21/0	Solicitor
Mary Ann Wheeler	3/6	Asst to father, Brick-maker, Nettlebed
Henry Shail	-	Ag lab, Inmate

Not summoned: Thos N Watts, Tailor and woollen draper, Chairman, Henley Union.

Dr Munro responded on 9 June: "Sir, I received your letter today and, without an instant's delay, hasten to give up my appointment with the Poor Law Board, either at once or at the end of this quarter, as may suit you. I cannot, however, but complain of the injustice that has been done me, as you will see from the enclosed letter, that some evidence that was not before the interested Guardians, when laid before the Editor of the Lancet, the answer was "that there was no conscious intentional neglect."

I intend remaining here until the end of September the 31st (sic) 1st and during that time I think the Guardians, as in former times, will find a difficulty in finding anyone to accept of their advertisement.

I cannot understand why this is one of the places that has changed its MO more frequently perhaps than any other in England in a very few years and I can only add that I am very sorry that I accepted the appointment after barely sufficient to keep one's … or come amongst such a wretched population.

PS You are aware that you have kept me from giving over my house for another quarter as your letter only reached me today, four days after I have entered on another fresh quarter."

Attached Letter: The Editor of the Lancet presents his compliments to Dr Munro and regrets that an answer to his questions, prepared for last week's Lancet, did not get admission for want of space. The Editor cannot of course decide the question of diagnosis, about which two competent practitioners… (missing). Possibly more visits to the patient by Dr Munro might have been advantageous but clearly there was no conscious or intentional neglect. The Editor is of the opinion that the maladministration by the Guardians should have been communicated with Dr Munro before asking the patient, at least before prescribing for him, altering Dr Munro's treatment.

5 July: From the Clerk, Henley Union to LGB: In reply to your letter of 3rd enquiring whether the Guardians have received from Dr Munro his resignation of the office of Medical Officer and if so, what steps they have taken for the appointment of his successor, I beg to forward to you on the other side extracts from the minutes of the proceedings for the Board relevant thereto.

13 July: The Clerk reported that Dr Munro had notified his resignation in the following manner at the foot of the District Medical Relief Book laid before the Board this day:

"I have sent in my resignation as MO to the Nettlebed District of the HoT Union to the LGB London."

27 July: No applications received from advertisement of the vacancy.
Resolved that Mr Baines of HoT (Mr Jeston's partner) be appointed to undertake the duties of MO of Nettlebed for one year at a salary at the rate of £80 a year and that, in the meantime, the consideration of further arrangements be referred to the Visiting Committee.

5 August HU Letter to Dr Munro: "Notwithstanding your resignation of your appointment to the office of MO of Nettlebed, I find from a certificate dated yesterday sent by you, you continue to issue certificates as a MO of that District.

Mr Baines is the Medical Officer appointed to supply the vacancy temporarily and Mr Glass only will issue orders for medical attendance.

I think it necessary to give you this information and to request that you will not repeat the irregularity, which can only occasion inconvenience to the Board and the newly appointed MO and RO."

Dr Munro replied on 9 August: "Sir, I received your semi-private letter about my appointment here. The facts are these. On 29 June I sent in a resignation of my appointment to the Board at London in either of two ways: first, that I should resign at once or, second, that I should (go) at the end of the present quarter.

My resignation at once was not accepted but you continued to receive my reports etcetera, and orders to attend cases have been done up to this time.

Under these circumstances I hold that there is no vacancy up to the 29th Sept, when I have to give notice (which I find I mooted namely to LGB) that I will resign also my appointment of Vaccination Officer for this District.

PS I will attend no new admission cases without a note."

Copy memorandum at the foot of District Medical Relief Book for the weeks ended 7 August 1875: "This is my last Relief Sheet and unless I am supplied with more, cannot make further reports to the Board."

Letter to Dr Munro, 21 August: "LGB have received a communication from the Guardians of Henley Union containing a copy of your letter to the Clerk of the 9th, from which the Board observes that you claim to hold the office of MO until 29 Sept.

"The Board in their letter of 28 June required you at once to place your resignation in the hands of the Guardians, and they were not aware until recently that you had not done so in a regular and valid manner. The Board's acceptance of your resignation was wholly unnecessary.

"The Board cannot consent to your continuing to hold the Office of MO until the end of the present quarter, as you propose. Unless you place your formal resignation, to take immediate effect, before the Guardians at their next meeting, the Board will be under the necessity of adopting severe measures to terminate your appointment." (Dr Mouat LGB)

24 August "I have the honour to resign my office of MO and Public Vaccination for the Nettlebed District of the HU." Sgd W S J H Munro.

Appendix G

Treatment of Tramps: A copy of a letter dated 1 December 1868 from J.S. Burn, The Grove, Henley-on-Thames

Received by Poor Law Board Dec 3 1868.

Sir

Your letter as to Tramps, was read at our Board today, and I made the following remarks upon the subject as a private individual, and not as a Guardian.

The Tramps applying for relief, are always searched but the regular <u>tramp</u>, has several dodges to prevent money being found on him – Our work and food is uniformly the same, and we always get those who refuse work, to be imprisoned by the magistrates – I think however the food and the work should be the same in all Unions; observations made by the Tramps to the Task Master confirm one in this opinion.

I think also that the Tramp should be kept in the Union longer than he is at present and under the present system he gets through his task and breakfast by half past 9, and so has a whole day to prowl about the country.

As to discrimination, I fear there is not so much as there ought to be, nor so much as there might be if a policeman were employed, and that he did his duty – At the same time we have but few <u>Wayfarers</u> – those we have are treated more liberally – the great bulk are professional Tramps, and this is the reason why the Ticket System was not adopted – I was in correspondence with Mr Baker of Gloucester, on the subject, I approved his plans and they would have been adopted I think, if we had had many Wayfarers to provide for.

Separate cells, as at Witney, would be very desirable instead of our present "social" assembly; but in our Union we have just built some Tramp Wards, and could not well alter them for the <u>Separate</u> System.

I should wish here to give my view respecting the punishment of the Tramps who destroy their <u>Clothes</u> – if they do this <u>outside</u> the Union, the police would take them up for indecently exposing themselves – If they do it in the Union, they should be kept in the nudity, <u>in which they had placed themselves</u>, until the Master obtained an order from a Guardian for clothing, or until they could be taken before the Magistrate. With the sanction of the Poor Law Board, this reasonable punishment might be tried.

The Board recommends a Book of the names, age, residence etc of the Tramps. Our Guardians keep such a Book, but the contents cannot be depended on, for "George Smith" at Henley, becomes "John Jones" at the next Union.

As to the Imprisonment of Tramps, and of refractory inmates of the Union, it seems to me, that Imprisonment is very little, if any, punishment – they are so well fed in Gaol, that we believe that many commit offences, by way of a change – as a break in the monotony of their life – They are taken before a Magistrate where they can lay their grievance before his "Worship" – they get a ride to Oxford, and spend their three weeks at the expense of the County, or rather at the expense of the Ratepayers, many of whom are not better fed and provided for.

I have entered into these details, because the London Board may get more information in this manner than if they got a formal report from the Union and because I have heard that the London Board desire to see the working of any system previously to their enacting any general Orders.

I remain Sir
Your mo. obedt. Servt.

(signed) John S. Burn

To A Fleming Esq

PLB annotated: Acknowledge and thank for the remarks contained in his communication – Bring back.
4 Decr 68

Ref: MH.12.9690. National Archives, Kew.

Appendix H

Henley Union Workhouse Census: Inmate Name and Birth Index of those in the workhouse on census nights 1841-1911

???	Daisy 1901, Henley	George Adams 1837, Bix
Adams	Edwin 1866, Uxbridge	William, 1817, St Giles, Northamptonshire
Adby	Fanny 1842, Eye and Dunsden	
Aldridge	Arthur 1880, Shiplake	Eliza 1847, Watlington
	H 1838, Grays	William 1840, Hambleden, Bucks
Allaway	D, 1809, Henley	George 1834, Henley
	Sarah, 1836, Henley	S, 1838, Reading
Allen	M A, 1796, Caversham	S, 1793, Watlington
Alleway	Daniel, 1810, Henley	
Alloway	George, 1843, Henley	Sarah, 1836, Henley
Allum	W, 1813, Eye and Dunsden	
Amer	Charles, 1778, Barvell???	H, 1855, Eye and Dunsden
Andrews	Ann, 1862, Not Known	Daniel, 1860, Not Known
	John Louis, 1866, Not Known	Mary Ann, 1867, Not Known
	Mary Julia, 1864, Not Known	
Appleby	Hannah, 1796, Greys	
Ashby	Eliza, 1855, Nettlebed	John, 1814, Nuffield
Atkins	Elizabeth, 1832, Henley	S, 1836, Hambleden, Bucks
	Sophia, 1836, Henley	W, 1861, Henley
	William, 1860, Henley	
Attwell	William, 1819, Shiplake	
Atwell	William, 1820, Shiplake	
Audery	Ada, 1873, Henley	Fredrick, 1875, Henley
Austen	H, 1858, Watlington	S, 1833, Watlington
Austin	A, 1857, Hambleden, Bucks	Alice, 1785, Hambleden, Bucks
	Daniel, 1838, Hambleden, Bucks	Mary A, 1837, Hambleden, Bucks
	Sarah, 1844, Russell's Water	William, 1841, Hambleden, Bucks
Avery	William, 1846, Henley	
Ayres	Henry, 1830, Henley	
Badwell	M, 1831, Shiplake	George, 1857, Shiplake
Bailey	Benjamin, 1838, Henley	Ellen, 1859, Henley
	G, 1790, Hambleden, Bucks	George, 1787, Aylesbury, Bucks
	Harriett, 1840, Henley	Thomas, 1842, Henley
Barcus	F, 1859, Henley	
Barnes	L, 1849, Cuxham	Louisa, 1849, Henley
	Mary, 1880, Hambleden, Bucks	Rebecca, 1876, Hambleden, Bucks
	William, 1797, Caversham	
Barney	S, 1809, Fawley, Bucks	Sarah, 1809, Henley
	Sarah, 1810, Henley	W, 1850, Henley
Barson	Frances, 1834, Henley	George, 1834, Cumnor, Berks

Bartlett	Elizabeth, 1829, other English County	James, 1781, other English County
Bateman	Ann, 1835, Watlington	Hephzbah, 1838, Watlington
Batten	William, 1841, Shirburn	
Bean	Eliza, 1868, Brentford, Middx	John, 1869, Brentford, Middx
Beard	Ann, 1845, Shiplake	Matthew, 1766, Oxon
Beckenham	Mary, 1845, Shinfield, Berks	
Bedford	Mary Ann, 1805, Henley	
Beechey	William, 1822, Fawley, Bucks	
Bell	Thomas, 1802, Watlington	W, 1816, Watlington
Bennett	Jane, 1779, Edinburgh, Scotland	
Benson	Henry, 1870, Brentford, Middx	
Betteridge	E, 1790, Watlington	
Bevan	Jacob, 1796, Oxon	Joseph, 1816, Oxon
Beven	Ellen, 1823, Henley	Mary A, 1844, Henley
Bishop	D, 1853, Peppard	John, 1861, Peppard
	Louisa, 1863, Peppard	M, 1855, Peppard
Blackall	E, 1852, Peppard	Ephraim, 1836, Wargrave, Berks
	Mabel, 1911, Henley	R, 1850, Peppard
	S A, 1848, London, Middx	
Blagrave	B, 1800, Sonning	
Blake	Ann, 1833, Oxon	Ann, 1834, Nuffield
	Elizabeth, 1816, Oxon	Thomas, 1838, Oxon
	William, 1835, Oxon	
Bolton	W, 1799, Glous	
Bond	Ann, 1843, Ipsden	Harriett, 1845, Ipsden
Boughton	Ada, 1893, Birmingham	Amelia, 1896, Caversham
	Bertha, 1891, Birmingham	Edwin John, 1899, Caversham
	Emily Ada, 1865, Chesterfield, Derbys	Nellie Emily, 1889, Nottingham
Bowden	R, 1780, Grays	
Bowler	Martha, 1777, Lower??? Wittenham???, Berks	
Bowling	James, 1820, Henley	
Bradford	Emily, 1826, Rotherfield Greys	
Brakspear	Florence, 1880, Nettlebed	William, 1901, Henley
Bramham	Ann, 1800, Henley	
Breakspear	Arthur, 1872, Not Known	Jesse, 1870, Not Known
Brewer	George, 1853, Turville, Bucks	James, 1864, Turville, Bucks
	Sarah, 1835, Turville, Bucks	Sarah, 1868, Turville, Bucks
	Thomas, 1862, Turville, Bucks	William, 1853, Turville, Bucks
Brinsdon	Alfred, 1880, Caversham	John, 1882, Caversham
Bristow	Mary A, 1826, Watlington	William, 1850, Watlington
Broadway	C, 1830, Watlington	E, 1854, Britwell
	E, 1860, Britwell	E S, 1852, Britwell
	Ellen, 1839, Britwell	R, 1855, Britwell
Brooker	E, 1823, Grays	Eliza, 1822, Peppard
	Emily, 1844, Peppard	H, 1849, Henley
	Henry, 1848, Henley	Henry William, 1833, Egham, Surrey
Brooks	Harriet, 1836, Lewknor	Leonard, 1844, Thame
	Thomas, 1767, Cuxham	
Brown	Harriett, 1863, Watlington	M, 1786, Watlington
	Martha, 1806, Greys	Martha, 1807, Rotherfield Greys
	Martha, 1811, Rotherfield Greys	William, 1795, Greys
	W, 1790, Sonning	William, 1861, Rye, Sussex

Bruckland	Elizabeth, 1862, London	Emily, 1867, London
	John, 1864, London	Sarah, 1828, London
Bryant	J, 1831, Shiplake	
Bucket	John, 1845, Henley	Mary Ann, 1848, Henley
Buckett	Ernest, 1877, Henley	George, 1843, Henley
	Harry, 1879, Henley	John, 1864, Henley
	Matilda, 1846, Henley	Susan, 1835, Henley
Bunce	Ann, 1805, Not Known	Frederick, 1897, Henley,
	Isabella, 1881, Henley	James, 1826, Rotherfield Greys
	William, 1785, Abingdon, Berks	William James, 1900, Henley
Burgiss	Daniel, 1823, Assendon	
Burnham	Ann, 1804, Henley	
Bushnell	Caroline, 1873, Rotherfield Greys	Fredrick, 1875, Rotherfield Greys
	William, 1786, Oxon	
Butcher	Elizabeth, 1834, Pyrton	Fredrick, 1876, Pyrton
	John, 1819, Watlington	Mary, 1863, Pyrton
	William, 1865, Pyrton	
Butler	Ashar, 1771, Oxon	E, 1844, Watlington
	E, 1855, Watlington	Edith, 1850, Hambleden, Bucks
	F, 1857, Watlington	John, 1836, Fawley, Bucks
	John, 1871, Hambleden, Bucks	Kezia, 1833, other English County
	Sarah, 1788, Henley	Sarah, 1836, Oxon
	William, 1838, Oxon	William, 1839, Not Known
Button	J, 1796, Sonning	
Camp	Alice, 1791, Oxon	Francies, 1828, Oxon
	William, 1829, Oxon	
Cane	John, 1837, Bramley, Hants	
Canning	George, 1845, Andover, Hants	
Carter	James, 1766, Cookham, Berks	
Caterer	Ann, 1821, Watlington	Ann, 1822, Cuxham
	Ann, 1881, Watlington	Mary Ann, 1862, Henley
	Mary Ann, 1862, Watlington	Mary Ann, 1864, Henley
Chamberlain	Emily, 1842, Cheltenham, Somerset	Thomas, 1824, Medmenham, Bucks
Chapman	Bertha, 1873, Not Known	James, 1828, Oxon
Chinnery	John, 1830, St. Marylebone, Middx	
Chipperfield	William, 1870, Brentford, Middx	
Clark	Fred, 1908, Henley	
Clarke	Alexander, 1830, Nettlebed	Beatrice Ada, 1900, Hurst, Berks
	Elizabeth, 1872, Brentford, Middx	Elizabeth, 1874, Reading, Berks
	Frances Elizabeth, 1898, Caversham	Lucy, 1860, Not Known
	Thomas, 1862, Not Known	William, 1761, other English County
	William Thomas, 1901, Lower Assendon	
Clements	Albert, 1862, Not Known	Alice, 1872, Rotherfield Greys
	Elizabeth, 1771, other English County	Emily, 1876, Rotherfield Greys
	Emily, 1878, Rotherfield Greys	Francis, 1858, Not Known
	George, 1874, Rotherfield Greys	George, 1875, Rotherfield Greys
	James, 1860, Not Known	
Clifford	Eliza, 1825, Watlington	Henry, 1846, Watlington
Cobb	William, 1837, Oxon	
Coker	Christophe D, 1846, Not Known	Elizabeth, 1841, Not Known Cole
	Alice, 1887, Eye and Dunsden	Arthur, 1884, Eye and Dunsden
	Kate, 1856, Eye and Dunsden	
Coleman	Ada, 1881, Henley	

Collings	George, 1865, Henley	
Collins	Elizabeth, 1869, Brentford, Middx	Henry, 1791, other English County
	Henry, 1876, Brentford, Middx	
Cook	A, 1858, Hambleden, Bucks	Ann, 1856, Henley
	J, 1854, Hambleden, Bucks	S, 1856, Hambleden, Bucks
	Sarah, 1856, Henley	Sarah, 1858, Hambleden, Bucks
Cooper	E, 1849, Henley	Elizabeth, 1799, Fawley, Bucks
	J, 1853, Sonning	John, 1773, Heckfield, Hamps
	Joshua, 1837, Henley	Joshua, 1844, Henley
	M A, 1830, Henley	Richard, 1772, Finghurst???, Fingest? Buck
Copas	Ellen, 1843, Pyrton	John, 1845, Pyrton
	Sarah, 1840, Pyrton	
Corby	Elizabeth, 1870, Henley	Mary Ann, 1848, Not Known
Cottrell	Leah, 1842, Watlington	
Cox	Elizabeth, 1870, Swyncombe	George, 1834, Henley
	George, 1868, Henley	John, 1784, Henley
	Sarah, 1857, Swyncombe	W, 1793, Henley
Coxen	Nina, 1876, Brentford, Middx	
Crane	Anne, 1876, Brentford, Middx	
Cranfield	Ethel, 1874, Henley	Stephen, 1829, Oxon
	Hilda, 1876, Henley	
Creed	Richard, 1773, Caversham	
Cresswell	Bridget E, 1848, Caversham	Eliza, 1846, Maidenhead, Berks
	Eliza, 1855, Caversham	James, 1847, Caversham
	Phoebe, 1801, Sonning, Berks	Samuel, 1796, Greys
Croft	John, 1854, Upfrd Magna, Shrops	
Cross	William, 1836, Hambleden, Bucks	
Croxford	George, 1859, Watlington	George, 1885, Watlington
	James, 1887, Watlington	
Crutchfield	E, 1841, Peppard	H, 1859, Peppard
Cusden	John, 1832, Eye and Dunsden	Martha, 1819, Eye and Dunsden
Darvell	Fanny, 1814, Cuxham	
Davis	Absolom, 1821, Hambleden, Bucks	
Dawson	Ann, 1838, Not Known	
Day	J J, 1849, Pyrton	
Deadman	Charles, 1836, Sonning	
Dean	John, 1840, Hambleden, Bucks	S, 1790, Grays
	Sarah, 1790, Greenwich, Kent	
Dell	Robert William, 1880, Henley	
	Denham W, 1854, Hambleden, Buck	
Denton	George, 1844, Bermondsey, London	
Dicker	Charles, 1817, Mortimer, Berks	
Dixon	E H, 1847, Henley	F, 1798, Henley
Dobson	William, 1775, Pyrton	
Dodd	William, 1766, Oxon	
Douglas	Dora, 1908, Henley	Elizabeth, 1877, Henley
Drewett	Thomas, 1833, Henley	
Duckett	Daniel, 1797, Eye and Dunsden	
Dunn	Betsy, 1781, Oxon	
Dyer	James, 1844, Watlington	James, 1849, Watlington
Eady	Anne, 1821, other English County	Elizabeth, 1826, other English County
	Elizabeth, 1828, Fulham, Middx	James, 1848, Henley
	Mary A, 1851, Henley	William, 1844, Henley

Ealey	Maria, 1858, Shinfield, Berks	
Earl	George, 1824, Swyncombe	J, 1788, Nettlebed
	Mary, 1826, Ox	
East	Sarah, 1778, Hambleden, Bucks	
Eden	E, 1791, Brightwell	Edward, 1790, Brightwell
Edgeley	Eliza, 1836, Henley	
Edson	Matilda, 1833, Oxon	
Eggleton	Louisa, 1826, Oxon	Priscilla, 1825, Ox
	Thomas, 1813, Henley	
Elliott	Sarah, 1871, Brentford, Middx	William, 1852, Watlington
Emery	Margrate, 1868, Henley	Samuel, 1870, Henley
	Thomas, 1858, Henley	
Emmett	Ada, 1870, Henley	Harry, 1872, Henley
	William, 1868, Henley	
England	Daniel, 1855, Harleston, Northants	
Evans	James, 1839, Shiplake	Robert, 1866, Henley
	Thomas, 1878, Henley	
Fawks	Eliza, 1880, Henley	Jane, 1863, Whitchurch
Fearton	James George, 1869, Uxbridge, Middx	
Finch	Charlotte, 1786, Oxon	
Fisher	Sarah, 1792, Not Known	John, 1797, Henley
Fletcher	M, 1848, Pyrton	Richard, 1793, Radnage, Bucks
Floyd	Fanny, 1876, Eye and Dunsden	Mary, 1872, Eye and Dunsden
Fluter	Charlotte, 1869, Hambleden, Bucks	George, 1867, Hambleden, Bucks
	Sophia, 1846, Hambleden, Bucks	
Foster	F, 1818, Henley	
Fox	Annie, 1878, Swyncombe	Harriett, 1881, Swyncombe
Francis	William, 1832, Caversham	
Franklin	Thomas, 1769, Ilsley, Berks	
Freebody	Ann, 1814, Not Known	Ann, 1850, Sonning, Berks
	Thomas P, 1844, Checkendon	
Freeland	Gilbert, 1830, other English County	Mary, 1828, other English County
Freeman	James, 1865, Watlington	
Freesey	George, 1820, Hambleden, Bucks	
Fuller	Ann, 1847, Caversham	Elizabeth, 1806, Leatherby, Dorset
	Emma, 1842, Caversham	Henry, 1811, Caversham
	James, 1843, Caversham	Walter, 1850, Caversham
	William, 1777, Caversham	William, 1837, Caversham
Gardiner	Thomas, 1780, Ewelme	
Garlick	Richard, 1793, Nettlebed	
Garner	Charles, 1834, Stratford upon Avon, Warwicks	
Garratt	William, 1845, Maidensgrove	
Gates	Sarah, 1793, Bix	
Gauntlett	J, 1786, Hambleden, Bucks	Joseph, 1782, Wantage, Berks
Gearing	Ann, 1828, Oxon	Eliza, 1827, Watlington
	Fanny, 1862, Watlington	John James, 1891, Henley
George	Matilda, 1846, Not Known	William, 1828, Watlington
Giles	Edward, 1815, Speen, Berks	
Gillatt	John, 1804, Swyncombe	
Gillett	James, 1816, Pishill	
Gilliard	Julia, 1860, Hackney, London	
Gillott	J, 1849, Reading, Berks	

Goddard	Edward, 1862, Henley	Eliza, 1832, Henley
	Emma, 1860, Henley	Owen Ronald, 1890, Henley
Godley	Ada, 1867, Henley	Albert Edwd, 1890, Greys
	Arthur, 1888, Henley	Ellen, 1895, Henley
	Geo Frederick, 1889, Greys	George, 1889, Henley
	Mary Ann, 1861, Theale, Berks	Nellie, 1895, Henley
Godwin	Martha, 1834, Pusey, Wilts	
Goff	Henry, 1853, Ipsden	
Gore	Lumtin, 1776, other English County	
Gould	George, 1813, Watlington	
Grainger	Alfred, 1858, Nettlebed	James, 1834, Henley
	John, 1864, Nettlebed	Thomas, 1861, Nettlebed
Granger	James, 1840, Remenham, Berks	William, 1842, Remenham, Berks
Grantham	Ellen, 1869, Reading, Berks	Ellen, 1871, Wallingford, Berks
Green	Elizabeth, 1812, Watlington	Jane, 1842, Barbican, London
	John, 1776, Oxon	John, 1780, Thame
	Mark, 1838, Peppard	Matilda, 1840, Watlington
	William, 1799, Henley	
Greenwood	Ann, 1848, Not Known	
Gregory	Caroline, 1869, Henley	Flora, 1868, Henley
Grey	John, 1795, Hambleden, Bucks	
Grimes	Hannah, 1836, other English County	Jane, 1816, other English County
Grubb	Elizabeth, 1802, Henley	
Gumm	Mary, 1811, Oxon	
Haines	Arthur Edwd, 1892, Henley	James Walter 1895, Winslow, Bucks
	Lilly, 1890, Emmer Green	Louisa, 1849, Emmer Green
	Louisa, 1854, Emmer Green	
Haines???	James, 1894, Caversham	Thomas, 1833, Shiplake
Hains	H, 1857, Lambeth, Surrey	M, 1824, Lambeth, Surrey
	M A, 1847, Lambeth, Surrey	
Halt	Thomas, 1816, Henley	
Hamblin	James, 1805, Swyncombe	Mary, 1804, Swyncombe
Hammond	Amey, 1845, Checkendon	Emily, 1833, Not Known
	Emma, 1837, other English County	George, 1842, Checkendon
	James, 1841, Checkendon	Sarah, 1816, Oxon
	Sarah, 1840, other English County	Sarah, 1841, Not Known
Hancock	C, 1849, Marlow, Buck	M A, 1853, Slough, Buck
Hanson	Annie Elizabeth, 1879, Hambleden, Bucks	Edmund, 1831, Oxon
	Eliza, 1834, Oxon	Ellen, 1877, Hambleden, Bucks
	Leah, 1811, Oxon	Lucy, 1835, Oxon
	Sarah Jane, 1881, Hambleden, Bucks	
Hardie	J, 1848, London, Middlesex	
Harding	Annette, 1864, Oxon	Georgina, 1865, Oxon
	Henry, 1822, Abingdon, Berks	William, 1756, Oxon
Harman	Ellen, 1850, Fawley, Bucks	Harriott, 1784, Hambleden, Bucks
Harmer	S, 1849, Bix, Oxon	
Harper	William, 1801, Oxon	
Harris	Elizabeth, 1756, Oxon	Francis, 1776, Not Known
	Frederick, 1831, Oxon	Henry, 1836, Henley
	Matilda, 1860, Henley	Sarah, 1826, Oxon
	Thomas, 1826, Oxon	Thomas, 1828, Oxon
	Thomas, 1831, Harpsden	Thomas, 1831, Oxon

Harting	Ann, 1837, Not Known	Anne, 1837, Oxon
	Caroline, 1829, Oxon	Elizabeth, 1832, Oxon
	James, 1828, Ox	Mary, 1834, Oxon
Harvey	Griffin, 1793, Nettlebed	
Hawkes	George, 1899, Henley	Hannah, 1865, Hambleden, Bucks
	Mark, 1859, Watlington	
Hawkins	Catherine, 1771, Oxon	John, 1791, other English County
	Lucy, 1834, Oxon	Mary A, 1841, Not Known
	Mary Ann, 1838, Oxon	Phebe, 1807, Oxon
Hawthorn	Fanny, 1869, Brentford, Middx	
Hayes	William, 1837, Not Known	
Heath	Ann, 1822, Nuffield	S, 1838, Bix
Heather	Charles, 1826, Oxon	
Henley	R, 1849, Henley	Rachael, 1849, Not Known
Herbert	E, 1836, Watlington	E, 1860, Watlington
Herbert???	Henry Thos, 1837, Dunsden	
Herridge	Elizabeth Ann, 1869, Peppard	Esther, 1850, Peppard
	William, 1870, Peppard	
Hester	A, 1823, London, Middx	G, 1852, London, Middx
	Sarah, 1831, Cuxham	W, 1860, London, Middx
Hewett	Agness, 1871, Caversham	Thomas, 1872, Caversham
	William, 1870, Caversham	
Hide	Marius, 1840, Not Known	
Higgins	H, 1843, Hambleden, Bucks	
Higgs	R, 1798, Reading, Berks	
Hile	John, 1766, other English County	
Hill	Bertie, 1911, Henley	Daniel, 1808, Eye and Dunsden
	Edwin, 1851, Bledlow Ridge, Bucks	
	John Henry William, 1863, Watlington	Emily, 1883, Chieveley, Bucks
	William, 1908, Binfield Heath	Leonard, 1909, Binfield Heath
Hilsley	Charles, 1839, Stratfield Saye, Hants	
Hine	Faith, 1835, Eye and Dunsden	
Hoar	Shadrach, 1828, Oxon	William, 1848, Watlington
Hobbs	D, 1826, Hambleden, Bucks	David, 1825, Hambleden, Bucks
	David, 1826, Hambleden, Bucks	George, 1833, Hambleden, Bucks
Holland	Thomas, 1811, Swyncombe	Thomas, 1813, Swyncombe
Holloway	Charles, 1844, Taunton, Somerset	Eliza, 1840, Reading, Berks
	Elizabeth, 1818, Reading, Berks	Francis, 1842, Dustton? (Dunster?) Somerset
Hone	George, 1862, Henley	Mary Ann, 1840, Henley, Oxon
Hooney	Sarah, 1872, Henley	T, 1792, Henley
	Thomas, 1792, Henley	
Hopkins	Alice, 1871, Pishill	Elzth., 1869, Pishill
	Emily, 1873, Pishill	J, 1790, Sonning
	Lucy M, 1850, Eye and Dunsden	Sophia, 1848, Eye and Dunsden
Hopkinson	Bertram, 1877, Henley	Elizabeth, 1868, Abingdon, Berks
	Rose, 1853, Rotherfield Greys	
House	Louisa, 1874, Caversham	Louisa, 1877, Caversham
Hughes	Elizabeth, 1841, Not Known	
Humphery	Jane, 1845, Watlington	
Humpherys	Emily, 1850, Not Known	Jane, 1845, Not Known
Humphreys	Joseph, 1771, other English County	
Humphreys???	George, 1847, Hambleden, Bucks	

Hunt	A, 1793, Lambeth, Surrey	R, 1789, Caversham
	Richard, 1826, South Stoke	
Hussey	M, 1794, Harpsden	Mary, 1796, other English County
Hutton	Richard, 1770, Grays	Richard, 1771, Oxon
Irving	Charlotte, 1859, Remenham, Berks	Fanny, 1834, Remenham, Berks
	Edward, 1862, Not Known, Berks	Frederick, 1859, Remenham, Berks
Ivermee	George, 1817, Henley	George, 1839, Henley
	Henry, 1841, Henley	
James	Charlotte, 1838, Faringdon, Berks	Harriett, 1830, Henley
Jeffries	Alexander, 1867, Uxbridge, Middx	
Jemmett	Ann, 1819, Barnet, Herts	Ann, 1819, Not Known, Bucks
Jerome	John, 1868, Henley	William, 1813, Caversham
Jimmett	Ann, 1819, Barnet	Arthur, 1866, Rotherfield Greys
	John, 1811, Hambleden, Buck	
Johnson	George, 1869, St. Pancras, London	William, 1834, Henley
	William, 1839, Henley	
Johnson II	William, 1838, Caversham	
Johnstone	Seymour, 1845, Henley	
Jokeway	Ellen, 1851, Cheltenham, Glous	
Jones	M, 1774, Ipsden	M, 1832, Henley
	S, 1858, Henley	Samuel, 1858, Henley
	Thomas, 1806, Henley	Thomas, 1812, Birmingham, Warwicks
Jordan	Anne, 1837, Oxon	Cassandra, 1866, Watlington
	Elizabeth, 1832, Watlington	Francis, 1864, Watlington
	George, 1811, Watlington	James, 1834, Oxon
	John, 1832, Oxon	Sarah, 1858, Watlington
Jupp	Emily, 1870, Brentford, Middx	
Keel	Charles, 1825, Reading, Berks	
Keeley	Charles, 1842, Hambleden, Bucks	Daniel, 1839, Hambleden, Bucks
	Edward, 1847, Hambleden, Bucks	Mary, 1826, Hambleden, Bucks
	Mary A, 1843, Hambleden, Bucks	Sophia, 1798, Eusdon???, Oxon
Keep	James, 1825, Great Marlow, Bucks	
Kelsey	William, 1819, Liverpool, Lancs	
Kemp	Alice, 1793, Henley	
Kempster	Mary, 1776, other English County	
Kimble	Anne, 1806, Oxon	
King	A, 1790, Watlington	Anne, 1801, Oxon
	Louisa, 1817, Watlington	Phoebe, 1814, Medmenham, Bucks
Knight	William, 1791, other English County	
Lambden	C, 1849, Sonning	E, 1847, Sonning
Lamborn	Charles, 1872, Bix	William, 1871, Bix
Launchbury	A, 1859, Henley	G, 1851, Henley
	H, 1848, Henley	J, 1819, Bix
	S, 1849, Henley	
Lane	John, 1800, Hambleden, Bucks	
Langford	Frances, 1876, Pishill	Lucy, 1828, Henley
	Sarah, 1849, Pishill	Sarah Ann, 1878, Pishill
Langhuish	Arthur, 1868, Remenham, Berks	
Larner	A, 1846, Nuffield	William, 1771, Oxon
Lawrence	Fanny, 1818, Medmenham, Bucks	George, 1795, Not Known, Berks
	Henry, 1829, Rotherfield Greys	J, 1853, Brightwell
Leaver	William, 1806, Shiplake	
Ledger	John, 1801, Oxon	

Legate	Emma, 1846, Remenham, Berks	
Lester	Alice, 1868, Not Known	Martha, 1870, Not Known
Lewin	Emma, 1827, Oxon	
Lewis	William, 1840, Knighton, Radnorshire, Wales	
Liddard	George, 1847, Caversham	
Liddiard	James, 1817, Wootton Bassett, Wilts	
Light	Martha, 1803, Not Known	
Linsey	William, 1870, Brentford, Middx	
Lloyd	Eliza, 1829, Watlington, Oxon	Eliza, 1830, Pishill, Oxon
	John, 1840, Not Known	
Looker	Tryphena, 1846, Caversham	
Lovegrove	Ellen, 1817, Henley	Ellen, 1819, Henley
	Martha, 1800, Caversham	Sarah Cicely, 1847, Henley
	Thomas, 1816, Oxon	
Lovejoy	Arthur, 1864, Henley	Henry, 1886, Henley
	Hughie, 1891, Henley	J, 1797, Sonning
	James, 1803, Hambleden, Bucks	John, 1887, Henley
	Mary Ann, 1849, Henley	
Low	John, 1798, Watlington	
Lunnon	John, 1779, Henley	
Machin	Elizabeth, 1832, Oxon	Henry, 1830, Oxon
	William, 1834, Oxon	
Major	C, 1847, Henley	Caroline, 1849, Henley
	L, 1822, Henley	L N, 1849, Henley
	Lucy, 1822, Henley	Mary E, 1846, Lambeth, Surrey
Mann	W, 1786, Chalgrove	
Mant???	Thomas, 1861, Henley	
Marcham	Ann, 1823, Not Known	John, 1830, Oxon
Marshall	Thomas, 1809, Bradfield, Berks	
Martin	Eliza, 1808, Watlington	Elizabeth, 1809, Watlington
	William, 1835, Bix	
Maskell	Nathaniel, 1829, Eye and Dunsden	
Mason	Edmond, 1789, Basingstoke, Hamps	
May	Edgar, 1898, Henley	Ellen, 1865, Swyncombe
	Ellen, 1870, Swyncombe	George, 1846, Caversham
	Hannah, 1844, Aldworth, Berks	
Medmore	Arthur, 1870, Uxbridge, Middx	
Mersom	Alice, 1820, Pyrton	Charles, 1850, Pyrton
	James, 1848, Pyrton	William, 1846, Pyrton
Merson	B, 1849, Pyrton	
Middleton	George, 1840, Eye and Dunsden	
Milliard	Matilda, 1831, Dudley, Staffs	
Mines	William, 1820, Hambleden, Bucks	
Mingay	J, 1845, Shiplake	Jane, 1844, Not Known
	John, 1846, Not Known	
Mole	Harriett, 1869, Brentford, Middx	J, 1791, Henley
Moles	John, 1826, other English County	
Money	T, 1790, Britwell	Thomas, 1836, Britwell
	Thomas, 1842, Britwell	
Monger	Annie, 1890, Wokinghan, Berks	J, 1852, Shiplake
	Reginald, 1911, Henley	S A, 1849, Shiplake
Moore	Elsie, 1897, Shiplake	Jessie Ellen, 1900, Shiplake

	Lucy, 1895, Shiplake	Robert, 1831, Maulford, Notts
Morgan	Francis, 1783, Hambleden, Bucks	Susan, 1770, Checkendon
Morris	Ann, 1839, Grays	Arthur, 1871, Uxbridge, Middx.
	E, 1850, Henley	John, 1840, Henley
	Shirley, 1869, Uxbridge, Middx	Thomas, 1841, Henley
	William, 1784, Warborough	
Morse	Thomas, 1787, Benson	
Mossiman	Eliza, 1829, Oxon	Harriet, 1835, Oxon
	John, 1801, other English County	Phebe, 1837, Oxon
Mossman	Harriett, 1852, Eye and Dunsden,	Harriett, 1854, Eye and Dunsden
	James, 1857, Eye and Dunsden	William, 1862, Eye and Dunsden
Moth	Ann, 1797, Henley	
Mott	Annie, 1826, Upton, Berks	
Munday	Alice, 1862, Caversham	Emily, 1859, Caversham
	George, 1864, Caversham	Henry, 1861, Caversham
	Joseph, 1870, Brentford, Middx	Thomas, 1822, Not Known, Oxon
Murphy	Elizabeth, 1842, Newfoundland, Canada	
Napper	William, 1830, London, Middx	
Nash	Rebecca, 1805, Watlington	
Neale	Ellen, 1891, Henley	Florence Ethel, 1886, Henley
	Lilian, 1892, Henley	Nellie, 1889, Henley
Neighbour	Edmond, 1772, Pyrton	John, 1856, London, Middx
	John, 1858, Not Known, London	Richard John, 1859, Not Known, London
	Thomas, 1793, Watlington	
Neville	David, 1827, Marlow, Bucks	Mary Ann, 1839, Eye and Dunsden
Newell	Mary, 1887, Watlington	
Newman	William, 1810, Henley	
Newport	William, 1871, Henley	
Newton	Sarah, 1868, Brentford, Middx	
Nicholes	William, 1839, Henley	
Nicholls	Alice, 1889, Shiplake	Emily, 1877, Shiplake
	George, 1830, Stratton, Somerset	William, 1807, Henley
Nichols	William, 1808, Nettlebed	
Noon	Margrate, 1835, Wantage, Berks	
Norcutt	Ann, 1877, Nettlebed	Fredrick, 1874, Swyncombe
North	James, 1776, Oxon	
Nunn	Emma, 1880, Little Shefford, Hungerford, Berks	Fred, 1868, Reading, Berks
	Gertrude, 1911, Reading, Berks	Rose, 1908, Caversham
O Neil	Edward, 1871, Brentford, Middx	
Oakley	Ambrose, 1828, Watlington	
Ormsby	Mary, 1832, Oxon	
Owen	Charles, 1850, Henley	John, 1816, other English County
	Martha, 1823, Henley	
Page	George, 1831, Sheffield, Yorks	
	Thomas, 1815, Watlington	J, 1806, Watlington
Pain	James, 1799, Eye and Dunsden	
Painter	E, 1790, Britwell	Mary, 1802, Mere, Wilts
Parson	Henry, 1794, Caversham	Henry, 1857, Reading, Berks
Payne	Alice, 1872, Caversham	Emily, 1861, Caversham
	Emma, 1832, Birmingham, Warwicks	James, 1834, Gallows Tree Common

	John, 1789, Not Known, Oxon	John, 1825, Caversham
	William, 1841, Lambeth, Surrey	
Peace	Fanney, 1833, Bix, Oxon	
Pearcy	John, 1818, Nettlebed	
Peppitt	George, 1827, Coleshill, Bucks	
Percey	Elizabeth, 1796, Oxon	
Pernen	William, 1793, Henley	
Perrin	F, 1856, Henley	J, 1852, Hambleden, Bucks
	T, 1848, Hambleden, Bucks	W, 1793, Henley
	William, 1831, Limerick, Ireland	
Pettifer	George, 1887, Henley	
Phaeby	George, 1835, Henley	
Phillips	E, 1846, Henley	George, 1877, Rotherfield Greys
	H, 1859, Henley	J, 1793, Bix
	Mary, 1833, Bix	
Pidgeon	Joseph, 1806, Shiplake	
Pike	Edith Mary, 1881, Henley	Ethel, 1886, Henley
	Frederick Wm, 1876, Henley	Mary Ann, 1846, Henley
Pinnock	Eva, 1878, Caversham	
Pitt	T, 1849, Shiplake	Timothy, 1849, Not Known
Plumridge	Anne, 1781, Oxon	
Pocock	Fredrick, 1868, Henley	
Porter	David, 1854, Sedgley, Staffordshire	
Pratt	Emma, 1816, Oxon	Fanny, 1840, other English County
	J, 1829, Bix	John, 1807, Henley
	Racheal, 1839, Ipsden	
Proctor	Emily, 1860, Yarmouth, Norfolk	
Province	Ann, 1845, Henley	Charles, 1839, Oxon
	Eliza, 1847, Henley	Jemima, 1817, Oxon
	Jemmima, 1820, Woodcote	
Quarterman	Charlott, 1816, Pyrton	Charlotte, 1816, Watlington
Randall	A, 1854, Pyrton	Charles, 1856, Watlington
	E, 1841, Pyrton	Elizabeth, 1824, Hambleden, Bucks
	Ellen, 1868, Watlington	James T, 1848, Henley
	Louisa, 1865, Watlington	Mary Ann, 1860, Watlington
	S, 1834, Pyrton	M, 1860, Pyrton
	Susan, 1834, Watlington	
Rawlings	George, 1840, Not Known	
Read	Dorothy, 1911, Caversham	
Reeves	Anne, 1827, Oxon	Mary, 1773, Forsell???, Warwickshire
Reynolds	Ada Louisa, 1892, Tilehurst, Berks	Ernest Charles, 1888, Leverton, Berks
	Florence, 1897, Burghfield, Berks	James Sidney, 1893, Burghfield, Berks
	Thomas Frederick, 1887, Burrwood, (Bearwood?), Berks	
Ridge	Jessie, 1864, Henley	Mary Ann, 1861, Henley
Rigsby	C, 1852, Not Known, Gloucs	S, 1850, Not Known, Gloucs
Rimes	J, 1857, Henley	M A, 1860, Henley
Ring	Ann, 1798, Watlington	Charles, 1841, Watlington
	Ellen, 1843, Watlington	Louisa, 1820, Watlington
Roberts	E, 1834, Swyncombe	F, 1853, Swyncombe
	H, 1857, Swyncombe	Mary, 1823, Romsey, Hamps
	Mary Ann, 1827, Eastwell Hoo, Hamps	Mary Ann, 1863, Swyncombe
	R, 1860, Swyncombe	Thomas, 1858, Swyncombe

Robinson	Eliza, 1860, Britwell Salome	
Rumball	Thomas, 1794, Nettlebed	
Rumble	Annie, 1827, Maidenhead, Berks	
Russell	Anne, 1864, Henley	George, 1808, Henley
	Hannah, 1867,	Harriet, 1820, Henley
	Jane, 1862, Henley	
Sadler	Agnes, 1833, Oxon	Ann, 1823, Bix
	George, 1851, Henley	J, 1793, Sonning
	Louisa, 1843, Henley	Mary Ann, 1859, Shiplake
	William, 1848, Pishill	
Sargeant	Annie, 1868, Greys	
Sargent	Elizabeth, 1852, Rotherfield Greys	Elizabeth, 1862, Rotherfield Greys
Sarney	Edward, 1840, Not Known	
Saunders	H, 1802, Shiplake	
Saundy	Frederick, 1879, St Andrews, Holborn, London	Alice, 1868, St. Andrews, Holborn, London
Sawyer	Eliza, 1845, Caversham	
Sergeant	Annie, 1872, Henley	
Seymore	Elizabeth, 1766, Oxon	
Seymour	Arthur, 1842, Not Known	John, 1825, Watlington
	W, 1851, Henley	
Shale	James, 1853, Ipsden	
Shane	William, 1824, Rotherfield Greys	
Sharp	George, 1838, Henley	
Sharpe	Alice, 1886, Caversham	Edward, 1902, Henley
Shaw	Ann, 1844, Not Known	Maria, 1789, Henley
Shepherd	William, 1834, Britwell Salome	William, 1835, Britwell Prior
Sheppard	T, 1847, Britwell	
Short	Henry, 1866, Not Known	
Shurvell	Mary, 1864, Greys	
Shurville	Emma, 1842, Henley	Mary, 1840, Henley
	Thomas, 1836, Stoke Row	
Simmonds	Ann, 1861, Henley	Elizabeth, 1865, Henley
	Jane, 1835, Henley	Robt, 1828, Oxon
	Thomas, 1841, Whitchurch	William, 1857, Henley
Simmons	J, 1811, Peppard	J, 1835, Henley
	W, 1857, Holborn, Middx	
Singleton	Mary Ann, 1829, Stonor	
Skettles	Eliza, 1847, Henley	
Slade	Richard, 1813, Shiplake	Richard, 1820, Shiplake
Slaughter	Ellen, 1830, Oxon	John, 1821, Oxon
Smith	Benjamin, 1832, Oxon	Benjamin, 1834, Henley
	C, 1853, Bix	Charles, 1870, Uxbridge, Middx
	Delilah, 1774, Not Known	E, 1848, Bix
	E, 1858, Bix	Edwin Richard, 1851, Henley
	Eliza, 1828, Watlington	Ellen, 1858, Not Known, Oxon
	George, 1823, Binfield Heath	H, 1851, Bix
	J, 1852, Watlington	J, 1853, Checkendon
	J, 1856, Bix	J, 1861, Henley
	Sarah, 1793, Greys	Susan, 1817, Bath, Somerset
	Susan, 1821, Not Known	Susan, 1824, Bath, Somerset
	Susan, 1848, St. Marylebone, Middx	T, 1804, Cuxham
	T, 1850, Watlington	W, 1797, Ipsden

	Walter, 1825, Caversham	William, 1797, Wallingford, Berks
	William, 1821, Bix	William, 1839, Sherborne
	William, 1840, West Bromwich, Staffs	
Soden	James, 1780, Watlington	
Spicer	John, 1803, Hambleden, Bucks	
Springrove	John, 1869, Brentford, Middx	
Spyers	John, 1779, Brightwell	Rhoda, 1840, Brightwell
Stacey	Alice, 1870, Brentford, Middx	Edith, 1874, Brentford, Middx
	Thomas, 1835, Henley	
Stakes	Elsie Emma, 1863, Pocklington, Yorks	
Stallwood	William, 1816, Medmenham, Bucks	
Standbrook	Elizabeth, 1811, Oxon	
Stanhill	Dinah, 1815, Watlington	
Statham	Henry, 1829, Uxbridge, Middx	
Steele	William, 1824, Ipsden	
Stephens	Charles, 1857, Henley	George, 1852, Henley
	Henry, 1806, St. George, Hanover Square, Middx	John, 1859, Henley
	Kate, 1856, Henley	Sarah, 1861, Henley
Stevens	Alfred, 1848, Britwell Salome	Alfred, 1868, Rotherfield Greys
	Charles, 1843, Sonning	D, 1789, Henley
	David, 1810, Shiplake	M, 1791, Watlington
	R, 1803, Sonning	Robert, 1803, Eye and Dunsden
Stevenson	Richard, 1826, Oxon	
Stockwell	Alice, 1872, Brentford, Middx	Charles, 1833, Henley
	Ellen, 1870, Brentford, Middx	Fanny, 1874, Brentford, Middx
Stone	James, 1814, Medmenham, Bucks	James, 1821, Hambleden, Bucks
Stones	William, 1761, Oxon	
Storrey???	Walter, 1897, Not Known	
Stradley	Martha, 1844, Shiplake	Sarah, 1838, Shiplake
	William, 1836, Shiplake	
Strange	Alfred, 1781, Oxon	Elizabeth, 1834, Pangbourne, Berks
	Elizabeth, 1869, Henley	Fanny, 1871, Henley
	Gertrude, 1871, Henley	James, 1873, Henley
	Mary Ann, 1869, Henley	
Street	Charles, 1844, Medmenham, Bucks	G, 1854, Henley
	M N, 1836, Peppard	Robert, 1775, Ipsden
	T, 1851, Grays	C, 1857, Ipsden
Strictiley	Richard, 1814, Shartiton???, Warwicks	
Strong	Ann, 1767, Checkendon	
Strudley	Isabella, 1860, Shiplake	Martha, 1858, Shiplake
	Walter, 1875, Henley	
Styles	Henry, 1845, Stokenchurch	Violet, 1909, Binfield Heath
Swain	John, 1860, Checkendon	
Talbott	John, 1776, other English County	
Taylor	S, 1811, Henley	Susan, 1811, Henley
	William, 1809, Henley	Susan, 1838, Oxon
	Thomas, 1843, Lower Assendon	William, 1806, Oxon
Terry	Charles, 1884, Henley	Daisy, 1882, Henley
	John, 1818, Upsgrove	

Thatcher	Charles, 1890, Hambleden, Bucks	George, 1889, Hambleden, Bucks
	George Henry, 1886, Hambleden, Bucks	Mary, 1885, Hambleden, Bucks
	William, 1887, Hambleden, Bucks	William James, 1886, Hambleden, Bucks
Thorn	Louisa, 1873, Brentford, Middx	
Thrupp	M, 1799, Cork, Ireland	Mary A D, 1838, Athlone, Ireland
Tombs	Ja???, 1852, Henley	Kate, 1908, Henley
	Rose, 1863, Henley	William, 1840, Watlington
Toomer	George, 1799, Henley	
Toovey	William, 1793, Hambleden, Bucks	
Town	Racheal, 1808, Britwell	William, 1848, Britwell
Towner	H, 1848, Grays	
Towns	John, 1806, Watlington	
Tredwell	Louisa, 1867, Shoreditch, London	
Tuck	Hannah, 1792, Dublin, Ireland	Timothy, 1784, Berrick Prior, Oxon
Tucker	Alfred, 1871, Uxbridge, Middx	
Turner	Charles, 1876, Henley	Emma, 1832, Caversham
	Harriett, 1873, Henley	Henry John, 1890, Emmer Green
	John, 1834, Rotherfield Peppard	Lydia, 1868, Henley
	Mary, 1830, Grays	Mary Anny, 1836, Henley
	Richard, 1826, Oxon	Sarah, 1850, Henley
	Thomas, 1871, Henley	
Vernon	Mary, 1847, Watlington	Mary, 1848, Watlington
Vicars	Joseph, 1796, Caversham	
Vidler	George, 1856, Rye, Sussex	
Wake	Francis, 1801, Oxon	
Walden	Richard, 1846, Lambourn, Berks	
Wallace	Thomas, 1788, Cholsey, Berks	
Walters	Harriett, 1858, Shiplake	
Ward	E, 1807, Checkendon	James, 1833, not known
	William, 1786, other English County	William, 1804, Eye and Dunsden
Warner	John, 1799, Henley	William, 1827, Henley
Watkins	Eliza, 1838, Caversham	
Watson	J, 1852, Pyrton	William, 1859, Pyrton
Webb	C, 1858, Bix	Charles, 1842, Henley
	E, 1860, Nuffield	Edmond, 1780, Assendon
	Fredrick, 1871, Henley	George, 1870, Pyrton
	Jane, 1837, Wallingford, Berks	M, 1840, Nuffield
	Martha, 1850, Pyrton	Walter, 1875, Henley
Welford	Elizabeth, 1875, Henley	Fredrick, 1873, Henley
	Harry, 1878, Henley	James, 1870, Henley
	Mary, 1841, Henley	William, 1837, Henley
Weller	Emma, 1840, Henley	
Wells	Elizabeth, 1787, Shiplake	
Welsh	James, 1867, Uxbridge, Middx	
Wenman	Sophia, 1824, Shiplake	
Wernham	E, 1853, Caversham	
Wetherall	Ann, 1828, Oxon	Mary, 1834, Oxon
	William, 1830, Oxon	
Wheeler	James, 1810, Pishill	John, 1839, Henley
	M, 1783, Watlington	

White	Ann, 1822, Eye and Dunsden	Cornelius, 1834, Oxon
	Elizabeth, 1835, Henley	Elizabeth, 1872, Eye and Dunsden
	Thomas, 1784, Watlington	W, 1792, Hambleden, Bucks
	William, 1830, Oxon	
Wicks	Charles, 1835, Henley	
Wilde	Sarah, 1791, Oxon	
Wilder	J, 1844, Grays	
Wilkins	Matilda, 1839, Not Known	
Wilkinson	A, 1813, London, Middx	Amelia, 1813, Not Known
Williams	Alfred, 1847, Henley	Maria, 1829, Oxon
	Mary, 1833, Oxon	
Willis	Ann, 1815, Alton, Hamps	Edward, 1761, Oxon
	Elizabeth, 1786, Oxon	James, 1808, Peppard
	Joseph, 1810, Rotherfield Greys	Sarah, 1789, Nuffield, Oxon
Willshire	Lavina, 1868, Not Known	
Wilson	E, 1848, Henley	George, 1858, Henley
	James, 1864, Henley	Nellie, 1821, Caversham
	Thomas, 1862, Henley	
Wiltshire	Edward, 1805, Wantage, Berks	Edward, 1807, Caversham
Wise	J, 1786, Grays	John, 1829, Henley
	John, 1833, Rotherfield Greys	Sarah, 1819, Rotherfield Greys
Wiswold	John, 1793, Henley	
Wix	Caroline, 1840, Not Known	
Wixon	George, 1826, Watlington	George Hall, 1847, Pyrton
Wood???	John, 1874, Henley	
Woodley	Eliza, 1843, Britwell Salome	Elizabeth, 1867, Britwell
	Ellen, 1863, Britwell Salome	Emma, 1865, Britwell Salome
	Henry, 1838, Wallingford, Berks	Mary, 1825, Hampstead Norris, Berks
	William, 1824, Henley	
Woods	John, 1879, Henley	William, 1813, Henley
Woodward	Caroline, 1848, Henley	Daniel, 1851, Henley
	E, 1850, Reading, Berks	Ellen Maria, 1878, Rotherfield Greys
	Emma, 1842, Brightwell	Henry, 1876, Rotherfield Greys
	John, 1873, Rotherfield Greys	
	Martha, 1822, Brightwell	S, 1821, Caversham
	W, 1851, Caversham	
Wright	Daniel, 1797, Not Known	George, 1790, Shiplake
	George, 1829, Oxon	Mary Ann, 1826, Oxon
Young	A, 1779, Hambleden, Bucks	A, 1851, Watlington
	A, 1853, Watlington	Alfred, 1873, Brentford, Middx
	Ann, 1839, Watlington	Edward, 1842, Pyrton
	Elizabeth, 1848, Pyrton	G, 1848, Watlington
	George, 1872, Brentford, Middx	Hannah, 1778, Not Known
	Hannah, 1813, Henley	J, 1853, Watlington
	Joseph, 1800, Mapledurham, Berks	Lizzie, 1841, Watlington
	Lucy, 1846, Pyrton	Martha, 1838, Pyrton
	Mary A, 1851, Pyrton	R, 1846, Watlington
	William, 1844, Pyrton	

Courtesy of Dr J.G.T. Jones, © Henley Census Group 4/8/2011.
See full census listings 1841-1911 at **www.henleycensus.info** for general search facility.

Bibliography

"The Workhouse – A Study of Poor Law Buildings in England", English Heritage, 1999.

"The Victorian Workhouse", Trevor May, Shire Publications, 1999.

"Upon the Parish Rate – the Story of Louth Workhouse", Bill Painter, Louth Naturalists', Antiquarian and Literary Society, 2000.

"The Workhouse Southwell", National Trust, 2002.

"A Poor Little House…" – the Story of Belford Union Workhouse, J M Bowen, Bell View (Bedford) Ltd., 2005.

"Workhouse", Simon Fowler, National Archives, 2007.

"Shadows of the Workhouse", Jennifer Worth, Phoenix, 2005.

"The Poor", David Hey, Oxford Companion to Family and Local History, OUP 2008.

"Henley on Thames Poor Law Union and Workhouse Records 1835 – 1851", Oxfordshire Black Sheep Publications, 2008.

"Henley on Thames Poor Relief Vol.1 1780 – 1821", Oxfordshire Black Sheep Publications, 2008.

"Henley on Thames Poor Relief Vol.2 1822 – 1835", Oxfordshire Black Sheep Publications, 2008.

"Henley Rural – The History of a Rural District Council in Oxfordshire 1894 – 1932", Brian Read, 2003.

"Henley on Thames – A History", David C Whitehead, Phillimore, 2007.

"Life in a Victorian Workhouse from 1834 to 1930", Peter Higginbotham, Pitkin Publishing, 2011.

"Illegitimacy", Eve McLaughlin, Varneys Press, 1999.

"Early Medical Services, Berkshire and South Oxfordshire from 1740", Margaret Railton, Polmood Publications, 1994.

"The English Poor Law", JJ & AJ Bagley, Macmillan, 1966.

"The Poor Law in Nineteenth Century England and Wales", Anne Digby, The Historical Association.

"Labouring Life in the Victorian Countryside", Pamela Horn, Sutton Publishing, 1976.

"A Social History of the English Working Classes 1815 – 1945", Eric Hopkins, 1979, London.

"Single Mothers in the Workhouse", Peter Higginbotham, Your Family History, December 2010.

"A History of the County of Oxford Vol XVI: Henley-on-Thames and Environs, Binfield Hundred, Part 1", edited by Simon Townley, Victoria County History, 2011.

"The Book of Henley-on-Thames", GHJ Tomalin, Barracuda Books, 1975.

"Down and Out in Paris and London", George Orwell.

"The Workhouse Encyclopaedia", Peter Higginbotham, History Press, 2012.

"Voices from the Workhouse", Peter Higginbotham, History Press, 2012.

See also www.henleycensus.info.

KEY DATES IN THE DEVELOPMENT OF TOWNLANDS

1601   Old Poor Law enacted under Queen Elizabeth I placing responsibility on Parishes to relieve the Poor. Parish officers appointed, including Overseer of the Poor.

1652   Land acquired by Henley Corporation per Richard Boult, known as "Town Land". "Parcel of arable land of three acres on N side of hill in Henley for use and benefit of the Poor of Henley", vested in Henley Corporation. Land rented out.

1727   Poor House in existence in New Street on site of Kenton Theatre.

1790   Larger premises needed so new Poor House for 150 persons built on Town Lands. (John Crocker recorded the Rules and Regulations pertaining for Master to exercise discipline).

1834   New Poor Law enacted to cope with GB's expanding population. Strict regulations enforced from London by Poor Law Commissioners.
Merging of 21 parishes to form Henley Union: from Caversham to Cuxham

June   First meeting of Board of 32 Guardians of Henley Union: mostly landed
1835   gentry, farmers, reverend gentlemen (all ratepayers!) Following first meeting of Guardians, the means of taking over existing Poor House discussed with Henley Corporation, who agreed a lease.

1835   Guardians obtained permission from London to enlarge from 150 to 250 places, costing £2500 for building + £1500 for equipment.

1841   Infirmary built x 4 wards, including water closets and bathrooms. Pest house for infectious disease cases erected. (Said to have housed Samuel Coleridge, sick after his Army unit left Henley.)

1847   Tramp Ward introduced at West Hill end of site.

1862   Purchase of 3 more acres of adjoining land at £700.

1871   New school building for 100 children at £2250.

1886   Upgrading of infirmary (with drains connected with sewers rather than middens), following demand by Medical Officer

1894   Responsibility for workhouses passed to Local Government Board. Boards of Guardians reconstituted (but remain the "old guard").

1908   Mortuary built.

1930   Power transferred to County Councils, who set up Public Assistance Committees to deal with the destitute.

1948   National Assistance Act ended the poor laws. National Health Act transferred hospitals to NHS.

1970s   Henley GPs moved their two surgeries on to Townlands site.

1980s   Peppard Hospital was closed. New ward built on Townlands site to accommodate; also beds from Henley War Memorial Hospital (closed 1984).

2015   Proposed opening of new Community Hospital on two acres and redevelopment of Workhouse/School etcetera for housing.

Index